P9-DGY-962

How to Identify Your Organization's Training Needs

How to Identify Your Organization's Training Needs

A PRACTICAL GUIDE TO NEEDS ANALYSIS

John H. McConnell

AMACOM

American Management Association

New York • Atlanta • Brussels • Buenos Aires • Chicago • London • Mexico City
San Francisco • Shanghai • Tokyo • Toronto • Washington, D.C.

Special discounts on bulk quantities of AMACOM books are
available to corporations, professional associations, and
other organizations. For details, contact Special Sales
Department, AMACOM, a division of American Management
Association, 1601 Broadway, New York, NY 10019.
Tel.: 212-903-8316. Fax: 212-903-8083.
Web site: www.amacombooks.org

This publication is designed to provide accurate and authoritative
information in regard to the subject matter covered. It is sold with
the understanding that the publisher is not engaged in rendering
legal, accounting, or other professional service. If legal advice or
other expert assistance is required, the services of a competent
professional person should be sought.

Library of Congress Cataloging-in-Publication Data

McConnell, John H.
    How to identify your organization's training needs : a practical guide
to needs analysis / John H. McConnell.
        p.   cm.
    ISBN 0-8144-0710-2
    1. Employees—Training of.   2. Employer-supported education.   I.
Title.

HF5549.5.T7 M3694 2003
658.3'124—dc21   2002008038

Printing number

10   9   8   7   6   5   4   3   2   1

*To Fred Voss, without whose support my career
would have been less successful*

Contents

List of Figures   *ix*

Acknowledgments   *xi*

1. Introduction   1

Part One   Assessing Your Present Training Function   **11**

2. Analyzing Your Training Department's Effectiveness   13

3. Analyzing Your Training Department's Organization   43

Part Two   Planning and Procedures for Needs Identification   **61**

4. Distinguishing Between Organizational and
   Employee Training Needs   63

5. Identifying Possible Areas in Which People Need
   Training   81

6. Planning to Identify Training Needs   103

7. Procedures for Identifying Training Needs   119

**Part Three   Implementing Specific Methods to Gather
                Information**   **135**

8. Standard Interviews   137

9. Job Analysis Grid Interviews   155

10. The Need-to-Know Process   171

11. Performance Standards   181

12. Meetings   191

13. Questionnaires   203

14. Tests and Assessments   217

15. Combination Methods   231

Part Four   Concluding a Needs Anaysis   **245**

16. Combining Inputs and Reporting Results   247

17. Transferring Training Needs to Training Objectives   279

18. Considering External Services and Products   291

    Procedures, Summaries, and Checklists   *299*

    Appendix: Forms   *325*

    Index   *349*

List of Figures

Figure 2-1. Training activities. 16
Figure 2-2. Your training activity perceptions. 18
Figure 2-3. Training department survey. 20
Figure 2-4. Training rating comparison form. 24
Figure 2-5. Completed training rating comparison
form. 26
Figure 2-6. Coded training rating comparison form. 27
Figure 2-7. Training rating comparison form showing
degree of agreement. 29
Figure 2-8. Training activity priority list. 32
Figure 2-9. Department employees' rating comparison. 35
Figure 2-10. A blank internal clients' rating comparison
form. 36
Figure 2-11. A completed internal clients' rating
comparison form. 38
Figure 2-12. Cost comparison-analysis. 40
Figure 2-13. Asset comparison matrix. 41
Figure 3-1. Key result areas. 47
Figure 3-2. Organization chart for a training
department. 49
Figure 3-3. Organization chart with lines of authority
and support positions. 50
Figure 3-4. Key result area/position form. 52
Figure 3-5. Position description preparation form. 53
Figure 3-6. Sample position description for a training
manager. 56

Figure 5-1.   Training department's annual review
              questionnaire.   84
Figure 5-2.   Annual employee performance survey.   89
Figure 5-3.   A sample follow-up questionnaire.   94
Figure 6-1.   Sample training needs analysis report.   112
Figure 6-2.   Training needs information planning form.   115
Figure 6-3.   Training needs information planning form
              with sample data.   117
Figure 8-1.   Interview planning form.   144
Figure 9-1.   Grid results combining form (Example 1).   165
Figure 9-2.   Grid results combining form (Example 2).   167
Figure 9-3.   Grid results combining form (Example 3).   168
Figure 9-4.   Grid results combining form (Example 4).   169
Figure 13-1. Orientation questionnaire.   206
Figure 15-1. Competencies and their definitions for an
              example financial services company.   234
Figure 15-2. Supervisory management competency
              questionnaire.   241
Figure 16-1. Information combination form.   251
Figure 16-2. Information combination form with sample
              values for two groups.   252
Figure 16-3. Information combination form with results
              calculated.   253
Figure 16-4. Information combination form with totals.   254

Acknowledgments

Every author discovers that his/her final product almost always depends on assistance from a number of others. Fortunately, most people are very generous with their time and thoughts. This is particularly true for a book of this type.

There is not a single method for identifying training needs. There are a number of procedures in general use as well as systems unique to individuals and organizations. My consulting experience has given me the privilege to work with many of these training professionals. And, through this work, I have been exposed to many of their methods for identifying training needs. A number of their contributions are included in this book.

Some of the people who have directly and indirectly provided technical and other assistance are listed below.

R. Brayton Bowen is president of The Howland Group, a human resources and change management consulting firm. He previously held senior human resources management positions with General Mills and Providian. He holds a B.A. and M.A. from Brown University. Mr. Bowen is a contributing faculty member for Seton Hall University on Systemwide Leadership Development and is co-featured on the management video series *Management Speaks*. He is also the host and co-producer of a five-part documentary on anger in the workplace and has several published articles in *Industry Week* and *Retail Review*. He is a member of the Institute of Management Consultants.

Ralph J. Brown is a management consultant specializing in human resources systems. His former positions have included director of employee relations for Philip Morris USA, director of management information systems for Flintkote, Inc., and director of personnel and administration for Wolverine Tube Division of Allied Signal. He holds a B.A. from Wayne State University and is a frequent speaker and seminar leader.

Brian Duffy is currently president of Alliance Insurance, a firm that provides administrative support and technology to the California insurance industry. He has held former positions as executive vice president of personal lines with Fireman's Fund Insurance Companies, senior vice president for Colonial Penn Group, and operations and industrial relations manager with Procter & Gamble. Mr. Duffy is a graduate of the University of Pennsylvania and the Wharton School of Business. He has conducted numerous management training seminars and provided extensive industrial relations consulting.

Leslye Fuller is educational program analyst for the chancellor for education and professional development in the Department of Defense, where she is developing academic quality standards for the department's civilian education institutions and professional development programs. Past assignments have included the development of distance learning and web-based and satellite-delivered courses for the Office of the Undersecretary of Defense; in addition, she served as comptroller at the Defense Business Management University, the team leader on Vice President Gore's National Partnership for Reinventing Government, and the head of the career management division of the Department of the Navy Acquisition Intern Program. She has a B.A. from Florida State University and is a frequent speaker at national conferences on the application of technology to education and training.

Russell A. Glicksman is currently president and CEO of The Beam Group, a human resources and management consulting firm. Prior to his current position, he was executive vice president of operations and senior vice president of human resources for Colonial Penn Group. Mr. Glicksman is a graduate of Gettysburg College with a B.A. in psychology. He is a member of the Human Resources Council for the Life Office Management Association (LOMA) and is a frequent speaker at human resources association conventions.

Roy J. Kahn is a management consultant specializing in organizational and management development and administrative services. Previously he was vice president of human resources for Washington Gas Company; a principal in the Personnel Services Division of F.R. Schwab and Associates, Inc.; vice president of personnel for John Wanamaker Department Stores; and corporate manager of personnel for Hertz Corporation. Mr. Kahn received a B.S. in industrial relations from Rider College and has authored several articles that appeared in *Management World*.

Kathryn Z. McMaster is currently vice president of human resources for Nobel Learning Communities, a not-for-profit operator of private schools. Prior to her current assignment she was vice president of human resources for Colonial Penn/GE Financial Services. She has a B.A. from Temple University and is a certified benefits specialist and compensation professional. She is a member of Penjerdel Employee Benefits Association and the Philadelphia Human Resources Planning Group and its Outreach Committee and Society for Human Resource Management, and she conducts a series of interviewing skills workshops.

Christine M. Morris is currently manager of human resources information services for ARVIDA, a real estate development firm. Prior to her current position she was director of human resources for Singer Asset Finance Company, LLC; director of human resources for Life Care Retirement Communities; vice president/director of administration for International Trade Systems, Inc.; and personnel administrator for the city of Boca Raton, Florida. She is a graduate of Barry University and is certified in human resources management information systems.

Robert A. Nowaczyk is currently vice president and director of administration for Oppenheimer Funds. Prior to joining his current company, he was vice president of human resources for Vanguard Group and held several human resources positions with a major financial services and insurance company. He has a B.S. from the University of Delaware and an M.B.A. from Widener University. He is past chairman of the Society for Human Resource Management Employment Practice Committee and past president and founding member of the Greater Valley Forge Human Resources Association.

Arthur E. Pearson is currently president of Management Development Services, Inc. His firm specializes in providing human resources services and products. Prior to his current position, he was director of planning and organizational development for M. Lowenstein & Company and the director of evening education programs for the American Management Association. He's also held several positions with Western Electric Company, Graybar Electric, and General Motors. He is a graduate of the College of Wooster and the author of several articles for The Conference Board and other publications on corporate aid to education.

Robert Ryan is the director of the Human Factors Life Cycle Office at the Internal Revenue Service. The office is responsible for transition management issues relating to impact on information technology professionals during a major business systems modernization project. Prior to his current assignment, he was director of the Naval Career Management Site, a principal adviser to the Secretary of the Navy, and a senior official of the Naval Postgraduate School. He holds a B.S. from the University of Dayton, an M.Ed. from Wright State University, and an Ed.D. from Auburn University. He has received a Distinguished Civilian Special Act Award, is past adjunct faculty member at Prince George's Community College and Pensacola Junior College, and conducts numerous workshops and seminars on career development.

Ferdinand J. Setaro is managing director of TLE Associates. The firm specializes in organizational development and improvement services. Formerly he was director of organizational and management development for Vanguard Group; director of organizational and management development for Colonial Penn Group; director of human resources for CPG Data Group; and director of supervisory development for the American Management Association. He has a B.A. from Columbia University and is a graduate of the Advance Program in Organizational Development. He is past president and chairman of the board of directors for the Association of Internal Management Consultants and is a prolific author and seminar leader.

Elizabeth N. Treher is co-founder of The Learning Key. The firm provides consulting and coaching to enhance and facilitate individual and organizational performance. Prior to establishing the firm, she held project leader positions in government, academia, and industry including management of Squibb's Center for Science Education and the design and implementation of a corporate college. She is a graduate of Washington University and also holds an M.A. and Ph.D. from the same school. She has more than sixty publications and patents to her credit, is past president of the Associations of Psychological Type, and was an invited member of the first United States delegation to China on human resources training and development.

Additional recognition needs to go to Adrienne Hickey, executive editor at AMACOM, who proved to be a friend as well as a colleague; Mike Sivilli, associate editor at AMACOM, who regularly improves my manuscripts; Rob Kaplan, my agent, friend, and colleague; and Ruth Long who finds and corrects my manuscript errors.

To all of you, thank you.

John H. McConnell

Introduction

The training function is becoming an increasingly important element of organizational and individual employee success. As jobs have become more technical and organization specific, there are fewer candidates whose qualifications meet such requirements. The need for a "pair of hands" is diminishing as the need for technological knowledge and abilities is increasing.

New jobs are continually being created, and new equipment and systems introduced to existing jobs. Some jobs are vanishing, and many whose jobs are eliminated do not have the needed skills for the positions that are now available. In addition, many organizations have found it difficult to locate people who possess what were previously considered the necessary basic English, communication, and mathematical skills. All of these conditions require the type of expertise training can provide, so training is called on to make available the types of employees required.

This increasing need for effective training is not limited to any industry or to the size of an organization. It may appear to be an obvious need for a large company involved with the latest technological developments, but it can also be a requirement in smaller, more traditional organizations. A two-person doctor's office and a ten-person retail store often utilize unique software that requires training, and an untrained employee in a small organization can have a significant impact on overall results. In a large organization, a single untrained employee has little impact, but one untrained employee in a four-person insurance agency is 25 percent of the agency workforce.

A change in the economy may also create different types of training needs. When the economy is strong and employment is increasing, a high level of new employee training is required. When the economy turns down, new employee training generally decreases, but the training needs of existing employees often increase as employers attempt to reengineer work, transfer people, and meet performance goals with fewer resources. However, economic conditions are cyclical. Whatever the current one is, it is only temporary, and the overall trend will continue to reflect more jobs with fewer qualified people available to fill them.

A 2002 article in *The New York Times* reported that current projections call for a short fall of 6,000,000 people to fill the jobs that will be available by 2006, and a seminar speaker recently commented that the majority of today's children will be hired for jobs that were not in existence when they were born. If anything, training's importance will intensify in the future.

As training has become increasingly important, it has also come under increased scrutiny. Employers demand specific measurable results for the resources expended. Simultaneously, training is becoming more of an individual activity. New and more effective training techniques and delivery methods are being developed, but to ensure successful training, it is still necessary to first identify what training is required both by the organization and individual employees.

An AMA Study

When the American Management Association developed a procedure to measure supervisory management competencies, it conducted a number of studies to ensure the procedure's validity and reliability. One of the studies was an evaluation of the management competencies of current supervisors before and after they participated in their company's supervisory management training course. An interesting byproduct of that study was the affirmation of the importance of conducting training to meet specific needs.

The study was designed to answer three questions:

❐ How valid are the procedure measurements of management competencies?

❏ How reliable are the procedure measurements of management competencies?

❏ Can the procedure measure changes in management performance that can be attributed to training?

How Valid Are the Procedure Measurements of Management Competencies?

To answer this question, current supervisors whose job performance was known and measured by an existing objective performance review process were selected to participate in the procedure, and a concurrent validity study was conducted. This was accomplished by comparing their actual on-the-job performance ratings as supervisors with the procedure overall ratings of their total management competencies. (The current on-the-job performance ratings of the supervisors were not known to the people conducting the measurement procedure.) The result was a significant correlation between the program measurements and their job performance. This indicated the procedure accurately measured management competencies as they related to current supervisory job performance.

How Reliable Are the Procedure's Measurements of Management Competencies?

To determine the procedure's reliability two calculations were made. Some of the supervisors participated in the procedure two times, and the results were compared. The two results were significantly similar and indicated the procedure produced consistent measurements when repeated.

The second calculations were based on comparing two sets of measurements from the same procedure. It was possible to use measurements from two halves of the procedure. When compared, the two results were almost identical. Based on these two measures, it was determined the procedure was reliable.

Can the Procedure Measure Changes in Management Performance That Can Be Attributed to Training?

The supervisors were categorized into two large groups. Each of these large groups consisted of several subgroups of twelve supervisors—the maximum number the procedure could measure at any one time. The groups were balanced with respect to their demographics: age, time in supervision, seniority with the organization, education, race, marital status, and current job performance ratings.

Both groups participated in the procedure and evaluations of their individual management competencies were obtained. Then one group (called the test group) participated in the organization's management training course and following the course was reevaluated by the procedure.

The other group (called the control group) did not participate in the organization's management training course after its initial evaluations. Instead, participants returned to their normal jobs, but when the test group was reevaluated, the control group was also reevaluated.

The study's designers theorized that if the test group members' reevaluation indicated changes in management competencies, but the control group members showed no significant changes in their management competencies, the changes in the test group could be attributed to the organization's management training course.

So, what were the results of the study?

There were no significant changes in either group's supervisory management competencies, so it initially appeared that the supervisory management training course had no impact on the participants' management competencies. However, on closer examination of the results, it was discovered that one subgroup of twelve supervisors in the test group had shown significant improvement in their management competencies. More interestingly, the improvements occurred in the management competencies in which their pretraining evaluations had indicated required the most improvement. Why this change in just a few participants?

The designers of the study had wanted to limit any effect the pretraining evaluation might have on individual performance. They had wanted the pretraining measurement to be an assessment and not an educational tool. They had not wanted the participants to learn from the experience, so no one in either the test group or the control group was to be informed of how they were evaluated by the pretraining test. By accident, members of that one subgroup had been given the results of their pretraining evaluations. Before the supervisory management training course, they were told which competencies were evaluated, which competencies reflected their evaluated strengths, and which evaluated competencies needed improvement. They knew their training needs before attending the course.

Several months later, a follow-up review of the participants' on-the-job performance was conducted. It discovered that the supervisors from the subgroup whose management competencies had been measured as improved, had also improved in their performance as supervisors. The other participants showed no significant job performance improvement.

The conclusion was that the supervisory management training course was effective when it was conducted to meet specific employee needs, and an equally important corollary was that the training was most effective when the employees recognized their development needs. It also suggested that training conducted other than to meet specific recognized needs was not effective.

One might reply, "So what's new? That has always been the case."

True, most professional trainers have long believed that training is most effective when designed to meet specific needs, or as one trainer commented, "In training, an aimed rifle at a specific target approach is more effective than a shotgun aimed in a general direction approach."

Even so, much training has been conducted without any predetermination of needs. There are numerous organizations in which training departments are measured by such things as the number of employees attending courses, the number of books purchased, and the percentage of time training rooms are utilized. These are useful statistics, but hardly the basis for determining the quality and effectiveness of training. Sometimes training has even been conducted without any thought to the needs of the organization or individual employees.

An Overheard Conversation

While riding on a commuter train, the following conversation between two training managers from two different organizations was overheard:

Manager #1: So, how are things going?

Manager #2: Great, we are very busy. In fact, In have added three new trainers to the department.

Manager #1: What training are you planning this year?

Manager #2: I don't know. I MBO'd them last year. Interviewing is currently a hot topic in the journals, but I am also considering something that is sexier—like quality customer service.

Another training director once confided that all managers in his company were allowed to attend one external training course a year, and they were encouraged to attend one at a "good" location. The reason was not to meet any development need. Instead, the training was viewed as cover for a trip somewhere—a reward for being in management.

Today's Training Objective

These types of approaches are no longer acceptable. Organizations assign a great deal of their assets to training, and like any other activity, it should get an acceptable return on its investment. Training is now an important element for organizational and individual employee success, and to succeed it must meet both the needs of the employees being trained and those of the organization as a whole. This book believes the ultimate mission of the training function is:

> To provide employees with the skills and knowledge required to ensure optimum performance results, develop a cache of employees qualified to meet the organization's operational needs and objectives, and contribute to positive morale, employee satisfaction, and development.

Professional Trainers

As training has become more important, so too have the requirements for trainers. Professional trainers today need an array of skills and abilities to fulfill their mission. Unfortunately, not all of them have fully grasped this fact, and not all have actually identified or understood their role in the organization.

A national association for trainers regularly offers seminars at its annual conference. One of the most requested seminars deals with selling training programs to top management. These seminars do not always deal with providing training that is needed. Instead, they often cover techniques for convincing top management to support training that has not been identified as required—a practice one participant described as "selling top management what is good for them rather than what is needed."

Another professional training organization once asked a consulting firm to develop a self-study course for trainers in the competencies required to be a successful trainer. Apparently, the organization had spent considerable time and money on a study to identify the competencies all professional trainers should possess. Now it wanted to make a method for improving in these areas available to its members.

When the competencies were reviewed by the consulting firm, it agreed that all of them represented the type of operational skills, abilities, and knowledge a trainer should have, but none dealt with providing training to meet the organization's or employees' needs and objectives. When this point was raised, the training organization told the consulting firm that a professional trainer should only be concerned with acquiring professional skills. What training was conducted was secondary and not a major concern of a professional trainer. (Based on that response, the consulting firm declined to develop the self-study materials.)

This Book's Approach

So much for horror stories. By acquiring this book, you have already identified yourself as someone who is interested in ensuring a professional training function designed to meet identified needs. This book has been written in a format to assist you in that effort.

It provides you with both an overview of the training function—including an analysis of your training function's current status—and the tools to fulfill the crucial first step for all training—identification of the organization's and individual employees' training needs.

It begins by leading you through an analysis and review of your training function. Next, it provides methods for identifying areas with possible training needs. Descriptions of various methodologies for identifying training needs are provided. Then this book details the procedures in a manner you can immediately put to use.

Actually, there are many procedures for identifying training needs, but there is no best one for all situations. This book reviews the ones most commonly used and supplies instructions for a number of specific procedures and combinations of several approaches.

Included are methods for combining inputs from several sources, reporting the results, and translating the identified needs into training objectives. In the process, information is also provided on how to evaluate training identification procedures and how to determine their value and cost to your organization.

The final product of identifying training needs is a description of exactly what training is required. In addition, the identified needs are then transformed into measurable objectives that a training designer or developer can use to select or create a training course to meet the identified needs.

A review of this book's chapters describes the approach and contents:

Analyzing Your Training Department's Effectiveness

Analyzing Your Training Department's Organization

Distinguishing Between Organizational and Employee Needs

Identifying Possible Areas That Need Training

Planning to Identify Training Needs

Procedures for Identifying Training Needs

Standard Interviews

Job Analysis Grid Interviews

Need-to-Know Process

Performance Standards

Meetings

Questionnaires

Tests and Assessments

Combination Methods

Combining Inputs and Reporting Results

Transferring Training Needs to Training Objectives

Considering External Services and Products

Procedure Summaries and Checklists

Appendix: Forms

The procedure summaries and checklists section includes the procedural steps introduced in the book along with checklists to ensure proper implementation. This provides you with a quick reference and guidelines for identifying training needs.

Various forms are introduced in this book. These forms are furnished in the appendix and also on an accompanying CD-ROM for you to copy and use.

By the book's conclusion, you will have analyzed the basic effectiveness of your training department, learned a number of procedures to identify training needs, discovered how to determine which procedure to use, and learned how to implement and report a training needs identification study.

Let's begin with an analysis and review of your current training function.

PART ONE

Assessing Your Present Training Function

2

Analyzing Your Training Department's Effectiveness

Any time you embark on something new, it is best to know from where you are starting. You need to know where you are before you can make a plan to go somewhere else, so in this chapter and in Chapter 3, you will spend some time analyzing and reviewing your current training function. In the process, you may also identify some needs the training function has for improving its performance.

The analysis will concentrate on how well the training function is perceived as meeting the organization's requirements. The review will identify the mission, structure, and key result areas of training and, as by-products, will create an organizational chart and initial position descriptions for training positions.

Definitions

Before beginning, there are a few definitions of terms used in this book that you should know:

❑ **Organization.** This term is used to describe the company, employer, division, association, or whatever else is the overall entity for whom you work.

❑ **Function.** Function is used to describe a major organizational activity—a key result area—of the organization such as human

13

resources, sales, finance, and training. In many cases this is a department, so at times the words function and department are used interchangeably.

❒ **Clients.** This word refers to the individuals and entities who use the services of the training function.

❒ **Internal Clients.** Internal clients are the individuals, departments, and functions within your organization that use the services of the training function.

❒ **External Clients.** These are the individuals and organizations that are not a part of your organization but who make use of the training function's services.

❒ **Manager and Supervisor.** These terms are used to describe positions accountable for managing other employees. Although they are used in this book somewhat interchangeably, supervisors are generally considered to be those who oversee non-management employees, and managers are those who survey management and professional employees.

Analysis

There are a number of ways your training function can be analyzed and its strengths and areas of needed improvement identified. Since a premise of this book is that the training function within an organization should have as a part of its mission the meeting of the organization's requirements, how successful the function is perceived as accomplishing that will be the basis for the analysis. This will be accomplished by obtaining comparisons of perceptions regarding the training function's performance. For that purpose the following twelve activities of training will be used:

1. Training organization
2. Training personnel
3. Employee training
4. Employee development
5. Remedial training

6. Organizational development

7. Communications

8. Training facilities

9. Identifying training needs

10. Training design and development

11. Training delivery

12. Assessment and measurement

In Figure 2-1 these activities are repeated along with their definitions. A short line also precedes each activity. Read the definitions and then indicate how important you believe each activity is to your training function. Do this by distributing one hundred points among the twelve activities. Write the number of points you are assigning to an activity on the line preceding it. If an activity does not apply to your training function, use a zero for that activity. The points you assign to all activities should total one hundred.

Your Performance Perceptions

We will be using your assignment of points later in this chapter. Now, let's determine how you and others perceive the effectiveness of the training function. To do that we will use the same twelve activities, but ask different questions and use a different form.

First, let's see how you rate the function in each activity and how you perceive others rate them.

There are two factors to consider before answering the above questions—training conducted by other areas and training activities that are outsourced.

In some organizations, training is conducted by other than a centralized training function. Often it is conducted by individual employees in operating departments who have been identified as trainers for those areas. If this situation exists within your organization, and your training function is accountable for the operating department trainers' results, you need to consider them in answering the questions. However, if they are seen as completely

Figure 2-1.
TRAINING ACTIVITIES.

_____ Training organization—the mission of the training function, its internal structure, and internal and external relationships

_____ Training personnel—the selection, qualifications, and motivation of department employees

_____ Employee training—training in requirements of specific job or organizational activities

_____ Employee development—training in requirements for future jobs and broadening of abilities for a current job

_____ Remedial training—training conducted to correct inadequate basic skills such as mathematics, reading, speaking, and writing.

_____ Organizational development—improving communication and understanding throughout the organization in order to produce effective, functioning teams; establishing or changing to a desired culture; and responding to changing conditions

_____ Communications—internal and external communication of the training department's abilities, results, and offerings

_____ Training facilities—the physical space and equipment allocated to conduct training

_____ Identifying training needs—determining the training required by individual employees and the organization

_____ Training design and development—creating, structuring, or obtaining a training program to meet specific objectives or outcomes

_____ Training delivery—implementation of training to meet specific needs and objectives (e.g., courses, programs, self-study, etc.)

_____ Assessment and measurement—using valid and reliable methods to determine the current abilities of an individual and the results of training activities

Total points = 100

separate from a centralized training function, you may want to consider treating them as different training functions by answering the above questions separately for each of them.

Outsourcing of training is a relatively recent development. In outsourcing, subjects, and at times the entire training functions, are assigned to an external organization. Most of the time this occurs when the external organization can supply unique skills or lower implementation costs. At other times, there may be considerations such as legal compliance, speed of delivery, specialized knowledge, and improving service. If training outsourcing is used by your organization, you can still answer the above questions for the portion of the training they perform. If only a portion of training is outsourced, you can treat that portion as a separate training function.

Answer three additional questions for each of the activities that are applicable to your training function. The questions are:

1. On a one to nine scale (one being low, five being typical, and nine being high), how well do *you* think the training function is performing in this activity?

2. On a one to nine scale (one being low, five being typical, and nine being high), how well do you think *employees* of the training function feel it is performing in this activity?

3. On a one to nine scale (one being low, five being typical, and nine being high), how well do you think the internal *clients* of the training function within the organization feel it is performing in this activity?

Figure 2-2 illustrates a form that you may use. It is a table in which you can record your answers to each question for each activity. At this point, you should answer the questions without consultation with others. *Your* perceptions are what's important here.

Write your numerical answers for the three questions in the second, third, and fourth columns opposite the appropriate activities. For activities not applicable to your training functions, place an X in the columns opposite the activity. Remember to use the nine-point scale for your answers (one being low, five being typical, and nine being high). When you have entered answers for the

Figure 2-2.
YOUR TRAINING ACTIVITY PERCEPTIONS.

Activities	Your Ratings	Your Perception of Department Employees' Ratings	Your Perceptions of Internal Clients' Ratings
Training Organization			
Training Personnel			
Employee Training			
Employee Development			
Remedial Training			
Organizational Development			
Communications			
Training Facilities			
Identifying Training Needs			
Training Design and Development			
Training Delivery			
Assessment and Measurement			
Overall Department			

twelve activities but not for overall department, turn to the page following the table for instructions.

After you have entered three ratings for each of the twelve activities, answer the following similar three questions for the overall training function:

1. On a one to nine scale (one being low, five being typical, and nine being high), how well do *you* think the overall training function is performing?

2. On a one to nine scale (one being low, five being typical, and nine being high), how well do you think *employees* of the training function feel it is performing?

3. On a one to nine scale (one being low, five being typical, and nine being high), how well do you think the internal *clients* of the training function within the organization feel it is performing?

Write your numerical responses to the above questions in the last row of the form opposite the "overall department" box.

Performance Perceptions of Others

Your recorded responses in the table featured in Figure 2-2 provide an overview of how you rate your training function's effectiveness and how you perceive others will rate it. However, these are just your perceptions, and although your own ratings should accurately reflect them, your sense of how the other two groups might answer may not be as accurate. In any event, you should know how those two groups rate training and if there are differences between their ratings and yours.

Since the basic mission of the training function is to assist in meeting organization requirements, knowing how employees of the training function and how internal clients perceive its effectiveness are very important. You can discover their perceptions by asking these same questions of the two groups. You can then compare your ratings with those supplied by training's employees and its internal clients. This will allow you to identify areas of differences that require attention as well as areas in which all are in agreement.

Figure 2-3 illustrates a sample communication that can be used to obtain answers to the questions from the two groups.

Why not just have a meeting, you may ask? Well, meeting discussions and group composition can sometimes affect individual ratings, so you will probably receive more accurate and independent perception ratings by unsigned responses in answer to your written inquiry.

Note, the sample communication form requests ratings for all twelve activities of training as well as the overall function, so it

Figure 2-3.

TRAINING DEPARTMENT SURVEY.

TO: (group or type of employee)

The training department is currently conducting an audit of its performance. As one of our (clients/department employees), your perceptions will be of considerable assistance with this project. Please take a few moments to complete this form and return it. No identification is requested.

The following are the categories of training and the definitions we are using. Read each one and then rate how well you feel our training department is performing in that category. The questions ask for your perceptions—what you think—not necessarily information based on an evaluation of factual performance criteria.

For your ratings, use a nine-point scale (1 = Low; 5 = Typical; and 9 = High). Select a single number from that scale for each rating. Write the number on the line in front of the category. If you do not have any idea as to how well training is performing in a category, place an "X" on the line for that category.

_____ Training organization—the mission of the function, its internal structure, and internal and external relationships

_____ Training personnel—the selection, qualifications, and motivation of department employees

_____ Employee training—training in requirements for specific job or organizational activities

_____ Employee development—training in requirements for a future job and broadening of abilities for a current job

_____ Remedial training—training conducted to correct inadequate skills, such as in math, reading, or writing

_____ Communications—internal and external communication of the department's abilities and offerings

_____ Identifying training needs—determining the required training of individual employees and the organization

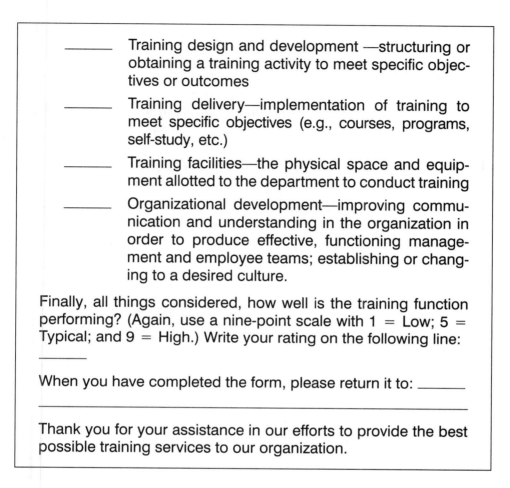

———— Training design and development —structuring or obtaining a training activity to meet specific objectives or outcomes

———— Training delivery—implementation of training to meet specific objectives (e.g., courses, programs, self-study, etc.)

———— Training facilities—the physical space and equipment allotted to the department to conduct training

———— Organizational development—improving communication and understanding in the organization in order to produce effective, functioning management and employee teams; establishing or changing to a desired culture.

Finally, all things considered, how well is the training function performing? (Again, use a nine-point scale with 1 = Low; 5 = Typical; and 9 = High.) Write your rating on the following line:

————

When you have completed the form, please return it to: ————

Thank you for your assistance in our efforts to provide the best possible training services to our organization.

can only be used with people who have knowledge of the department's performance in all categories. If you wish to use it with people who only know performance in some of the categories, you need to revise the form to include just those categories. However, in all cases request an overall rating of the department's performance.

Even though identification of the individual completing the form is not required or requested, you need to know from what group of employees or department a completed from is received. You need to know if a completed form is from an internal client or a department employee. You may also want to know whether a completed form is from management, professional, or nonmanagement employees. You can accomplish this by asking on the form for information to identify an employee group or area (not individual employee identification), using different colored paper for the form you send to each group, or referring to the group in the address or text.

Do not use numerical or alphabetic coding on the form for identification. Such coding is obvious and tends to make people question whether or not they can be individually identified. Hidden coding can destroy your ability later to obtain information.

> An Ohio-based company's training department wanted to obtain performance evaluations from operating managers. It felt that by having unsigned replies to a supplied form, the managers would be more forthcoming with their responses. However, the training department wanted to know from what areas it was receiving input.
>
> The department decided to state in the accompanying letter that the form was not to be signed—no identification was required. However, each form was coded with pinholes located beneath the staple. The coding was discovered and the department was never able to obtain input in the future. Its reputation of honesty had been destroyed.

Combining Responses

When you have received all of the completed training department survey forms, the next step is to combine the individual responses by group. To accomplish that, first sort the responses into two areas: training department employees and internal clients. Then, total the rating for each group in each category and divide that total by the number of ratings received for the category. (You are calculating an average rating for each category.)

For example, assume you received the following ratings from five internal clients regarding training personnel. Each client represented a different function within the organization. They and their ratings are:

Client Function	*Rating*
Human resources	7
Accounting	5

Scheduling	8
Administration	6
Marketing	4

The ratings total thirty. Since there were five responses, the average internal client rating for training personnel is six. However, all clients may not respond to all activities. For example, if only four of the five internal clients responded to the question about facilities, then the average rating is based on just the four responses.

Client Function	*Rating*
Human resources	6
Accounting	4
Scheduling	5
Administration	5
Marketing	No response

Here the total ratings from internal clients is twenty. Dividing the total by four (the number of internal clients who actually responded) results in an average rating of five.

Figure 2-4 shows a training rating comparison form that can be used for recording your ratings and the averages from department employees and internal clients in each activity. Column one lists the activities. Column two is for your ratings. Column three is for the average ratings of the training department's employees, and column four is for the average ratings of training's internal clients.

To complete the form, you first enter your ratings for each activity from the second column of your training activity perception form (see Figure 2-2) into the second column of the Training Rating Comparison Form (Figure 2-4).

You next enter the average activity ratings you calculated for each group. (Again, the training department employees' average ratings are entered in column three, and the internal clients' average ratings are entered in column four.)

Figure 2-4.

TRAINING RATING COMPARISON FORM.

Activities	Your Rating	Average Department Employee's Rating	Average Internal Client's Rating	Degree of Agreement
Training Organization				
Training Personnel				
Employee Training				
Employee Development				
Remedial Training				
Organizational Development				
Communications				
Training Facilities				
Identifying Training Needs				
Training Design and Development				
Training Delivery				
Assessment and Measurement				
Overall Department				

If all the ratings for an activity (whether good or poor) are the same, that is a positive result. All groups perceive the activity the same way. Where there are significant differences among ratings, you need to perform some additional investigation to learn why those ratings differ. In our example, average ratings for training function employees are from a group of four employees, and average ratings for internal clients are from a group of five.

Figure 2-5 is an example of the form with all ratings entered. Note that the ratings have been entered to the left side of each column.

Note that the columns are quite wide, so there is room to write another number to the right. That second number is obtained from the following table:

Rating Number	Coding Number
1, 2, 3, or 4	1
5	2
6, 7, 8, or 9	3

To use the table, find the rating number for the activity and then enter the corresponding coding number in the same space. Enter it to the right of the space. For example:

Identifying Training Needs	5	2	5	2	3	1	

The rating number is the one on the left in each space, and the coding number is on the right. If a rating number is in decimals or fractions, round if off to the nearest whole number.

Figure 2-6 shows the same example form with all coding numbers entered.

The last column, degree of agreement, is for you to indicate the amount of agreement between the three ratings for each activity. For that you are first going to code the ratings.

With the ratings coded and entered, it is possible to identify the degree of agreement between all three. That is determined by the relationship between the three coded ratings for each activity.

(text continues on page 28)

Figure 2-5.

COMPLETED TRAINING RATING COMPARISON FORM.

Activities	Your Rating	Average Department Employee's Rating	Average Internal Client's Rating	Degree of Agreement
Training Organization	7	5	5	
Training Personnel	7	8	6	
Employee Training	6	8	5	
Employee Development	7	7	6	
Remedial Training	5	5	5	
Organizational Development	4	4	3	
Communications	7	4	3	
Training Facilities	7	5	8	
Identifying Training Needs	5	5	3	
Training Design and Development	6	8	5	
Training Delivery	8	9	7	
Assessment and Measurement	5	5	4	
Overall Department	7	8	6	

Figure 2-6.

CODED TRAINING RATING COMPARISON FORM.

Activities	Your Rating		Average Department Employee's Rating		Average Internal Client's Rating		Degree of Agreement
Training Organization	7	3	5	2	5	2	
Training Personnel	7	3	8	3	6	3	
Employee Training	6	3	8	3	5	2	
Employee Development	7	3	7	3	6	3	
Remedial Training	5	2	5	2	5	2	
Organizational Development	4	1	4	1	3	1	
Communications	7	3	4	1	3	1	
Training Facilities	7	3	5	2	8	3	
Identifying Training Needs	5	2	5	2	3	1	
Training Design and Development	6	3	8	3	5	2	
Training Delivery	8	3	9	3	7	3	
Assessment and Measurement	5	2	5	2	4	1	
Overall Department	7	3	8	3	6	3	

Use the table below to determine degree of agreement and enter the appropriate number in the last column of the form.

Coded Ratings	*Number to Enter*
If all the coded ratings are the same number enter	100
If two of the coded ratings are the same but one differs by one number, enter	85
If two of the coded ratings are the same but one differs by two numbers, enter	50
If all three numbers differ, enter	40

The following is an example:

Identifying Training Needs	5	2	5	2	3	1	85

Figure 2-7 shows the same example form with the degree of agreement column entries. The next step is to identify areas of agreement and disagreement, and activities identified as needing improvement.

Analyzing Differing Levels of Agreement

Activities with eighty-five and one hundred degrees of agreement indicate you and the other two groups perceive the training function as performing in the relatively same way. However, a forty or fifty-degree agreement indicates there is a significant difference in perceptions for that activity. Those differences should be investigated. You need to discover what is causing the varying perceptions and what actions are required to obtain similar perceptions.

Actually, discovering differing opinions regarding the training department's performance identifies a training need in itself, but instead of an organization or an individual employee training need, it recognizes a need for improvement of the training function—a valuable piece of information to have.

In Figure 2-7, communications is the only activity that is rated forty or fifty. It shows what can happen when your ratings are

Figure 2-7.

TRAINING RATING COMPARISON FORM SHOWING DEGREE OF AGREEMENT.

Activities	Your Rating		Average Department Employee's Rating		Average Internal Client's Rating		Degree of Agreement
Training Organization	7	3	5	2	5	2	85
Training Personnel	7	3	8	3	6	3	100
Employee Training	6	3	8	3	5	2	85
Employee Development	7	3	7	3	6	3	100
Remedial Training	5	2	5	2	5	2	100
Organizational Development	4	1	4	1	3	1	100
Communications	7	3	4	1	3	1	50
Training Facilities	7	3	5	2	8	3	85
Identifying Training Needs	5	2	5	2	3	1	85
Training Design and Development	6	3	8	3	5	2	85
Training Delivery	8	3	9	3	7	3	100
Assessment and Measurement	5	2	5	2	4	1	85
Overall Department	7	3	8	3	6	3	100

significantly higher than those of both training department employees and internal clients. In such a situation, the questions you want to answer are:

❒ What are the reasons for the ratings of the department employees and internal clients?

❒ What is the basis for my rating?

❒ What actions are required to produce similar ratings?

Asking these questions may produce performance facts of which you are unaware. The answers may also uncover incorrect information about the training function. Whatever the answers, you will have information that will allow you to take corrective action.

Analyzing Low Ratings

Next, you need to identify those areas of agreement (areas rated with eighty-five and one hundred degrees of agreement) where the ratings on activities are basically the same: low. These are areas where there is agreement among the three groups—agreement that the activities require improvement. If this occurs, you have identified another need of the training function.

In our example, organizational development received a coded rating of one from all three groups. You need to determine why this happened. Here you must ask:

❒ What is the basis for the ratings of the department employees and internal clients?

❒ What is the basis for my rating?

❒ What actions are required to produce higher ratings?

If the answers you receive are similar, they probably identify the problem. However, you may discover that although you all rated the activity as requiring improvement, you each did so for different reasons. If that is the situation, you have two steps you must take: First, take action to ensure all groups have the same correct information. Second, take action to improve performance in the activity.

Prioritizing Areas for Further Investigation

So, what do you investigate first? Do you investigate the basis for differing perceptions of an activity or do you investigate why an activity is rated as needing improvement?

There is no one correct answer. Both areas are important to a successful training function, and if either or both are identified through your analysis, they should be investigated and corrected before moving on. However, you need to decide which area to tackle first.

For example, if your training department's delivery is rated as needing improvement, that will probably be the first area you will want to investigate. It implies the training function's primary activity is not effective. On the other hand, if your facilities are rated as needing improvement, and there is very low agreement on the ratings for the overall department, you will probably want to first resolve the rating differences for the overall department, and handle the training facility difference later.

An approach that can provide assistance is to review the points you earlier assigned each activity to indicate how important it was to the training function's success. (See Figure 2-1.)

Any training activity to which you assigned more than twenty points was identified by you as a significant contributor to training's success. If any of the activities you assigned twenty or more points to received low ratings or low levels of agreement among ratings, they might be the ones to first investigate.

Using your knowledge of the organization and the training department, prioritize any areas of low ratings and low levels of agreement. Prioritize them in the order to be further investigated. (You can use the training activity priority list form shown in Figure 2-8.)

The top half of the form should list the activities rated as needing improvement along with their individual ratings. These should be listed in their descending order of importance—the sequence in which you believe they should be further investigated.

The lower half of the form is for listing the activities in which there is significant disagreement among ratings. Again, list them in their descending order of importance—the sequence in which you believe they should be further investigated.

(text continues on page 34)

Figure 2-8.
TRAINING ACTIVITY PRIORITY LIST.

Activities Requiring Improvement   Rating

1. _____   _____

2. _____   _____

3. _____   _____

4. _____   _____

5. _____   _____

6. _____   _____

7. _____   _____

8. _____   _____

9. _____   _____

10. _____   _____

Activities with Low Rating Agreement   Agreement

1. _____   _____

2. _____   _____

3. _____   _____

4. _____   _____

5. _____   _____

6. _____   _____

7. _____   _____

8. _____   _____

9. _____   _____

10. _____   _____

Activities Requiring Further Investigation   Agreement   Rating

1. _____   _____   _____

2. _____   _____   _____

3. _____   _____   _____

4. _____   _____   _____

5. _____   _____   _____

6. _____   _____   _____

7. _____   _____   _____

8. _____   _____   _____

9. _____   _____   _____

10. _____   _____   _____

11. _____   _____   _____

12. _____   _____   _____

13. _____   _____   _____

14. _____   _____   _____

15. _____   _____   _____

16. _____   _____   _____

17. _____   _____   _____

18. _____   _____   _____

19. _____   _____   _____

20. _____   _____   _____

By completing this first page of this form, you have an initial plan for the order in which to investigate activities, but it is comprised of two separate lists. They should be combined into one list, so you have to decide which activity from both lists to consider first. You can then combine them into one list. The second page of the form provides a format for that. Here again you should base your prioritizing on the importance of each activity to the success of the training function, your knowledge of the organization, and the training function.

Further Analysis

Once you have identified activities requiring further investigation and prioritized them in an order for consideration, there are several additional pieces of information that can be of assistance. Figures 2-9 and 2-10 provide you with forms you can use to examine the degrees of agreement between your perceptions of the training department employees' ratings and the ratings of training's internal clients.

As with the previous forms, use the average ratings from each group. However, for these forms use your perceptions of each group's ratings. Your perceptions of the department employees' ratings are in the third column of the form in Figure 2-2. Your perceptions for the internal clients' ratings are in the fourth column of the form in Figure 2-2. For example, when entered on the form in Figure 2-9, they would appear as:

Activities	Your Perception of Department Employees' Rating	Average Department Employee's Evaluation	Degree of Agreement
Employee Training	8	4	

Degree of Agreement

With the forms in Figures 2-9 and 2-10 the fourth column, degree of agreement, indicates the relationship between your perception of how the other group will rate an activity and how that group

Figure 2-9.

DEPARTMENT EMPLOYEES' RATING COMPARISON.

Activities	Your Perception of Department Employees' Rating	Average Department Employee's Evaluation	Degree of Agreement
Training Organization			
Training Personnel			
Employee Training			
Employee Development			
Remedial Training			
Organizational Development			
Communications			
Training Facilities			
Identifying Training Needs			
Training Design and Development			
Training Delivery			
Assessment and Measurement			
Overall Department			

Figure 2-10.

A BLANK INTERNAL CLIENTS' RATING COMPARISON FORM.

Activities	Your Perception of Internal Clients' Ratings	Average Internal Client's Evaluation	Degree of Agreement
Training Organization			
Training Personnel			
Employee Training			
Employee Development			
Remedial Training			
Organizational Development			
Communications			
Training Facilities			
Identifying Training Needs			
Training Design and Development			
Training Delivery			
Assessment and Measurement			
Overall Department			

actually rated it. When the ratings are on the same side of five, you both see the activity as above or below typical but to slightly different degrees. However, when the two ratings are on both sides of five, one of you is seeing the activity as requiring improvement and the other is seeing it as above typical.

The following table provides a method of presenting the two ratings with a single degree of agreement number:

Ratings	*Number to Enter*
If the two ratings are the same number, enter	100
If the two ratings are different, but on the same side of five, enter	85
If one rating is at five and the other below or above five, enter	50
If the two ratings are different and on both sides of five, enter	30

If any of the degrees of agreement are rated thirty or fifty, it means there is a significant difference between your perception of how the other group rates a training activity and how that group actually rates it. That information should assist you in further investigating the earlier prioritized areas.

Figure 2-11 shows how a completed form for internal clients would look. Two activities on that form received a thirty in degree of agreement: communication and employment development, and three activities received a fifty: organization, employee training, and assessment and measurement.

You can also review the range of ratings for each group. For example, the group average rating may be five, and the range of ratings from four to seven. In such an instance, the average of five well represents all ratings. However, if the ratings of six individual group members were five, one, nine, five, eight, and two, the average might still be five, but that average is not as representative of the range of the ratings (which went from one to nine).

Figure 2-11.

A COMPLETED INTERNAL CLIENTS' RATING COMPARISON FORM.

Activities	Your Perception of Internal Clients' Ratings	Average Internal Client's Evaluation	Degree of Agreement
Training Organization	6	5	50
Training Personnel	7	8	85
Employee Training	7	5	50
Employee Development	6	4	30
Remedial Training	6	6	100
Organizational Development	7	7	100
Communications	7	4	30
Training Facilities	6	7	85
Identifying Training Needs	5	5	100
Training Design and Development	7	6	85
Training Delivery	8	7	85
Assessment and Measurement	5	4	50
Overall Department	7	6	85

Methods of Further Investigation

If you have identified any activities that require further investigation because of differences in ratings or low ratings, you need to revisit the people who initially provided the information. This can be accomplished through the use of a follow-up questionnaire, individual meetings, and group meetings.

If there are just one or two activities that are rated low or inconsistently, and it appears all you require is some explanatory information, a follow-up memo may do. At other times such a memo may be the first step, and information obtained from it is used to develop interview questions or meeting subjects. A sample of such a memo follows:

To: _____

As a part of our recently conducted training department analysis, we discovered there are differences in the perceptions of how well the training function is performing in the following activities:

(List activities with definitions.)

It will be of considerable assistance if you will provide a few comments or examples to indicate the basis for your perceptions in these activities.

Another approach is to interview people. In an interview you will be asking similar questions:

❒ What are examples of the basis for your rating of (activity)?

❒ What can be done to increase your rating of (activity)?

❒ Has your rating of (activity) changed recently?

The advantage of the interview is that it allows you to ask follow-up questions based on the answers you receive. Interview preparations and guidelines are covered in Chapter 8 later in this book.

If you have a number of people to revisit, a group meeting may be a more practical approach. Like interviewing, meeting procedures are dealt with later in this book.

Other Insights

You can also gain additional insights into the effectiveness of the training function by using a number of other standard calculations and measures that can be of assistance. For that purpose Figure 2-12 and Figure 2-13 can help.

The cost comparison analysis (see Figure 2-12) provides standard information. It can be compared with other training departments if the information from them is available. Sometimes, such information is collected and published by industry groups and professional associations, and some of the information such as total employees, sales, and total assets is available in annual reports. It also can provide a yearly comparison that you can use to identify any changes in training's operation.

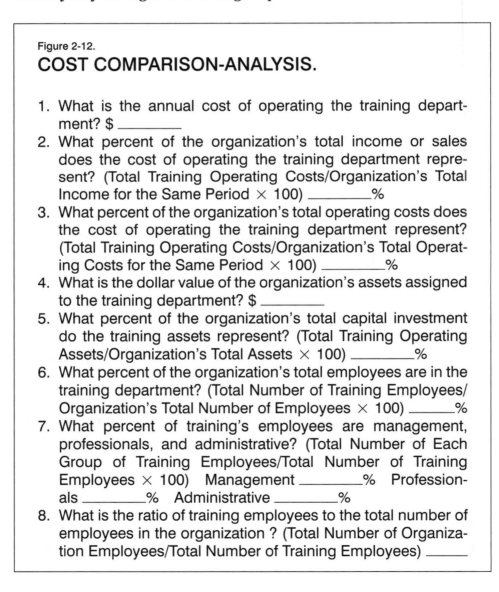

Figure 2-12.

COST COMPARISON-ANALYSIS.

1. What is the annual cost of operating the training department? $ _____
2. What percent of the organization's total income or sales does the cost of operating the training department represent? (Total Training Operating Costs/Organization's Total Income for the Same Period × 100) _____%
3. What percent of the organization's total operating costs does the cost of operating the training department represent? (Total Training Operating Costs/Organization's Total Operating Costs for the Same Period × 100) _____%
4. What is the dollar value of the organization's assets assigned to the training department? $ _____
5. What percent of the organization's total capital investment do the training assets represent? (Total Training Operating Assets/Organization's Total Assets × 100) _____%
6. What percent of the organization's total employees are in the training department? (Total Number of Training Employees/Organization's Total Number of Employees × 100) _____%
7. What percent of training's employees are management, professionals, and administrative? (Total Number of Each Group of Training Employees/Total Number of Training Employees × 100) Management _____% Professionals _____% Administrative _____%
8. What is the ratio of training employees to the total number of employees in the organization? (Total Number of Organization Employees/Total Number of Training Employees) _____

Figure 2-13.

ASSET COMPARISON MATRIX.

For this analysis your assets are considered to be employees, budget dollars, equipment, and time. Use numbers for employees, dollars for budget, numbers for equipment, and hours for time, or you may use percents for any or all.

If an activity does not apply, place an X on the appropriate lines. If some people, budget dollars, equipment, or time is assigned to more than one activity, use partial numbers. For example, an employee assigned to both remedial training and employee training could be entered as 0.5 in each. You may want to enter the actual time consumed by the activity rather than the time assigned.

Activity	Employees	Budget	Equipment	Time
Organization	_____	_____	_____	_____
Personnel	_____	_____	_____	_____
Employee training	_____	_____	_____	_____
Employee development	_____	_____	_____	_____
Remedial training	_____	_____	_____	_____
Organizational development	_____	_____	_____	_____
Communications	_____	_____	_____	_____
Facilities	_____	_____	_____	_____
Identifying training needs	_____	_____	_____	_____
Training design and development	_____	_____	_____	_____
Training delivery	_____	_____	_____	_____
Assessment and measurement	_____	_____	_____	_____

The asset comparison matrix (Figure 2-13) allows you to compare the relationships between training's various assets and how they are assigned. Are they assigned where they are needed? Are some areas overstaffed and some understaffed? Does the budget assigned to an activity support that activity's contribution? Is there a proper relationship between the assets assigned to each activity?

All of the approaches suggested in this chapter are meant to give you a better understanding of training's real and perceived effectiveness to help you take any corrective actions that are required. You want to ensure your current operation is performing as it should before initiating new activities such as identifying additional training needs.

You should also be knowledgeable and comfortable with the training function's organization, which is discussed in Chapter 3.

3

Analyzing Your Training Department's Organization

So far we have analyzed how your training function is perceived within the organization. Now we are going to turn our attention to obtaining all of the information required to operate the training department. Much of this information may already be available. If so, then this is only a collecting activity. However, if information is not available, you need procedures for creating it. This information includes:

❏ The training department's organization and positions

❏ The type of training delivery systems used

❏ The type of personnel conducting training

❏ Methods currently used to identify training needs

❏ Parties responsible for identifying training needs

The Training Function's Organization and Positions

Many training departments will have an organization chart and position descriptions. Even if you have such items, you should review the principles introduced in this chapter to determine how well they apply. You may want to make some revisions. If you do not have such items, then the instructions and forms in this chapter will help you to produce an organization chart for your department and basic descriptions of training department positions.

However, this book does not attempt to provide details of all possible organization structures, position description formats, and organization chart types. It is merely meant to give you a procedure to create basic ones to use with this book.

Training's Mission Statement

The first step in creating an organization chart and position descriptions for training is to state the training function's objective or mission—why it exists within the organization. What is its primary purpose? What makes it unique? Why is it different from every other function of the organization? The mission statement should be a direct, simple, and easily understood. If you already have one, that's great. If not, you need to create one.

Here's the mission statement offered as the basis for this book:

> To provide employees with the skills and knowledge required to ensure optimum performance results, develop a cache of employees qualified to meet the organization's operational needs and objectives, and contribute to positive morale, employee satisfaction, and development

Your training function's mission statement does not have to be the same. There may be other factors to consider within your organization. Your organization may even have a format for mission statements.

A review of a number of training department mission statements identified some common elements, among them:

❏ Providing employees with the skills and knowledge required for their jobs

❏ Contributing to meeting the organization's performance objectives

❏ Assisting with maintaining employee morale

❏ Ensuring the availability of qualified employees to meet future needs

❐ Meeting specifically identified employee and organization needs

❐ Operating within approved budgets

❐ Improving relationships with internal and external clients

❐ Providing measurable results

If you already have a training mission statement, review it to ensure it describes the function's purpose. If it does not, perhaps it needs revision. If you do not have a mission statement, now is the time to write one. In doing so, you might find it helpful to meet with employees in training, internal clients, and whomever training reports to. These individuals can provide valuable insights as to what they believe training should accomplish.

When you are ready, write what you believe the mission statement is or should be on the following lines. Write it in one sentence (beginning with the word "to").

To _____

_____

_____

Key Result Areas

Next, you need to identify the key result areas that training is required to fulfill in order to meet its mission, or its objective. Key result areas are the major activities assigned to training. For example, the key result areas of a human resources department usually include activities such as recruiting, compensation, benefits, and employee relations. The key result areas of the finance department include accounts payable, accounts receivable, payroll, credit, and budgeting and analysis activities.

To identify your training department's key result areas, consider the major activities the department is supposed to accomplish. Consider also the mission statement. Fulfilling the key result areas should ensure the department's mission statement is also fulfilled.

The list of activities provided in Chapter 2 may be of assistance in identifying your training department's key result areas. However, you may have some that are not listed, and you may not have all on the list. These activities include accountability for:

- ❐ Training organization
- ❐ Training personnel
- ❐ Employee training
- ❐ Employee development
- ❐ Remedial training
- ❐ Organizational development
- ❐ Communications
- ❐ Management and maintenance of training facilities
- ❐ Identification of training needs
- ❐ Training design and development
- ❐ Training delivery
- ❐ Assessment and measurement

Figure 3-1 is a short form on which you can write the key result areas you have identified for your training department.

The Organization Chart

Now let's construct a training department organizational chart based on the mission statement and key result areas you have identified. There are many theories on what makes for the best organization chart format. For our purposes, we are going to use a traditional approach. Here are the basic guidelines for that approach:

- ❐ Every position should have a separate box on the organization chart, with the position's title written within the box.
- ❐ If there is more than one job with a similar title, the job title should be shown in one box with the number of such jobs written beneath the job title.
- ❐ Every position box should indicate a reporting relationship. There should be a line connecting either the top or side of the

---

Figure 3-1.

KEY RESULT AREAS.

On the lines below, write the key result areas you have identified for your training function, but include only the eight most important ones. There may be more, but limiting the number will ensure the most important are listed. Each should be a descriptive phrase or single sentence. List them in descending order of importance for the department's success.

1. _____

2. _____

3. _____

4. _____

5. _____

6. _____

7. _____

8. _____

---

box to the position to which it reports. Even the top position box on the organization chart should have a line going upward to indicate that it, too, reports to another position.

❏ Positions that supervise other positions should have a line from the bottom of their position boxes to the boxes of the other positions. In some cases, the line may be from the side of the position box.

❏ Positions should be shown at their relative levels of accountability within the department. Those with the most accountability should be higher on the organization chart than those with lower accountability.

Let's assume a training department consists of the following positions:

- ❐ Training director
- ❐ Facilities manager
- ❐ Training delivery manager
- ❐ Training design manager
- ❐ Four skill trainers
- ❐ Two management trainers
- ❐ Scheduler
- ❐ Administrative assistant
- ❐ Two designers
- ❐ Researcher

Now, let's list these positions again, but this time in descending order of accountability by levels, so each row represents a different level on an organization chart, as follows:

Training Director		
Facilities Manager	Training Delivery	Training Design
Skill Trainers (4)	Manager	Manager
Scheduler	Management	Designers (2)
	Trainers (2)	
	Researcher	

You'll notice the administrative assistant position is not shown at a level of accountability. This is because it is a staff support position; its chart position will be described in a moment.

Drawing the Organization Chart

A completed organization chart for this department is shown in Figure 3-2. Observe how it agrees with the organization chart guidelines.

The lines connecting the boxes are called lines of authority (also sometimes referred to as lines of communication) since they indicate how authority is delegated from one position to another (or how formal communication flows through the organization).

As mentioned previously, the administrative assistant is a staff support position, so it is not in the line of authority for the depart-

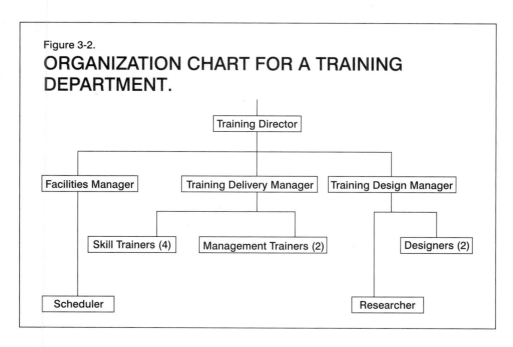

Figure 3-2.

ORGANIZATION CHART FOR A TRAINING DEPARTMENT.

ment. Its level is therefore based on the position to which it reports. In our example, the administrative assistant reports to the training director, so it will be shown at that level but to the side rather than directly beneath the training director's position box. Figure 3-3 shows the organization chart with the administrative assistant position added.

You may have heard of or seen dotted lines on an organization chart. Dotted lines indicate there is a relationship between positions for some portion of a job. For example, a small business such as a fast-food franchise may have a marketing manager who reports to the store manager. That is a typical solid line relationship. However, the same marketing manager may be accountable to the franchiser's director of marketing for the contents of all advertising. That relationship could be shown by a dotted line. However, organization charts with solid and dotted lines can be very confusing, so for our purposes, stay with solid lines.

There are also some organizational charts that use multiple solid lines from one position to more than one other position. In some cases, a single position may be accountable to more than one position for different responsibilities of its job. (See the concept of *unity of command* described later in this chapter.) Generally, these are forms of matrix organizations, but they represent a more complex chart than required for our purposes.

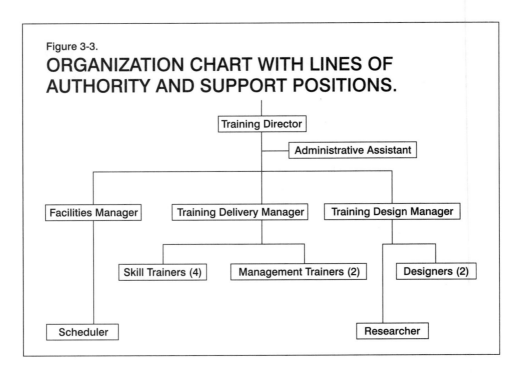

Figure 3-3.

ORGANIZATION CHART WITH LINES OF AUTHORITY AND SUPPORT POSITIONS.

If you do not already have a training organization chart and cannot complete one as described, you may have to obtain additional information. Again, meeting with the department's employees, as well as with those in the company to whom the training function reports, may furnish the information required. You may even discover that the department's organization is unclear.

A New Jersey electric motor manufacturer contracted a consulting firm to produce organization charts and position descriptions. The company employed 2,000 people at two locations in the state. It had fourteen departments or functions. The consulting firm was asked to document the existing organization.

As the consulting firm began to collect information, it discovered there was a completely different and unrecognized organization within the company, and it was this organization that actually operated the company. The company's senior management was surprised by the discovery. The consulting project was put on hold until an organization could be determined that met the company's operating objectives.

Key Result Area Assignments

A training department organization chart displays all positions and all the reporting relationships. However, you need to ensure that all positions have the proper assignments and that all of the key result areas have been assigned to positions. One way to accomplish this is to list the key result areas along with the position title primarily accountable for accomplishing that key result area. For this exercise you can use the form in Figure 3-4.

The form has lines for the eight key result areas you previously identified, but two lines are provided in the position title column opposite each key result area. This is because there may be more than one position assigned to a key result area. In such a case, each position should be accountable for a different element of the key result area.

If you are unable to identify a position accountable for a key result area, you have identified an activity that is probably only accomplished by accident. In such an instance, an assignment needs to be made. On the other hand, if you have more than one position opposite a key result area, be sure two or more positions have not been given the same assignment. That can lead to confusion and performance problems.

It is possible, however, that the key result area has been subdivided—with different positions accountable for different elements of it. If more than one position is assigned the same key result area, you need to investigate. Perhaps they are different elements of the same key result area. For example, let's say you identified the need to "Train all employees for job requirements" as a key result area. This activity may actually have two significantly different parts:

❏ Train all production workers

❏ Train all supervisors

In such a case, each element of the same key result area could be assigned to a different position.

Position Descriptions

The next organizational requirement is to write a position description for each job in the training function. Position descriptions

Figure 3-4.
KEY RESULT AREA/POSITION FORM.

Key Result Area	Position Title
_____	_____

may be written for a number of reasons (e.g., hiring, evaluation for compensation purposes, or job measurements). What we are concerned with is a position description that is written to describe exactly what the job is expected to accomplish.

Figure 3-5 is a form that provides a structure and guide for creating a position description. The first step is to write the position' s title, the date, and department name at the top of the form

Figure 3-5.

POSITION DESCRIPTION PREPARATION FORM.

Position Title: _____   Date: _____

Department: _____   Reports to: _____

Supervises: _____

Position Objective:

To _____

_____

Responsibilities:

1. _____

_____

2. _____

_____

3. _____

_____

4. _____

_____

5. _____

_____

6. _____

_____

7. _____

_____

8. _____

_____

on the appropriate lines. The date is important since it identifies when the position description was written, and that information is often necessary when comparing descriptions written for the same position at different times.

Next, you need to indicate the position's reporting relationships—that is, whom it reports to and any positions reporting to it. List these relationships by position title as well.

Using our earlier example from the training department organization chart, the training delivery manager's position description would appear as follows:

Position Title: Training Delivery Manager   Date: (today's date)
Department: Training   Reports to: Director of Training
Supervises: 4 Skill Trainers and 2 Management Trainers

Next, write the position's mission or objective. As with any mission statement, it should be direct, clear, and simple. It should describe the primary purpose of the position within the organization and department, what makes it unique, and why it is different from every other position.

> A Vermont real estate office employs a part-time individual (a local high school student) to clean its offices every weekday evening. He empties the wastebaskets, dusts the desks, vacuums the carpet, and mops the lobby floor. Once a week he cleans the windows.

> The mission statement for this job is simple, direct, and clear: To clean the real estate offices. This statement accurately describes what the position was created to accomplish and what makes it different from every other position in the organization.

Staying with our training delivery manager example, if you were to write the position's mission statement in one sentence (beginning with the word "to") it might read as follows:

> To manage the training delivery services of the department and implement all scheduled training courses

Once you have written the mission statement for a position, refer back to the assignment of key result areas. Ensure the key result area you identified as assigned to the position is covered by the mission statement.

The final portion of the position description preparation form calls for the position's responsibilities—the activities the position is to accomplish. List only the eight most important responsibilities, and list the responsibilities in descending order of importance for meeting the position's objective. Each responsibility should be written in one sentence beginning with a verb. For example:

❐ Supervises the department employees

❐ Processes new client applications

Often the most important responsibility reads very similar to the position's objective. For example, a position whose objective is "To represent the company to clients and prospective clients and sell the company's products" might have as its first responsibility: "Sells the company's products to clients and prospective clients."

Figure 3-6 is an example of a completed position description form for the training delivery manager.

You now have completed the steps for creating a basic position description for each job in the training department. However, additional work is required to develop a more comprehensive position description if it is to be used for other purposes such as salary evaluation, selection, and succession planning.

Actually, you may not be able to write all the training department's position descriptions without assistance. At the very least, the supervisor of each position should be involved. As a rule, the people in the positions and their supervisor should be in agreement on the position descriptions. However, if they cannot agree, it is ultimately the supervisor who must determine the contents of the position description. The supervisor is ultimately accountable for department results and what each position contributes to accomplishing the desired results.

There are three guidelines that can assist in determining the

---

Figure 3-6.

SAMPLE POSITION DESCRIPTION FOR A TRAINING MANAGER.

Position Title: Training Delivery Manager   **Date:** (today's date)

Department: Training   **Reports to:** Director of Training

Supervises: 4 Skill Trainers and 2 Management Trainers

Position Objective: To manage the training delivery services of the department and implement all scheduled training courses.

Responsibilities:
1. Manages training delivery services within approved budget.
2. Implements all training courses as scheduled.
3. Supervises employees reporting to her/him to ensure they meet performance standards.
4. Creates individual development plans for each employee reporting to him/her.
5. Serves as an active member of the Training Department's management team.
6. Assists the Training Director in developing annual budgets and plans.
7. Works with the Training Development Manager to create new courses and evaluate existing ones.
8. Recommends necessary revisions to existing training courses and possible areas requiring training courses.

---

effectiveness of an organization structure: delegation, unity of command, and span of control.

Delegation

Delegation is the passing of authority from one position to another. Authority is the power to take action—to make decisions. However, with delegation of authority comes responsibility. Responsibility is a statement of what a position is expected to do with the delegated authority. Authority should never be delegated without an accompanying responsibility, and responsibility must have a corresponding authority.

For example, you do not want to assign a position the authority to spend money without a responsibility as to how it is to be spent. On the other hand, if you hold a position responsible for maintaining a full workforce but do not delegate the authority to hire, it is impossible for the responsibility to be fulfilled.

Some position description formats require the authority for each responsibility to be listed opposite the responsibility. We have not required that, but ensuring there is a correct match between authority and responsibility is an excellent check on a position's ability to fulfill its responsibilities and objective.

The following is such a check on two of the training delivery manager's responsibilities:

Responsibilities	Authorities
Manages training delivery services within approved budget	To approve all budgeted expenditures To plan all training delivery services To maintain a full complement of trainers
Implements all training courses as scheduled	To assign trainers to scheduled courses To ensure all training materials are available To ensure qualified trainers are available for each scheduled course

Each responsibility has more than one authority. That is not uncommon, but sometimes a responsibility may have only one authority. Also, sometimes an authority may apply to several responsibilities.

One of the most common complaints recorded on employee opinion surveys is that employees are responsible for activities for which they are not given the necessary authority to accomplish. It is good to ensure that is not the case in your training department.

Unity of Command

Unity of command states that every position should report to no more than one other position for a single key result area.

A trainer should not be accountable to both a training manager and a design manager for the same key result area, such as quality of training delivery. There needs to be one clear accountability. When employees are accountable to two different positions for the same activity, sooner or later problems develop. A perfect example is a child living with two parents. The child quickly learns which parent to ask for what, and how to play them against each other.

However, it is possible to have a position report to two other positions if it is for two different key result areas or two different elements of a single key result area. For example, a skill trainer can report to a training manager for program delivery and to a training design manager for program evaluation.

Span of Control

Span of control refers to the number of key result areas one position is assigned, and accompanying it is the number of other positions for which it is accountable. A training manager may easily be able to supervise ten trainers who are conducting standard courses on a regular basis, but a training designer may have difficulty with two designers dealing in many separate areas.

Final Analysis

You should now have all the basic pieces of organizational information regarding your training department that are required before beginning a study of how to identify training needs. Perhaps most important is your review and analysis, which may identify some basic questions about the training department that should be addressed:

❐ In what areas is training performing well and in what areas is improvement required?

❐ How well do your perceptions of how the training department is performing compare with those of department employees and clients?

❏ Does the function have a clear workable organization?

❏ Are job assignments understood?

❏ Do position descriptions agree with the principles of good organization such as delegation, unity of command, and span of control?

You also have the basis for conducting a more in-depth analysis of the training function—though keep in mind that any analysis should be accomplished with the organization's objectives and mission as a guide. You want to be able to answer questions such as:

❏ Is the training department providing the organization the services it desires and needs?

❏ How well is the training department performing?

❏ How well is the training department perceived by its organizational clients to be providing services?

❏ How well is training using the assets its been provided with?

❏ How well does the training department compare with similar departments in other organizations?

❏ What should be done to improve the performance of training?

With the last question in mind, it is time to move on to procedures for identifying the training needs of your organization and individual employees.

PART TWO

Planning and Procedures for Needs Identification

Distinguishing Between Organizational and Employee Training Needs

Now that you have completed an analysis and review of your training function, it is time to introduce the actual procedures and methods for identifying training needs. A logical starting point is to consider the type of training need identification procedures, if any, that are currently being utilized in your organization.

Since you are reading this book, you are interested in identifying training needs, but perhaps your organization has identified training needs in the past and initiated training courses to fulfill those needs. As a first step, answer the following question: What percent of the training conducted in your organization is based on identified training needs?

Perhaps your answer is none. From what has already been discussed, you know the ideal answer is 100 percent. All training should only be conducted to meet specific identified training needs. Nevertheless, it is rare that an organization can provide that answer, and in fact, most organizations can only estimate an answer.

If you answered 70 percent or more, your organization is doing better than most. An answer in the 50 percent to 70 percent range is typical, and an answer below 50 percent means that more than half your training is being conducted for no specific identified need. This raises the question of whether or not such training is required.

Whatever the percentage, hopefully some training is conducted to meet identified needs, so that means somehow those needs were discovered. Do you know:

❒ Who initiates the identification of training needs?

❒ How someone requests the identification of training needs?

❒ Who conducts the identification of training needs?

❒ What procedures are used to identify training needs?

These are all questions for which you should know the answers. If you were unable to answer any of them, you should discover the answers before continuing.

Who Initiates the Identification of Training Needs?

Training should be designed, offered, and conducted for some purpose—to meet some objective—to fulfill some identified need. So, who initiates the process that identifies a training need? The usual sources are:

❒ **Managers**—who recognize possible training needs due to department performance results, individual employee performance reviews, future plans, and new equipment and systems.

❒ **Employees**—who recognize possible training needs to improve their current performance or prepare for other jobs.

❒ **Staff departments**—who recognize possible training needs based on activities such as employee opinion surveys, external consultant evaluations, succession planning, budget reports, and exit interviews.

❒ **Training employees**—who recognize possible training needs through conducting existing training courses and regular training performance surveys.

❒ **External consultants**—who recognize possible training requirements as part of other projects such as organizational studies, performance assessments, and management assessments.

Actually, anyone associated with the organization should be able to suggest the need for possible training and thus initiate the identification of training needs.

How Does Someone Initiate the Identification of Training Needs?

Sometimes training needs are given to the training department with a request to fulfill them. Other times training is asked to assist in identifying a possible need. Sometime it is an outgrowth of other activities. However, the ideal approach is to have in place, and communicated throughout the organization, a formal process that can be used to initiate the investigation of possible training needs. Generally such procedures take the form of:

- ❏ A published procedure (often including some type of request from) that anyone within the organization can use to indicate a possible training need

- ❏ An annual survey conducted by the training function to determine where there are possible training needs that require investigation

- ❏ A requirement that all appropriate activities such as annual performance reviews, purchase of new equipment, and employee opinion surveys include communication to the training function of any possible training needs

Who Conducts the Identification of Training Needs?

This varies by organization, but is best when it is someone trained in the appropriate skills to obtain adequate and reliable information. Most often it is someone in the training function. However, at times it is an external consultant or operating department employee.

What Procedures Are Used for Identifying Training Needs?

There are many procedures for identifying training needs, and as mentioned earlier, there is no best one for all situations. The procedures used should be selected to fit the situation, to be valid and reliable, and to be implemented by someone trained in their use.

If you can answer this question and the previous three questions, you have the basic knowledge on which to build an effective identification of training needs process. The answers to all these questions are the basis for the balance of this book.

First, let's take an overall view of exactly what the major types of training needs are.

Training Needs

For our purposes a training need is a gap between actual performance and desired performance or between current abilities and job requirements that can be closed by training.

Training needs fall into two basic categories:

❑ Training needs of the organization

❑ Training needs of individual employees

Sometimes organizational training needs and employee training needs are identical, but not always. The training needs of the organization have to do with the requirements to meet the organization's objectives. For example, a new employee orientation program is something the company wants all new employees to attend. It meets an organizational need of ensuring all employees have similar and correct information about the organization, its policies, and its benefits.

The unique skills required for jobs within a company are organizational training needs. For example, providing new employees on a job with the ability to operate the organization's customized PC-based system is an organizational training need. It is a specialized ability—unique to the job—that typical new employees cannot be assumed to have learned elsewhere. However, the basic skills required of an individual employee (not all employees) in a job are not usually classified as organizational training needs.

Individual employee training needs are those not required by typical employees. Individual employee training needs have to do with training required by a specific employee to improve performance, to be eligible for other jobs, or to acquire specific skills or abilities that most employees already have. For example, if only one employee in a department requires training in basic mathematics, that is an individual employee training need, not an organizational one. However, it is sometimes true that several employees may have the same individual training need.

> When jobs were relatively scarce and unemployment high, a New York accounting firm was able to increase requirements for its administrative assistant positions. When unemployment was reduced and jobs became more plentiful, the firm had to decrease its requirements and hire people without some of the skills previously demanded. The result was that its training department had to initiate a training program in basic skills that were formally possessed by people entering administrative assistant positions.

Training Needs of the Organization

Organizational training needs can be broadly classified into two general categories:

- ❏ Recognized training needs
- ❏ Requested training needs

Recognized Training Needs

These are the needs identified as required by all of the organization's employees, and all employees in specific jobs and departments. Sometimes they are called planned training needs since the organization knows that all employees have them, and plans can be made in advance for fulfilling these needs. They include such things as:

- ❏ The need to know the organization, its structure, policies, procedures, and benefits

❏ The need to know a department, its policies, rules, operating procedures, and personnel

❏ The need to have specific job skills and knowledge not generally possessed by most new employees in their jobs

The Need to Know the Organization, Its Structure, Policies, Procedures, and Benefits

Most new employees require basic information about their new employer, the structure of the organization, its policies, procedures, and conditions of employment (benefits, general rules, etc.). Some type of individual or group orientation training course generally supplies this during the first few days of employment. At other times orientation training is divided into several units. Each unit is conducted at the time the employee has the greatest need of its information.

> A New York City mutual funds company identified three basic areas of its orientation program. A new employee needed each area at a different time. General information including payroll, hours, and key personnel was needed immediately. Benefit information including insurance coverages and retirement plans was needed about one month later when most of the benefits went into effect, and development information on promotions, educational assistance, and job posting was needed about three months after hire.

> The company rescheduled its orientation into these three units at the three different times. They discovered the employees gained more from the sessions, had fewer follow-up questions, and made more informed decisions.

> Again, this is an affirmation of improving training's effectiveness by meeting identified needs.

Orientation training needs can be determined by several approaches. They can be identified by querying a number of internal sources. Human resources can provide descriptions of what rules, policies, procedures, and benefits should be known. (Often this is the same information covered in an employee handbook.) Supervisors of new employees can provide valuable input, but the most valuable sources of such information are recently hired employees. They can tell you what they discovered they needed to know during their first few weeks and months of employment. Information from these sources can be used to develop the specific objectives for an orientation program.

Consider your own organization. Do employees need some type of orientation and is one conducted? If such a program is required, does it cover specific identified needs of new employees? If yes, are those needs regularly reviewed to ensure they are still pertinent? Has consideration been given to offering orientation in stages, as its information is needed?

The Need to Know a Department, Its Policies, and Personnel

These needs are similar to those of new employees, only here the concern is with individual department requirements and working conditions. They represent what is required to be known by all employees in a department (rules, operating procedures, schedules, personnel). The sources for information are also similar—the supervisors and managers of a department, employees, and recently added new employees.

Often organizations that have identified needs for organizational orientation training fail to do the same for individual departments. This is unfortunate because in many ways initial department orientation training can be a major contributor to new employee success. If the information needed by new department employees has not already been determined, this is something that should be accomplished. Even if the needs have been earlier identified, they should be checked on a regular basis for any changes.

The Need to Learn Specific Job Requirements Not Generally Known by Most Employees

These are training needs required for specific jobs, and they are needs that the majority, if not all, new employees in those jobs (hired, promoted, and transferred) will probably possess. They are the activities and responsibilities unique to a job.

For example, most retail stores have customized selling systems. Experience at another retail store assists a new employee, but all new employees in selling jobs still need to be trained in the store's selling system. Most large retail stores hire new employees to start on a specified day and begin their employment with up to three days of training. Smaller retail stores often have self-study programs for employees hired one at a time.

An Illinois pharmacy that branched out into general merchandise employed an average of ten people at each of its forty stores. Individual stores could not afford a training professional, but operating personnel were never able to conduct effective orientation training.

The company commissioned a training design firm to develop self-study units for each of its key jobs: cashier, stock clerk, food and beverage sales, nonprescription medicine sales, camera and film sales, jewelry sales, and maintenance. A general store and company orientation self-study unit was also developed.

Now when new employees are hired, they complete the appropriate self-study unit, and after the unit meet with the store manager with any questions they may have. The self-study units are also used when existing employees change jobs or stores.

The programs worked so well that supervisor and management units were later developed.

Jobs that require skills with unique equipment are similar. For example, a fast food company may utilize a pressure cooker developed solely for its use. It has to train all new employees in its safe operation. A metals fabricator may have a piece of metal forming equipment designed for its own use. These are training needs the organization knows all new employees will have, so there are generally planned courses that are conducted as people enter these positions.

A Minnesota-based fast food chain requires all new store managers to attend a two-week training course at its home office. The course acquaints the managers with all aspects of a store's operation and how to perform all store jobs.

There are a number of possible information sources for specific job information: position descriptions, standards of performance, supervisors, and employees in the jobs. One often-overlooked source is the exit interview—an interview conducted with an employee as he/she is leaving the organization.

Exit Interviews

Exit interviews can provide information not otherwise obtainable. Employees leaving often feel freer to say things they might not say while employed. However, since many times employees are leaving because they did not like their jobs, the information tends to be negative. Even so, it can identify training needs as well as other working condition problems. Such information can yield insights into training needs that will contribute to employee retention.

Exit interviews should be conducted by other than the departing employee's supervisor or manager. A more neutral person trained in the approach will obtain the most useful information.

Some organizations do not conduct exit interviews but instead mail questionnaires to employees after they have left. These also can provide useful information, but people tend to be less explicit in writing than they are in person.

Some organizations use follow-up telephone calls a month or so after the employee has left the organization. They feel these provide better information than questionnaires, and they also report the information received at that time is more helpful than an exit interview conducted at the time of departure.

Requested Training Needs

These are needs that are not planned. They result from activities such as department performance, operating and job changes, and employee and organizational morale. They are brought to the attention of the organization when they occur rather than being early identified. Typically, they are brought to training's attention by such activities as:

- ❑ Changes in jobs and/or systems
- ❑ Addition of new equipment
- ❑ Department performance reviews
- ❑ New and revised government requirements
- ❑ Employee opinion surveys, organizational studies, department meetings, and focus groups
- ❑ Exit interviews conducted with departing employees

The common element in each of the aforementioned activities is the potential for calling attention to the need for training that might otherwise have been overlooked. Sometimes on examination, recognized needs can turn out to be individual employee training needs rather than organizational ones.

Changes in Jobs and/or Systems

These are changes made to current methods of operation. They are usually initiated by the organization, and they almost always require some degree of retraining. Here you generally have to look to the people initiating the change for information on what training is required. Many times you will have to conduct studies with existing employees to determine what training they require in order to fulfill the changed jobs or systems.

Addition of New Equipment

This is basically the same as a change in systems or jobs. The difference here is that a new piece of physical equipment is being added. Often such equipment comes from the equipment manufacturer with recommended training but other times, the organization must determine the training required for its employees. Even when a manufacturer recommends training, the training usually requires some degree of customization for the organization.

New equipment may also require different levels and types of training. For example, a new packing machine may require different training for groups such as: repair personnel, department supervisors, inspectors, and machine operators. This must be considered in deciding from whom to obtain training need information.

Department Performance

If department performance is not meeting its established standards or objectives, there can be a number of factors responsible. The department may have a high percentage of new employees. Its employees may need either retraining or training on changes that were not recognized. Employees may not be operating in the most efficient fashion, or the problem may not be solvable by training.

Here, as with identifying job training requirements and department training needs, an investigation must be conducted of the department employees, supervisors, and managers. However, training may not always be the solution. Other factors may be causing the problem—other factors that training cannot correct. For example, the performance standards for the department may have been improperly increased or external economic factors may be reducing product demand that affects department performance.

Government Requirements

Revised or new government rules and regulations can require employee training. For example, when the Occupational Safety and Health Act of 1970 was passed, many employers had to conduct training in the administration of the act's requirements and compliance by operating personnel with the act's regulations.

In the 1960s, when testing requirements were established as a part of an equal employment effort, many organizations were faced with the necessity to redo their selection and evaluation programs and train employees in the changes.

Opinion Surveys, Organizational Studies, Department Meetings, and Focus Groups

Activities conducted for other purposes may also identify training needs, even though that is not their primary purpose.

A Washington-based utility firm conducts an employee opinion survey each year. One year, it discovered the employees did not understand the company's new cafeteria benefit program. The company had initiated the program the previous year and believed it was something the employees would perceive as favorable, but the employees did not see it that way. They felt the program had reduced their benefits. The company was confident the difference was due to a lack of understanding on the part of the employees, so they requested the training department to initiate a new benefit training program.

Organizational studies may recommend restructuring of the entire organization or an individual department. Such restructuring often requires retraining of existing employees to meet new requirements. Other times organizational studies uncover problems with the current structure that can be solved through training.

Department meetings and focus groups called for other than the identification of training needs can still uncover such needs. For example, a meeting to introduce a new workflow may discover training is required to make the change work.

It is important that all employees be aware that when such needs are discovered through activities of this type that they be brought to the attention of the training department. Then a formal investigation can be conducted to identify the specifics of the need.

Training Needs of Individual Employees

We have reviewed some sources of organizational training needs identification. For individual employees, the sources are somewhat different since here you are dealing with the individual, not the job. A job's requirements are the same for everyone who fills it, but the qualifications of the jobholders will differ.

These are generally more similar to organizational requested training needs than recognized ones. They are needs that are not known in advance. They are initiated through activities such as:

❏ Performance reviews

❏ Selection process

❏ Testing and assessment

❏ Employee career objectives

❏ Succession plans

Performance Reviews

These are probably the most common sources for identifying individual employee training needs. Most useful are performance reviews based on a comparison of an employee's actual job performance with predetermined standards or objectives. In such reviews, results below standard can be identified and in most cases, quantified.

The difference between actual performance and desired performance is classified as a performance gap. Performance gaps need to be closed in order for the employee to perform to standard or objective, as required by the job, so performance gaps identify required training for an individual employee.

> A Michigan-based manufacturer requires all supervisors to develop and implement plans to assist their employees in closing any performance gaps. These become one of the supervisor's annual objectives, and a portion of the supervisor's annual performance review is based on the supervisor taking action to assist the employees to close any performance gaps.

> Perhaps most interesting of all is a California company that refers to the gaps not as performance gaps but as development gaps. "We want to reinforce the concept that such gaps can and should be closed through training," states the company's president.

The supervisor can deal with some performance gaps, but others may require the assistance of the training function. Many organizations require the training department to be notified when any performance gaps are identified, so if a problem is widespread training can develop courses to meet all similar needs.

A Texas petroleum firm requires all identified employee performance gaps to be reported to the training department at the time performance reviews are conducted. The training department combines all such information and where there are enough similar training needs, develops the appropriate programs.

Selection Process

The selection process is not typically viewed as a source for identifying training needs. However, it can produce a great deal of important training information. In the selection process, candidates (whether internal or external) have their qualifications compared with a job's requirements. A candidate's qualifications do not always meet all of the job's requirements. This is true even of the candidate selected for the position.

Communicating such training needs of a selected candidate to the candidate's supervisor and the training department allows both to immediately initiate actions that will assist the new employee in developing in the required areas.

A Connecticut company requires the hiring manager and the human resources professional involved in the selection process to identify any training needs and assign them as objectives to the new employee and her/his supervisor.

Sometimes the selection process can identify training needs that are more organizational than individual employee needs.

A Montana-based transportation company discovered that most otherwise good candidates for positions lacked the necessary PC skills. This information was communicated to training, and a course was designed to provide new employees with required PC skills.

Testing and Assessment

The selection process often includes testing and/or some other form of assessment. Their results can be further sources of identifying any training required for a new employee, and if the test is properly selected and implemented, it produces valid and reliable evaluations. For example, candidates for a quality control techni- cian's position may all be tested for the level of their statistical ability. If the candidate eventually hired tested as needing im- provement in one area, that is a training need that can be ad- dressed. Sometimes such programs are conducted for other purposes.

> An Ohio consumer products company conducts a supervisor assessment program quarterly. Employees desiring to be- come supervisors and employees recommended by manage- ment for consideration as supervisors can participate in the program. The program identifies the employees' strengths and areas of needed improvement as a supervisor. The train- ing department then offers a series of courses (some self- study) for the employee in areas assessed as needing im- provement before the employee is moved into a supervisor's position.

Career Objectives

Employees with identified career objectives often approach train- ing or their supervisors for assistance in meeting those objectives. The previously described supervisor assessment program is par- tially conducted to assist employees with management career ob- jectives.

Some companies, but not all, assist employees in identifying their individual training needs and some further assist the em- ployee in obtaining the type of training required. Counselors and testing are provided in these instances, and employees with spe- cific career objectives are encouraged to make them known.

Succession Plans

Many organizations prepare annual succession plans to identify the internal potential it has for filling management or other key jobs. These plans often include the identification of required train- ing. Usually this information is communicated to training.

Typically, succession plans are displayed on an organizational chart. The following is a portion of such a chart indicating two positions and possible internal candidates for each. The first entry beneath each position indicates an internal employee who can immediately fill the position. The next two names are other possible candidates. The number following the candidates' names indicates the amount of time required to prepare the person for the position.

Customer Service Manager   *Product Manager*

Alice Smith—Ready now   No one—Ready now

Joe Maxwell—3 months   Al Jones—8 months

Joan Peters—7 months   Shirley Boggs—12 months

In our example, there is an internal replacement for the customer service manager but none for the product manager. If the organization wants to ensure internal replacements are available for all its management positions, it needs to either hire someone or begin to develop Al Jones. Assuming it elects to develop Al Jones, the succession plan has identified an employee with a training need.

> A Canadian security firm conducted its annual management succession plan and discovered it had no internal candidates ready to be moved into a regional manager's position. From experience, the company knew at least two such openings would occur during the next year. The succession plan did identify the most likely candidates for such a position along with the amount of training required. Training was notified and the employees placed into a formal training program for the position.

There is one caution about using succession plans to identify training needs. In some organizations, succession plans are prepared solely to ensure that backups exist for management and key professional positions, but when a management or professional position requires filling, the succession plan is rarely used as a guide. If that is the situation in your organization, developing and training an employee for another job the employee has little chance of obtaining is not a good use of resources. It can also lower employee morale. However, in organizations where succession plans serve as a guide for future transfers and promotions, they should regularly be reviewed for training needs.

Procedure for Identifying Training Needs

Now that the categories of training needs have been introduced, let's consider the methodology for identifying specific needs. Although there are differences in the training needs of individual employees and the organizations, the identification procedures are basically the same:

1. Identify possible areas requiring training.
2. Plan and conduct a training needs investigation.
3. Analyze and report the obtained information.
4. If training is required, prepare behavioral objectives.

5

Identifying Possible Areas in Which People Need Training

The first step in the procedure for identifying training needs is to determine the areas that might have such needs. In most organizations, it is impossible to simultaneously examine all functions and employees, so the areas with the greatest or most urgent needs should be discovered and prioritized for further investigation. Some of these areas can be discovered through actions you initiate. Others may be brought to your attention by nontraining activities and employees.

Unanticipated Requests

Sometimes, you will receive an unsolicited request to investigate a possible training need. Activities such as the addition of new equipment, new laws, and changed department and job assignments can create possible training needs. Senior management may request training in an area identified by an employee opinion survey, or a supervisor may inform you of an employee's performance gap. Other times, you may discover areas of possible training needs through feedback from exit interviews and selection procedures, or as a by-product of training courses and counseling sessions.

These unanticipated requests can occur anytime, and they generally are the types of situations that require immediate attention. However, you should always have a planned approach for identifying areas of possible training needs. If your organization has not previously identified its training needs—in all or in part— you should probably begin by dealing with the organization's required (planned) training. Even if your organization's required training needs have already been identified, and training to meet those needs is being conducted, there still should be regular reviews to identify any needed changes. The important element is to ensure that the training department is in the communication loops regarding all such possible inputs.

The Need for Communication

Many training departments assign training professionals to various operating departments. The assignments involve them in the ongoing department operations through a continual dialogue with that department and its personnel. These professionals receive appropriate department communications. They attend department meetings, and they consult with department management. This approach provides early information on training requirements and ensures that the training function is in the loop.

A Maryland insurance company of 2,000 employees has a training department consisting of ten professionals and managers. The company has eight major operating divisions. A training professional is assigned to each operating division. In most cases, the assigned training professional is the person who conducts the majority of training for that division's employees. The training professional attends all division-level staff meetings and receives copies of all division reports and plans.

Since initiating this approach, both the training department and the operating divisions feel that training's response time to need has improved, training is more knowledgeable of operating division requirements, and the training courses are more useful.

Some training functions hold regular meetings with operating managers to review training and possible areas requiring additional training.

A California bank conducts an annual off-site meeting for all senior managers. The meeting normally lasts three days. Each meeting includes a two-hour session facilitated by the training department. That session is designed to identify upcoming training requirements and to evaluate the effectiveness of existing training activities.

Some companies include training in system changes or new equipment purchases.

In Alabama a nonferrous metals fabricator requires that teams created to consider the feasibility of new equipment or systems changes include a training representative. If the team's efforts lead to the purchase of new equipment or systems changes, the same training representative is assigned to the team that is implementing the purchase or design change.

All of the aforementioned examples involve the training function in the continuing operations of the organizations. They are ideal approaches for the early identification of training needs and for providing the appropriate courses. However, another method for discovering areas of possible training needs is a regular formal review.

The Training Survey

The questionnaire is probably the most used approach for identifying training needs. Usually the training department sends a questionnaire to all management within the organization. This is often an annual activity, conducted at the same time each year with all managers. However, in some organizations such a questionnaire is sent to different departments and divisions at different times of the year. (A typical questionnaire is illustrated in Figure 5-1.)

Figure 5-1.
TRAINING DEPARTMENT'S ANNUAL REVIEW QUESTIONNAIRE.

The Training Department is currently reviewing all existing training activities to ensure they are meeting their objectives and to identify additional training requirements. Your input will be of considerable assistance in this effort, so please answer the following questions and return the completed form.

1. List below the courses the Training Department is currently conducting for your department and employees, and then indicate how satisfied you are with the results of each course. Use a three-point scale to indicate satisfaction (1 = Not Satisfied; 2 = Satisfied; 3 = Very Satisfied).

Training Course	Satisfaction with Results
_____	_____
_____	_____
_____	_____
_____	_____
_____	_____
_____	_____

2. List below any of your department's individual employees who have specific training needs to improve current job performance.

_____

_____

_____

_____

_____

3. List below any additional training that you or your employees require. Please list in order of need (the most needed first, and so on).

_____

_____

_____

_____

_____

4. List below any training requirements you believe will develop within the next year.

_____

_____

_____

_____

_____

5. List below any other areas in which training can be of assistance to you and your employees.

_____

_____

_____

_____

_____

Although the questionnaire is presented as an annual review, the same questions can form the basis for a first-time questionnaire. The questionnaire can be sent to all management at the same time of year, or it can be sent to different groups, locations, or divisions at varying times.

The questionnaire requests information on:

1. How well existing training courses are meeting management's requirements

2. Employees who may have individual training needs

3. Additional training that may be required

4. Training requirements that are projected for the near future

5. Other areas that training can assist

Question One—Satisfaction with Existing Training

Responses to the first question indicate how well existing training courses are perceived as meeting management's needs. They quickly identify where there are concerns or dissatisfaction as well as what training courses are fully meeting requirements. In addition, they communicate information that can assist in improving existing training courses.

If management is not satisfied with any existing training course, that requires immediate attention. It may be that the needs for such training have changed, and the training course requires revision. On the other hand, you may discover the training is not being delivered as designed. Whatever the case, discovering the reasons for management not being satisfied becomes your first priority. You do not want to be conducting incorrect or unnecessary training.

At the very least, such inputs should be followed up with a meeting, as soon as possible, to obtain more detailed information.

> In the 1960s, a New York utility began a training course on how to install and weld steel pipe. All employees promoted to pipe installer were required to take the one-week course. In 1996, the classroom, which was basically a welding workshop, was completely updated at considerable expense. However, the company had discontinued using welded pipe a decade earlier. Its pipe installers were no longer required to weld steel pipe—something the training department did not discover until 2000.

Question Two—Individual Employees

Question two is designed to discover whether or not the supervisor believes he/she has employees with individual training requirements. The supervisor, through performance reviews, observation, employee initiation, or organizational planning, may have identified these requirements.

Generally, the responses to this question do not provide much more than names for further investigation.

Questions Three, Four, and Five—Future Training Needs

Questions one and two deal with current training requirements. Their responses demand your immediate attention. Questions three, four, and five indicate future training needs and other services that training may provide. These responses are important but usually do not require immediate action. Responses to these three questions should be considered in the order of the questions.

Responses to question three (additional training requirements) can reflect both department training needs and individual employee training needs. They may identify the need for new courses and employees who are being considered for other positions or who have stated career objectives.

In reviewing responses to this question, the order of importance is vital. A new training course may demand immediate action while training to assist with a career objective may not.

Question four projects future training needs within the next year. Due to the short time frame, additional information about any described training should be quickly obtained.

Question five is a general question designed to obtain information on how else the training function can assist a department. Sometimes the responses will focus on areas that fall outside of the training department's area of accountability, however, valuable suggestions are often made that can improve training's effectiveness.

One thing about these last three questions: Managers generally are very specific in their responses to questions one and two, but with these questions responses can sometimes become a wish list. At other times responses may appear as something to write rather than a real need. At other times, responses may appear to be an attempt to provide some type of an answer to the questions rather than the identification of a real training need.

Performance Survey

Another often-used approach is to annually survey managers regarding the training needs of their employees as identified through performance reviews. These surveys are usually distributed at the time annual employee performance reviews are conducted. As mentioned earlier, in some organizations such a report is required to be submitted to the training department by all supervisors and managers at the completion of their employee performance reviews. Such a report form appears in Figure 5-2.

The upper portion of the form is for recording employees with performance gaps—measured gaps between actual performance and desired performance. The lower portion of the form is to record employees who might have training needs other than those required to close performance gaps. In both cases, the urgency of providing such training is requested.

When forms are received from a number of supervisors and managers at the same time, the inputs for the two areas can be combined and then ranked by priority. Generally, you will want to deal with the performance gaps first.

Training Review Analysis

If you have only surveyed one or two supervisors, you can immediately move ahead to determine what type of training needs investigation is required. However, if the questionnaires were sent to a number of supervisors and managers, combining their responses and prioritizing is a next step.

If you used the annual training review questionnaire (Figure 5-1) or a similar survey, begin by listing training courses mentioned in responses to question one that were rated a one—not satisfied. As you are doing this, you may discover more than one supervisor or manager mentioned the same course. If that occurs, indicate next to the course title the number of supervisors mentioning it and their individual ratings. If they all rate it as a one, the course is apparently not meeting anyone's objectives. However, at times, the same course may be given different ratings by different

Figure 5-2.

ANNUAL EMPLOYEE PERFORMANCE SURVEY.

To: (Manager/Supervisor)

With the annual performance reviews of your employees now completed, the Training Department is interested in learning of any areas in which it can be of assistance to improve employee performance. Please complete this form by identifying such individuals in need of assistance. Upon its receipt, someone from the Training Department will contact you for more detailed information.

In the space below, list any employees in your department who have performance gaps that training might be able to assist in closing. After each name, indicate what you believe to be the urgency of obtaining such assistance. Use this rating system: 1 = Most urgent; 2 = Sometime in the next three months; 3 = Sometime in the next six months.

Employee	Urgency
_____	_____
_____	_____
_____	_____
_____	_____
_____	_____

During your performance reviews you may have also learned of employees with career or other objectives who could be provided assistance through training. Please indicate those employees on the following lines. Once again, indicate how urgent you believe it is to receive such assistance.

Employee	Urgency
_____	_____
_____	_____
_____	_____
_____	_____

managers. In those instances, you need to concentrate on the supervisors and managers giving it the low ratings.

Next make a separate list of employees mentioned in response to question two of Figure 5-1. These are employees who may require training in order to perform their current jobs as they should.

Just as you investigated differing perceptions regarding department performance, you will need to investigate to determine why different supervisors and managers are rating their satisfaction with a course differently. The answer could be that the course has application to the needs of some departments but not all. Other times it may be that some departments are currently using the course, but others are not.

You now have your two primary lists of possible training needs. One concerns current training courses and one covers current employee needs. You should then combine responses to questions three and four.

In question three of Figure 5-1, responses are in order of importance, so in combining them indicate their various rankings. For example, let's assume three supervisors listed report writing as a need course. One listed it first. One supervisor listed it second, and one listed it fifth. You can write those rankings after the course subject. That tells you how many supervisors mentioned it and how important it was to each.

Question four responses have to do with courses required during the next year. Here you want to identify how many times the same or similar course was mentioned. Finally, list any training mentioned to assist employees in obtaining other positions or meeting career objectives.

Question five asks for additional areas in which training can assist operating departments. List any suggestions indicating the number of times each was mentioned.

You now have four lists:

❐ Existing courses rated one by at least one supervisor or manager

❐ Employees who require assistance to close performance gaps

❏ Additionally required courses and their importance

❏ Any additional areas in which training can be of assistance

You next need to prioritize the lists for action. There is no single set of rules to establish priorities, but generally you should rank the training courses rated one and the employees who need assistance with current job performance as the first priority. (The training courses attended by the largest number of employees should be considered first. Next, rank the additionally required courses. And, finally, rank the courses required during the next year.)

The last two lists you need to make concern employees who need development assistance and any additional areas in which training can be of assistance to the various departments.

The appropriate supervisors and managers can consider these lists. For example, when you contact a supervisor regarding a one rating given to an existing course, you can also raise questions about another of the supervisor's responses.

Additional Information

So you now have a list of priorities for action. Sometimes, you will have all the information required to conduct a training needs analysis, but in most cases you will need further information. You need to know things such as:

❏ Why a current training course was rated a one (i.e., a not satisfied rating)

❏ What specific performance gap an employee has

❏ What additional training courses are required and by when

Why a Current Training Course Was Rated a One

To determine whether this is a training course no longer needed or one that requires revision, you need to know:

❏ What is the basis for the rating as one?

❏ How often is the course used?

❏ Is the course required for employees?

❏ What could be done to make the course meet employee and department needs?

❒ Have the needs changed?

❒ Has the subject matter changed?

What Specific Performance Gap an Employee Has

Here you need information about an individual employee:

❒ What is the specific gap?

❒ What appears to be causing the gap?

❒ Has there been a change in the employee's performance?

❒ Has the employee's job changed?

What Additional Training Courses Are Required and by When

To obtain the information required for additional and future training courses, you should find out:

❒ What is the subject?

❒ By when is the course required?

❒ How many employees will require training?

Methods for Obtaining Additional Information

When you need additional information regarding employee performance gaps you generally have only the supervisor or the supervisor and employee to query. In both cases an interview is the typical approach. To get additional information for possible organizational training the interview is just one approach.

When there are only one or two supervisors or managers from whom to obtain additional information, an interview with each may be the quickest and simplest approach. Interviews are also best for obtaining extra information regarding individual employee training needs. Where there are more than one or two supervisors and managers to contact, other methods such as follow-up questionnaires and group meeting are usually more efficient.

Questionnaires are useful when the population is in several locations and/or the information needed is straightforward. If the supervisors and managers are at the same locations and/or there may be disagreement among them, then a meeting may be more suitable.

Later chapters describe in detail how to prepare for and conduct interviews, questionnaires, and meetings. However, here are some brief ideas for using these methods to obtain additional information.

The Questionnaire

A simple questionnaire is best, and direct questions are most effective. Also, you should keep in mind that the resulting responses have to be somehow combined, so a structured response scale or objective responses are easiest for that purpose. However, the subject may not always lend itself to such approaches.

Assume you received several reviews that indicated dissatisfaction with a customer service training course. However, there were also a few managers who indicated they were satisfied with the same course. Here you want to discover:

❒ What is the basis for the dissatisfaction?

❒ Why are there differences?

❒ Is the course being used and, if so, when and for whom?

❒ What needs to be done to improve the course?

Figure 5-3 illustrates such a questionnaire. You can see how the questions have been structured to produce responses relatively easy to combine and provide a way for a respondant to provide any additional information.

The Interview

To be successful, an interview should be planned and the areas to question identified. You do not want to approach someone by saying, "Why are you dissatisfied with training?" That type of approach will probably be perceived as threatening. You are demanding justification of an opinion. Instead, your objective should be to obtain whatever additional information you need to determine whether or not an area needs an identification of training needs.

Figure 5-3.

A SAMPLE FOLLOW-UP QUESTIONNAIRE.

To: (Manager/Supervisor)

In response to our recent request for information on our existing training courses, a number of comments were received regarding customer service training. To better understand these comments and to determine if the course requires any revision, please take a few moments to answer the following questions and return the completed questionnaire.

To answer the first four questions and question nine, please use a nine-point scale (1 = Poor, 5 = Typical, and 9 = Excellent). You may use any point on the scale for your answers. For the remainder of the questions, please write in a response.

1. How do you rate the quality of the customer service training course's content? _____

2. How do you rate the course's ability to meet the training needs of your employees who attended it? _____

3. How relevant is the content of the course to your employees' work? _____

4. All things considered, how do you rate the overall value of the course to your employees? _____

5. When was the last time you had employees who attended the course? _____

6. How many of your employees attended the course during the past twelve months? _____

7. Do your employees have a need for this type of course?

   _____

8. How relevant is the content of the course to your employees' work? .

9. All things considered, how do you rate the overall value of the course to your employees? _____

10. What could be done to improve the course? _____

    _____

    _____

11. In the space below, please provide any additional information about the course that you feel will contribute to its use and effectiveness.

    _____

    _____

    _____

    _____

The Interview Objective

The most important element of your preparation for an interview is to identify the objective of the interview. Possible areas for investigation have been identified from the information you have already received. Your objective for a follow-up interview should clearly define why such an interview is necessary.

For example, perhaps the questionnaires indicated that a department is dissatisfied with the training provided to its new employees on how to operate a specific piece of equipment. In that case the interview objective should discover the basis for dissatisfaction with operator training.

If the interview accomplishes that objective, you will be able to decide whether or not an identification of training needs is required. You may discover that the problem is not a training problem. For example, the employees leaving training may be given assignments on machines for which they were not trained, or some machines may have received design modifications not covered in training.

Who to Interview

In most cases this is the individual who completed the questionnaire. There are some instances in which a comment on a questionnaire may really require an interview with someone else. For example, a manager completing a questionnaire may state that another department is not completing its work correctly, and it is affecting his/her department. In such an instance, you may also want to interview the manager of the mentioned department. Also, if you have received different ratings for the same course, you want to speak with both types of raters.

When you are identifying who to interview, keep in mind that if you need to talk to a number of people, it may be more efficient to hold a meeting with all of them at one time.

Information Required

The next step is to identify the specific information you require. You want to determine if this is an area to further investigate and if so, to obtain the information needed to plan such an approach.

You have identified the objective, so now list the key elements to question. For example, you should try to discover:

- ❐ The basis for possible new training or dissatisfaction with current training
- ❐ The changes that may have occurred to produce a training need
- ❐ The factors that brought the need to attention
- ❐ The problems caused by the lack of training
- ❐ The urgency of training

Question Development

You can now develop a series of questions. Keep in mind at this point you are only trying to identify areas where training needs may exist. You are not attempting to identify the specific needs. However, at times your inquiries may in fact identify the training need, and at other times you may discover there is no need to investigate.

Your questions should not be answerable in one word. If they are, it puts you in the position of pushing for an explanation. So instead of asking, "Do you feel the current course is too long?" You might ask, "How long do you feel an employee should spend in this course?" Write your questions in the order you plan to ask them. (This will ensure not forgetting one.)

Prepare your questions to obtain the information you require. Here is a series of questions prepared for a follow-up interview with a manager who indicated dissatisfaction with the results of a customer satisfaction course:

- ❐ On your questionnaire you indicated some dissatisfaction with the current (name of training course). What results do you feel that course should be achieving that it is not?
- ❐ How does the course's content relate to the needs of your employees?
- ❐ What length do you feel such a course should be?
- ❐ What do you feel will improve the course?
- ❐ How often do you feel changes occur that may affect course content?

You may discover that the operating manager has completely different objectives for the training than you do. The important point is to be neutral and open to any comments. Don't argue; don't indicate disagreement or agreement with answers. Accept the information given. Training's role is to provide the training required for the organization to meet its objectives. Its role is not to defend courses that are not perceived as helpful.

Often such interviews can clear up misunderstandings as well as provide information for training. Whatever the case, conclude the meeting by explaining what will occur next and by answering questions such as:

- ❏ Are you going to talk with other involved managers?
- ❏ Are you going to review the training course's objectives, content, and length?
- ❏ Are you going to begin a training need identification investigation?
- ❏ Do you feel the problem is not one for training?

Who Conducts the Interview?

So far we have dealt with the interview content and who to interview. Another important consideration is who should conduct the interview. Ideally, it is someone who is perceived as positive, neutral, nonthreatening, and interested. In addition, it should be someone with knowledge about the area. If a training professional is identified or assigned to the area, he/she may be the logical one to conduct the interview.

However, do not have a champion of the current training conduct the interview. Sending the course developer or leader to do the interview usually does not work. The developer or leader may defend the course rather than obtain information.

Meetings

When you have a number of people from whom to obtain information on the same subject, a meeting is often the most efficient method to use. The major difference in preparation is determining who should attend, and if there is to be more than one meeting, who should attend which meeting.

Meetings of this type are most productive when the participants are at the same level within the organization. Mixing levels can dramatically affect the outcome. Clerks from a department might not want to be as open if a senior manager is present, and senior managers might not accept differing opinions from those at lower levels in the organization. You also want to have people with similar degrees of knowledge attend the same meeting. If there are major differences between people and departments, it is better to hold separate meetings for the different departments.

Include all appropriate people. If you received mixed evaluations of a course from managers (some good and some poor) invite all to the meeting. This may allow you to resolve the differing perceptions and discover what, if any, are the real problems.

In conducting the meeting, follow this basic procedure:

❒ State the objective.

❒ Be sure everybody knows everybody.

❒ Begin with a nonthreatening, information-gathering exercise.

❒ Encourage equal participation.

❒ End with a summary of the information and a statement of what you will do next and when the participants will receive information from you.

If you were to follow these steps in an actual meeting, you might begin the meeting by saying something similar to this:

First, thank you for the valuable input you provided for our recent training review. Based on your responses, I wanted to meet and discuss with you the ways in which our training functions can be more effective and of greater assistance to you and your employees.

Today, our objective is to review the effectiveness of (name of course). It is a course that all of your employees attend.

Let's begin by having each of you write on a piece of paper what you believe the course's objective should be. Do that in one sentence.

Give the participants time to write their one-sentence answer, then say:

> Now, write beneath the objective how satisfied you are that the course met it. Use a scale of one to nine for that purpose. One is dissatisfied, five is neither dissatisfied nor satisfied, nine is very satisfied, but you may use any point on the scale. Try not to use fractions or decimals.

Give the participants a moment to again write their responses before continuing as follows:

> Finally, write at the bottom of the page how important such a course is to your operations. Write down whether it is not important, important, or very important.

In some instances you can have the participants read their answers as you request them, but in most cases the following statement seems to work better:

> Now, fold your paper in half and give it to me.

Shuffle the papers—mix them up—and randomly redistribute the answers. This is the point where you see where you are. Have the participants read the objective on their piece of paper. As they read the objectives, write the keywords from each on a chart pad or chalkboard. If there are differences, allow discussion by using overhead questions such as:

❏ What are the differences?

❏ What are the similarities?

Next, have each participant read the rating number. Write these in a column. Then have each person read the importance. Have these numbers read in the same order so the importance can be written in a second column next to the ratings. Depending on the answers you receive, ask questions such as:

❏ What are the major points of dissatisfaction? (This question is relevant if most people are dissatisfied with the results of the training courses under review.)

❒ What results do you feel we should be achieving that we are not?

❒ What can be done to improve the course?

❒ What are the differences?

❒ What are the similarities?

❒ What is the basis for the differences?

❒ What will make this course more effective for you?

❒ What are your needs that you want this course to fulfill?

If no one feels the course is important, you need to discover the reasons a course is being conducted if the managers apparently do not want it. You can ask questions such as:

❒ Have your training needs in this area recently changed?

❒ Is there another course that will better meet your current needs?

❒ Can this course be revised so it can meet your current needs?

You need to remain flexible. You are conducting the meeting to obtain information. Sometimes the information may lead to subjects other than the course. You want to allow free discussion if it relates at all to the course.

With the above information, you will know whether a training needs analysis is required, the course should be eliminated or revised, or the course should be offered to different employees.

Individual Employee Training Needs

The issue with individual employee training needs is different. Here you are dealing with only one employee and his/her supervisor. The starting place is the supervisor. Generally, this should be an interview. You want to ask:

❒ What is the basis for identifying the employee as requiring training?

❒ Is the training for improved performance on the current job or preparation for a future job?

❏ Does the employee know of your request?

Sometimes you may discover that there is no training need and the request was made for other reasons. For example:

> A Texas company's training department received repeated requests for training to improve a specific employee's performance. All the requests were from the same supervisor.
>
> Each time the request was investigated, the training department determined there was no training need. Eventually, they discovered the supervisor was being criticized for failing to meet department performance objectives. The employee was very vocal and continually told the supervisor what he should be doing. It was the supervisor's frustration with the situation that motivated the requests.

Prioritizing Possible Areas of Training Needs

You now have an idea of how a training needs identification investigation should be conducted and the basic information needed for planning one. You may have eliminated some areas as possible training issues, and you have additional information for the other areas. You still need the areas to investigate categorized into two groups: organizational training needs and individual training needs, since different approaches are used for each.

Once that is done, you need to reprioritize the areas and pinpoint which you should investigate first to identify training needs.

To prioritize the areas, first list all of them in two groups—organization training needs and individual employee training needs. Then rank the items in each group in order of importance to implement. In ranking, consider:

❏ The probable time necessary to conduct the study

❏ The number of potential employees to be trained

❏ Any deadlines that have to be met

❏ The probability a training need exists

❏ The number of people available to conduct a training needs analysis.

You will have then identified the areas that require an identification of training needs. Chapter 6 deals with planning the investigation, and Chapter 7 introduces methods for conducting the investigations.

6

Planning to Identify
Training Needs

Once you have determined the areas and employees of the organization that appear to have training needs and prioritized them for investigation, the next step is prepare plans for conducting the training needs analysis. How to prepare and plan for that analysis is the subject of this chapter.

In the process of identifying the areas and employees that may have training needs, a good deal of information is usually obtained. That information can serve as a basis for your preparations, and the analysis will identify exactly what those needs are. However, an analysis does not always identify training needs. It may reveal that what initially appeared to be a training issue is something else entirely.

> At a Colorado-based computer software firm, a supervisor requested training for his employees because of their failure to meet production goals. The supervisor cited the employees' unfamiliarity with the company's programming system as the reason for the failure. However, a training needs analysis discovered the problem was in the company's programming software. Corrections to the software eliminated all poor employee performance.

You must always remain flexible and prepared to recognize a nontraining problem if it surfaces; however, in the planning stage, try to ensure you are investigating a real training need and not some other problem or symptom. Sometimes, though, you have to begin your analysis before it becomes apparent the issue is not training-related.

Deciding What You Need to Know

A correctly conducted training needs analysis will yield specific information describing the required training, its timing, and the training population. That, then, becomes the basis for a training course designer to either create a new training program, identify an existing one that can fulfill the need, or obtain one externally. In some instances, it may be impossible to fulfill the need, but that is not the decision of the person conducting the training needs analysis.

Actually, knowing exactly what elements of information are required can serve as a guide—a road map—for your analysis.

Assuming you will be conducting an analysis for a real training need, the following are the elements the analysis should produce in its final report:

- ❏ Training subject(s)
- ❏ Importance of the training
- ❏ Urgency or time requirements
- ❏ Current training population
- ❏ Potential training population
- ❏ Frequency of training
- ❏ Subject review and update
- ❏ Required results of the training
- ❏ Content information sources

Training Subject(s)

In identifying areas of possible training needs, the general subject or subjects for training are usually identified. However, when the analysis is completed, it needs to describe in detail each subject and sub-subject. You want to know exactly what the training is to cover

For example, the first step may have identified a possible need for training in customer order taking on the telephone. In the final identification of that training need, the subject and sub-subjects may be:

1. *General Subject:* Telephone order taking (how to complete a product order form from an incoming customer telephone call)

2. *Sub-Subjects:*

   ❐ Understanding telephone order procedures

   ❐ Understanding shipping procedures

   ❐ Researching problem orders

   ❐ Handling customer complaints and objections

Another example is a training needs analysis conducted for a new employee orientation program. Your initial efforts may have identified the orientation program as the subject for new employees. Now you need to be more specific. You want to know exactly what to cover in the training. Sub-subjects could be:

❐ Company history

❐ Company structure

❐ Key personnel

❐ Pay procedures

❐ Company policies and rules

❐ Performance reviews

❐ Benefits

And of course, within each of the sub-subjects there could be further sub-subjects. For example, benefits could have as sub-subjects such as:

❑ Vacation

❑ Paid time off

❑ Retirement plan

❑ Insurance

Individual employee training needs are often expressed in a different fashion. Instead of subjects, you may identify differences between actual performance and desired performance, or between current qualifications and job requirements. You will then have to determine in what subjects training is required to close those gaps. For example:

> An employee's production standards may be to produce 200 parts per hour, but the employee produces only 150 parts per hour. There is a performance gap of 50 parts produced per hour. The subject is production improvement, but the sub-subjects may be machine operation, machine set-up.

Importance of the Training

In Chapter 17, we will examine methods for determining the value of training, but in the investigation step, you need to convey the importance of the training. For example, if the training involves how to operate a unique company system, and all employees need to know how to operate the system, the need for the training is very important. Employees cannot perform their job until the training has occurred. On the other hand, training an employee in subjects related to career goals may not have as great an importance.

A scale can be used to describe importance. That standardizes the responses. If you are going to use one, establish it in advance. Then you will be consistent. The inputs will be on the same scale, and you will be prepared with your questions.

A typical scale will appear similar to the following:

Very Important	Somewhat Important	Neither Unimportant nor Important	Somewhat Unimportant	Not Important

├───┤

Importance can also be described in terms of monetary value. For example:

❐ This training can save the organization $50,000 a year by reducing mistaken deliveries.

❐ Failure to provide this training will require an additional two weeks of on-the-job experience for each new employee at an approximate cost of $2,500 per employee. Sixteen new employees are projected to be hired each year, so the additional cost per year will be $40,000.

Each of these statements expresses the importance of the training need in a quantitative way. The importance of the training, along with its urgency, can then be used to prioritize the order in which to fulfill training needs.

Urgency or Time Requirements

Related to importance is urgency. Here, time is a good indicator. How soon must the training occur? For example:

❐ This training needs to be conducted before the arrival of the new production equipment on January 15.

❐ The training is required to be completed by October 3, when the new law goes into effect.

Current Training Population

You want to know what number of positions or employees are to be trained. In our new employee orientation training example, the positions and numbers to be trained are all new employees. In the case of a claims-processing training course, it could be all new claims adjusters. If the training need is for a single employee who is encountering difficulties in performing his job or an employee who wants to develop skills required for another position, the population may only be one.

The number of people to be trained can have a significant impact on the training program design. Is it just one or two employees, a whole department, or the whole organization? The number to be trained—combined with the importance and urgency of the training and type of content—will determine whether the training should be designed and conducted by the organization, contracted to an external firm, purchased as an existing program, or not done at all. If there are only one or two employees, an individual self-study program may be considered; for a large number of employees, a group course is more likely.

Potential Training Population

Consideration needs to be given not only to the current training population but to any future trainees as well. For example, assume the company was purchasing a new operating system for inventory control. The immediate need is to train four current employees in its operation. However, within the next two years an additional sixty employees will be hired and will require training. Thereafter, on average, ten new employees who require the training are projected to be hired each year.

All information on current and potential training populations should be reported by position titles, department, and numbers of employees. It should be shown by years. In our example, the training population would be shown as:

Employees to Be Trained	Year One	Year Two	Year Three	Each Year Thereafter
Inventory Control	4	30	30	10

Frequency of Training

How often the training course is to be conducted depends on several factors, including:

- ❑ Employee availability
- ❑ Total number of current employees to be trained
- ❑ Maximum size of training classes and method
- ❑ Required time to conduct training
- ❑ Projected future training population

Employee availability, for example, has a direct effect on training course design. For example, if a department has ten employees, all of whom require training, it may not be possible to train them all at one time. Having everyone in a training course might "shut down" the department's operation. In such a situation, perhaps only four employees can be released for training at any one time, or if only one can be trained at a time, individual training methods must be considered.

Sometimes the only available time for training is outside regular business hours.

A New Jersey chemical manufacturer initiated a supervisor training course. It was a group course requiring between ten and fifteen participants per session. The company selected that approach because it felt the supervisors would benefit from the resulting group discussions.

However, due to the nature of their jobs and the manufacturing process, no more than three supervisors could by away from their departments at any one time. Training had to be conducted outside of normal scheduled hours, so sessions had to be scheduled in the evening and on Saturdays.

The other consideration here is how long an employee can be away from the job at any one time.

A Delaware mutual funds administration company can allow its entire clerical staff to be away from their jobs between 8:00 A.M. (starting time) and 10:00 A.M., but they must be on their jobs the balance of the day.

An Ohio fund management company can allow supervisors to be away from their jobs on Tuesday through Thursday for up to four hours in any one week, but they cannot be away at any time on Monday and Friday.

Similar factors must be considered for future training populations. However, with new employees it may be possible to schedule their training prior to their reporting to their job assignments, so there are then fewer limits on their availability.

Subject Review and Update

There are few, if any, subjects that are not affected by change, or as someone once said, "The only thing that is constant is change."

Organizational training subjects can be affected by several types of changes, such as:

❐ Organization realignment and restructuring

❐ Revised job assignments

❐ Purchase of new equipment, systems, and materials

❐ Revised job qualifications

❐ External factors such as government rules and regulations

❐ Methods improvement

Although many of these are unanticipated changes, some changes can be projected. It may be possible to predict potential changes on the basis of experience or knowledge. Your investigation should indicate an approximate timetable for reviewing training subject content to ensure it is still current and relative.

Required Results of the Training

What someone most needs in order to develop or design a training program is a statement of exactly what the training is to accomplish. Sometimes the specific outcomes cannot be stated in detail until the training design has begun, but there should be some type of general statement resulting from your investigation.

For example, the subject for training may be the processing of new client applications. A general statement of the required results may be:

To learn how to process new client applications

A more specific and useful statement would be:

At the conclusion of the training, employees are able to process forty-five new client applications per hour with no more than 2 percent errors.

Content Information Sources

The identification of training needs does not usually include in-depth content detail. Discovering that is one of the training program designer's responsibilities. However, identifying sources for content can be easily accomplished at this step and can provide considerable assistance to the program designer. Typical sources of content are:

- ❐ Performance reviews
- ❐ Supervisors or managers of the people to be trained
- ❐ The people to be trained
- ❐ Senior managers (for organizationwide training)
- ❐ Department heads (for departmentwide training)
- ❐ A vendor (if training relates to equipment or systems)
- ❐ Someone with operational experience in a particular area (if training relates to a specialized area within the organization)

These sources can be further enhanced by indicating what specific type of information each can offer.

Training Needs Analysis Report

Figure 6-1 shows a sample training needs analysis report for an investigation of the training needs for a new product pricing system. The form supplies all of the information just reviewed. Use it as a model for how to structure reports based on your company's training needs analyses.

Deciding Who Should Conduct the Training Needs Identification Process

Consideration has to be given to the knowledge and skills someone must have to identify information in each area. For example, having someone with no order-processing experience attempt to identify order-processing training needs will probably be unsuccessful. That individual won't understand the information being offered. Another consideration is credibility. You want to use someone with whom the information providers will feel free to be open.

Figure 6-1.
SAMPLE TRAINING NEEDS ANALYSIS REPORT.

Training Subject(s)
    How to operate the new product pricing system from a PC
Content Information Sources
    The company from which the system was purchased
    Managers of the product pricing department
    Information-processing technicians
Importance of the Training
    Will reduce individual order pricing by 10 percent and increase
    order processing and invoicing speed by 30 percent, for annual
    company savings of $220,000.
Urgency of the Training
    New system to be delivered May 12 and available for training June
    12; will go online August 12. All order processing employees must
    be trained by August 12.
Current Training Population
    47 order processors
    6 order-processing supervisors
    2 order-processing managers
    3 information systems technicians
Potential Training Population
    Based on turnover and projected sales, the following employees
    will be added each year for the next five years. All require training.
    7 order processors
    1 order-processing supervisor
    1 order-processing manager
    1 information systems technician
Frequency of Training
    After initial training of current employees, all newly hired employ-
    ees will have to be trained before reporting to order-processing
    assignments. Due to small numbers of future trainees, consider-
    ation should be given to an initial group training course for current
    employees and a self-study version for later training.
Subject Review and Update
    Subject should be surveyed annually and in-depth every two
    years. Also, procedures should be established to communicate
    any systems changes to the training department.
Required Results of the Training
    Order processors can price products via their PCs at a rate of fifty
    per hour, with no more than a 2 percent error rate.

An Iowa manufacturer wanted to identify the training needs of machine operators. It selected people from the industrial relations department to conduct the investigation. The machine operators being questioned assumed there was a hidden agenda—was the company really looking for information to reduce the number of employees? The result: The information obtained was unreliable and the study a failure.

Chapter 5 described the practice of assigning a training professional to interact with a specific department on a regular basis. If this is a practice at your organization, that person is probably the best one to conduct a training needs analysis in that department. There is already an established relationship, and the training professional has considerable knowledge of the management, employees, and procedures of the department.

Sometimes a team is used consisting of a training professional (who knows how to structure and implement information gathering) and a department employee (who has the necessary knowledge and skills required in the area). When teams are used, it is important that they work well together, agree on what information is required, and trust each other's abilities and motives.

The Investigation

The last steps in preparing for the training needs investigation are:

❏ Deciding who to contact and in what sequence

❏ Determining the information sought from each contact

❏ Selecting the method(s) of information gathering

Your Contacts List

The process of identifying possible areas of training probably includes some of the people who possess the information you require. That is a starting point. What you need to do next is determine whom you need to see for each item of information you want to obtain. Sometimes it will be a single individual. Other times it may be several different people. The important consideration is that you have a source for all required information.

If you know there are different views on the possible training, it is better to include people with differing opinions. They will provide a fuller understanding of the situation. You also want to ensure you see enough people to obtain all the details you need.

Once you have decided who you need to contact, you then need to place them in a logical sequence. Consider going first to those people who can provide basic information, then moving on to people with more detailed knowledge to share. Another approach is to start with those directly involved and then move to those with less involvement in the subject at hand.

For example, assume you are seeking information about an employee's performance gap. The first person to talk to is probably the employee's supervisor. The supervisor most likely brought the situation to your attention—that is, it is the supervisor who identified the performance gap.

The second person to see is the employee. The employee can provide additional information about individual performance and the reasons the gap exists.

These two people may deliver information that indicates you should meet with others as well, such as coworkers, the supervisor's manager, or employees in other departments who work with the employee. This is a logical sequence of interviews. You begin with the basic and move to the more detailed.

If you are seeking information for a new employee orientation training course, you might begin with senior management to discover their objectives. From there a meeting with middle management could identify generally subjects to include, and a meeting with employees might produce details of what a new employee needs to know.

Then individual areas such as human resources can be contacted for specifics of the various topics to cover, and finally sources such as exit interview reports can be reviewed. Again a logical sequence.

Planning Form

Figure 6-2 is an information planning form for training needs. The first column is used to list the information you seek. The second

Figure 6-2.

TRAINING NEEDS INFORMATION PLANNING FORM.

Training Subject: _____   Date: _____

Information	Who to Contact	Sequence	Method

column is for listing the people you'll seek the information from. The third column is used to indicate the sequence of information gathering (i.e., the first person to contact; the second, and so on). The fourth column is for identifying the information-gathering method to use.

Figure 6-3 is an example of the same form, only it has been completed to illustrate how you might go about seeking information for a new employee orientation training course. In this example, the numbers one through five indicate the order in which you will contact the people listed as contacts. Also, Q is for questionnaire; M is for meeting; and I is for interview technique.

Investigation Methods

We have already introduced general investigative methods to use for information gathering—the interview, the questionnaire, and the meeting. Within each of these general classifications are a number of specific approaches. Chapter 7 gives an overview of the most commonly used approaches, as well as some that are unique. It includes information to assist in selecting which approach to use. Subsequent chapters will provide implementation details on a number of procedures.

Figure 6-3.

TRAINING NEEDS INFORMATION PLANNING FORM WITH SAMPLE DATA.

Training Subject: New Employee Orientation Training Course   **Date:** November 7

Information	Who to Contact	Sequence	Method
Overall course objectives	President and 3 senior VPs	1	I
General subjects to include	14 middle managers	3	M
What new employees need to know	22 middle managers	2	Q
Reasons employees left company	10 new employees	5	M
Employment conditions details	10 employees with one year plus seniority	4	Q
	Exit interview reports	7	NA
	Human resources	6	I

Notes:

Q = questionnaire
M = meeting
I = interview

7

Procedures for Identifying Training Needs

There are many methods you can use to gather information for identifying training needs. They basically fall into three categories: interviews, questionnaires, and meetings. Interviews are generally procedures used with individuals. Questionnaires and meeting are used with larger groups of people.

Interviews and meetings are in-person information-gathering procedures. Questionnaires are most often handled through some type of mail, e-mail, or fax distribution although sometimes they are completed in meetings.

Each type of procedure has its advantages and disadvantages, and each tends to lend itself better to certain situations than to others. Often to improve results, involve large groups in the process, and improve reliability of the collected information, more than one procedure is used to collect information in an investigation.

In this chapter the methods in each category will be described along with their uses. In subsequent chapters, detailed step-by-step implementation instructions will be provided for a number of the procedures.

Individual Procedures

Individual training needs analysis procedures are one-on-one methods. They involve the information gatherer and the information provider and primarily use oral communication. The ones most typically used are interviews and performance reviews. However, there are a number of varieties within these two techniques. These are described below along with several other sources of information that can assist in a training needs analysis.

Interviews

The interview is a one-on-one, in-person, planned, and structured meeting. It is designed and conducted for the specific purpose of obtaining required information. Interviews are generally used when there are relatively few (sometimes only one) person from whom to obtain information. However, there are times when interviews are conducted by one person with several interviewees, and other times when a single interviewee is interviewed by a panel (i.e., more than one interviewer).

There are several advantages to an interview. It provides a method that allows for immediate follow-up on the information provided. It is flexible enough to be readjusted as it proceeds, and it is a two-way communication process. Its disadvantages are that it requires relatively more time to conduct with several people than written and group procedures.

Interviews are best suited to situations in which there is no clear-cut structure for the possible training need and specific detailed information is not what is required. For example, if you are seeking a list of equipment an employee operates or a copy of department rules, a questionnaire is probably the most efficient approach. However, if you are trying to determine how performance standards are set and performance reviews conducted, an interview provides a better approach. For this reason they are often used as a first step to clarify directions, and then other procedures initiated.

Interviewing several people at one time (no more than three) can be useful if the information sought is noncontroversial and fairly straightforward—you want specific information. However, such interviews are really small group meetings and are usually better prepared for and implemented as per the guidelines for successful meetings described later in this chapter.

Panel interviews (during which several people interview one

or two interviewees at the same time and in the same room) are not generally successful as information-gathering approaches. By their very nature and structure they tend to be intimidating and not conducive to full exchanges of information. As a general rule for identifying training needs, panel interviews should be avoided.

Chapter 8 provides guidelines and instructions for preparing for and conducting interviews.

Performance Reviews

Performance reviews are the best and most used sources of information for identifying the training needs of individual employees. They are evaluations of an individual employee's performance for a specific period of time. Most often performance reviews are conducted by an employee's direct supervisor on a monthly, quarterly, or annual basis. When based on some type of objective criteria, they provide accurate information of the employee's job performance. They identify areas in which the employee is performing well and areas in which an employee requires improvement.

The main advantage of performance interviews is that they are measures of actual employee job performance as it relates to the department's and organization's objectives. Another advantage is that they usually have already been conducted, so only a review of the results with follow-up interviews with the supervisor and employee are required. Good performance reviews include the employee and the employee's supervisor together identifying the employee's training needs.

The disadvantage of performance reviews is that they are often not based on measurable criteria for the job. In some organizations performance reviews are a series of questions asked once a year about an employee's performances with no predetermined standards to measure them against. In such a situation the results are rarely accurate.

Another disadvantage is that if reviews are only conducted once a year, considerable time can pass before an employee's training needs are identified. And at times, there is no set procedure for gathering performance information during the year.

In the introductory chapter to this book, an AMA study of a procedure for measuring management competencies was mentioned. When the procedure was being tested, a general letter was sent to a hundred organizations requesting assistance with a validation study. Forty organizations responded positively and indicated an interest in being part of the study.

The next letter described the criteria for participation. One of the criteria was that the organization had to have an objective, measurable performance plan in effect. Thirty-six of the organizations responded that they had such a plan. However, when reviewed, all but three of the plans were discovered to have no objective or measurable base.

Typical was an organization that annually sent a list of traits to each supervisor and requested the supervisor to evaluate the performance of her/his employees in each trait. That evaluation was used to determine any increase in compensation. However, the traits had been selected from a management textbook. There was no evidence they were in any way related to the jobs at that company, and the supervisors had been given no training in how to evaluate employee performance in the traits.

When there is an objective, measurable description of desired results, and actual results are collected over a specified period of time and compared with the desired results, any differences are quickly identified in measurable terms. These differences are called performance gaps, and when actual performance is less than desired performance, the gaps reflect the training needs of the employees.

Chapter 11 provides guidelines and instructions for establishing measurable job measurements and conducting performance reviews.

The Need-to-Know Process

The Need-to-Know Process is an interviewing technique designed to identify exactly what a typical learner will need to know in order to be successfully trained. The approach identifies the specifics actually requiring training, areas that do not require training but require either review or reinforcement, and elements that require no training or reinforcement. A further benefit is that the process often produces the basic design for a training course to meet the identified needs.

The Need-to-Know Process is an effective procedure for assisting in the design of efficient and practical training courses. Its disadvantage is that it is very labor intensive due to its one-on-one nature and the requirements of using it with a number of people. However, recent studies have indicated the same technique can be used in small groups. The process also requires the interviewer to be knowledgeable and skilled in both the procedure and the specific job for which the training needs are being identified.

The Need-to-Know Process is described in detail in Chapter 10.

Job Analysis Grid

Job Analysis Grid is another structured interview process. It was developed from behavioral analysis techniques and is used when the interviewer wants to collect information without the subject contaminating it.

For example, a supervisor may tell an interviewer what she believes the organization wants to hear or what makes her look good rather than the truth, or an employee may describe job requirements in terms of his abilities rather than what is necessary for the job. The Job Analysis Grid technique limits such contamination.

Its main advantage is its ability to produce information that is free of any attempt, conscious or unconscious, to control it. Like the Need-to-Know Process, its disadvantage is that the procedure requires more time than a regular interview. It is often used as a first step in identifying training needs for large populations. The procedure is detailed in Chapter 9.

There are other individual procedures that can provide useful information for identifying training needs. Some of these require skilled practitioners. Others only provide background information or are used as a part of other procedures.

Job Analysis

Job analysis is the formal process of identifying the specific requirements of a job—the qualifications, skills, and competencies.

Such information is valuable for comparing an employee's qualifications to job requirements. It is also the first step in designing tests and other assessment devices. Actually, some of the previously mentioned information-gathering techniques are often used for this purpose. However, there are specific job analysis—structured interviews and questionnaires. Other techniques such as task analysis and job sampling can also be used.

Generally, job analysis does not identify training needs. Its focus is what is required for a job rather than what an employee needs. Job analysis often includes task analysis or job sampling.

Task Analysis

Task analysis is a form of job analysis. It identifies through observation, testing, or sampling the tasks and subtasks of a job. It is often used as a first step in identifying job requirements by determining the activities to be performed. To be successful it requires a trained observer.

Job Sampling

Job sampling is the selection of one or more individual events from work being performed. Usually, such sampling is on a random basis, but there are some job sampling approaches that require the total job to be reviewed for a specified period of time. Very much similar to task analysis, it is used to identify job requirements through the activities performed. To be successful the procedure requires a trained observer.

Group Procedures

The most frequently used group procedure is the meeting. However, there are a variety of meeting types:

❐ **The Conference.** This is a meeting of individuals, generally with similar interests, experience, or knowledge, to exchange and provide information under the direction of a facilitator.

❐ **The Focus Group.** This is a relatively small meeting (generally six to twelve participants) convened for a specific purpose under the direction of a facilitator.

❐ **The Classroom.** The classroom meeting involved a group that is assembled to receive information from a lecturer, teacher, or content-based media.

❐ **The Workshop.** This is a meeting generally used to develop skill or common understanding through some type of application.

❐ **The Teleconference/Audioconference.** This is a two-way electronic communication (an e-meeting) between two or more groups in separate locations. It may be conducted over the phone only (audioconferencing), or in a specially equipped room (teleconferencing), or potentially from the desktop (videoconferencing). Generally the approach works best as an information-providing meeting. However, out of necessity it can be used for information gathering, provided that a facilitator attends each group.

For purposes of training needs analysis, the first two meetings (the conference and the focus group) are most often used. They are information-gathering meetings rather than information-providing meetings. Also, they are led by a facilitator rather than a subject matter expert or lecturer.

Their advantages are that they bring together a number of people at one time, so they make better use of the information gatherer's time. They also allow for a discussion that can produce more insight than might be obtained through individual interviews.

Their disadvantages are that the participants must be available at the same time. This means participants in different locations may not be able to attend in person, and sometimes, not all participants can be away from their jobs at the same time. There is one other possible disadvantage to meetings, although it is a disadvantage that a skilled facilitator can usually avoid. Information-gathering meetings are to obtain information on a predetermined subject from a number of people at the same time. The participants in such a meeting are brought together to share their thoughts, opinions, and suggestions, so you want to be able to hear from all of them. However, studies have shown that such meeting outcomes can be the controlled by one participant rather than being the product of the entire group.

> A study of employee evaluation meetings conducted at a San Francisco–based company discovered that the meetings always favored the opinion of the most senior manager in the group.
>
> Another study at a New Jersey company discovered that even when management levels within a group were the same, the strongest personality most often determined the meeting's outcome.

As mentioned, this situation can be avoided by carefully monitoring the composition of the group and by having a skilled meeting facilitator present. Guidelines for meetings are provided in Chapter 12.

The number of participants at a meeting is also significant and can affect the results. Information-gathering meetings work best with no more than fifteen participants. However, with proper planning and direction the number may be increased to twenty. More than twenty significantly limits the possibilities of full participant involvement. However, if subgroup procedures are used it is sometimes possible to deal with a larger group.

An information-gathering meeting requires a skilled facilitator. Although not a content provider or an expert, the facilitator leads the participants to provide the type of information required, ensures full participation, and keeps the meeting on schedule. A facilitator is more skilled in the meeting process than in its subject.

Chapter 12 will examine how to lead or facilitate information-gathering meetings of two basic types. The first will be a meeting where there is no predetermined content other than identification of the area for which information is required. The other will be for a meeting that expands on already identified information.

Meetings are most successful when the participants have similar degrees of knowledge about the subject. However, numbers, geography, and availability can be a major consideration in their use. For example, if there are 240 logical participants for a meeting and only twelve of them can be handled at one time, that would require twenty meetings. If the participants are located in seven different countries, bringing them together for a two-hour meeting may not be practical. If all participants cannot be available at the same time, a meeting may not be the correct approach. Actually, these situations can sometimes be solved by combining methods (an approach that will be considered later in this chapter).

Written Procedures

For our purposes, written procedures include any method that primarily requires written responses. The most typical is the questionnaire. However, tests, assessments, self-reports, and succession plans also can provide valuable information for identifying training needs, and in today's electronic age, e-mail can replace traditional paper-and-pencil approaches.

The main advantage of written procedures is that they can be used with a large number of people at many different locations without the necessity of bringing them together. They also demand relatively little time of the information gatherer.

Their disadvantages are that you cannot be confident as to who is supplying the information. They are easily ignored, and they demand a structure that reduces their flexibility. Also, many people tend to hedge when they have to communicate in writing. There are several types of questionnaires used in identifying training needs: information-gathering, behavioral, surveys, online, and self-reports.

Information-Gathering Questionnaires

Some information-gathering questionnaires are structured in a format that controls the form of responses. Others are open-ended and allow someone to communicate whatever she/he wants in whatever fashion.

These questionnaires are best used when there is a large number of people from whom to obtain specific information. They also provide a basis for credibility by allowing for inputs from all people within the same population group. For example, if you are identifying training needed for employees throughout the organization, by sending questionnaires to all appropriate parties they all feel they have contributed to the final program. This can make the final result far more acceptable.

Earlier in the book, we examined a simple questionnaire that can be used to identify possible areas requiring your attention. For identifying training needs a more detailed and structured questionnaire is used. This type of questionnaire is meant to obtain specific information, so a direct approach is best. Using objective response or multiple choice questions produces answers that can be easily combined. However, sometimes you will have to ask questions that require longer, written responses. Even in a fully-structured questionnaire, providing an opportunity for such written comments is desirable.

Behavioral Questionnaires

Behavioral questionnaires are used to identify desired and undesired job behaviors. They can provide a description of various acceptable and unacceptable behaviors in job competencies. The end points of each scale represent the extremes of possible behavior in each competency. One end is poor behavior, and the other end is desirable behavior. They are often used in conjunction with other procedures to assist in identifying training needs. Their design and use are covered later, in Chapter 13.

Surveys

Surveys are also information-gathering questionnaires but tend to be in a more formal and standardized format. They often include internal reliability questions and are designed to meet specific criteria. Generally, surveys are developed by external experts, provided by external services, or purchased from appropriate publishers.

Online Questionnaires

Online questionnaires are gaining in popularity. They are easy to complete and easy to distribute over a company's e-mail system. And they often have a built-in system for combining results. Online questionnaires have the same advantages and disadvantages of more traditional questionnaires. However, they require access to computers for responses and some degree of computer literacy on the part of those responding.

Self-Reports

Self-reports are a form of questionnaire in which an employee is asked to evaluate his/her own performance and abilities. The approach can be useful for gaining insights into individual employee training needs, but studies have indicated they are often less than accurate.

Generalizing, many excellent employees tend to evaluate themselves lower than they are. Poor-performing employees tend to evaluate themselves higher than they are. One study indicated that self-evaluations tended to be fairly accurate when the employees knew there was also some form of objective evaluation with which the self-evaluations would be compared.

Tests and Assessments

Testing and assessment are standardized measures. They cover a wide range of procedures: assessment centers, paper-and-pencil tests, psychological interviews, and job simulations. There are also a number of PC-based tests in use.

When job-related, valid, and reliable, these are excellent sources of information. However, they require professional development, implementation, and interpretation.

Any of these devices needs to be based on elements required for a job, so the first step is to have an accurate job analysis. The second step is to obtain or develop a test that measures the identified job requirements. Then the test must be determined to be valid and reliable for the purpose it is being used.

Standard tests and assessment devices are available from commercial test publishers. Psychologists and psychological services firms offer psychological interviewing and assessments devices. Guidelines for selecting and using tests and assessment devices are covered in Chapter 14, as are considerations for using external sources of evaluation.

360-Degree and Peer Reviews

360-degree and peer reviews are evaluations of an employee completed individually by the employee's peers (in the case of peer reviews), and by employees at various levels who know the employee's performance (sometimes people external to the organization such as vendors and customers are also asked to complete such reviews).

These approaches have their critics as well as their supporters. They can provide valuable information for identifying employee training needs, but they are generally conducted with little control and have little evidence of reliability and validity.

Other Procedures

There are several other procedures that are valuable for obtaining information. They include the use of experts, combination methods, and other specially developed techniques.

Experts

The use of experts, often external, who have specific procedures for obtaining information is another possibility. These individuals tend to be used with highly technical subjects or when the internal personnel are not available. If the subject is controversial, experts may serve a purpose as neutral information collectors. Their great advantage lies in their experience in gaining such information. They are able to do this quickly and with a great degree of accuracy. Their primary disadvantage can be their cost.

Specialized Techniques

There are numerous other devices and procedures for obtaining the information. Some may be internally developed and others are available from external sources. Some may be variations on procedures reviewed, and others may be unique. They may be applicable to your use, but before considering, you need to ensure that they accomplish what they claim, and that they are valid, reliable, and cost-effective.

Combinations

It is often advantageous to combine procedures. For example, an interview can be used to identify possible training needs, a meeting to expand on the information for the interview, and a questionnaire to provide an opportunity for all appropriate personnel to participate and contribute. This will be described in further detail in Chapter 15.

Which Procedure to Use?

With so many procedures available, which should you use? Here again is a question with no one correct answer and no simple formula. However, here are some considerations that can guide you to a correct answer:

❏ **If you are analyzing training needs for a single individual employee, you are probably going to need to interview the employee's supervisor and perhaps the employee.** If it concerns a performance gap, you will also need the employee's performance review.

❏ **If the training need has to do with an employee's current abilities and the requirements of another job, you will want to discover those requirements and then compare them with the employee's qualifications.** You need to select which approaches will give you that information. You will want to review such items as job descriptions to identify what the job requirements are and use such procedures as tests, assessment, and performance reviews to determine the employee's current qualifications. Very possibly you will also want to conduct some interviews.

❏ **If you have a number of people from whom to obtain information, consider meetings and questionnaires.** Meetings are generally better but require more time and preparation. Consideration has to be given to the number of people from whom to obtain information and their locations and availability.

❐ **If the need is based on a new procedure or equipment, get to know what the procedure or equipment is.** Then consider the Need-to-Know Process.

❐ **If you are considering the use of procedures that require a certain level of professional training and expertise, be sure that expertise is available to you.** Do not use procedures you are not qualified to implement. For example, a specific measurement device such as a psychological test should only be used and interpreted by someone qualified to do so. Using devices without proper training can lead to faulty results.

And of course, there are cost considerations. You should estimate how costly a procedure is in both dollars and time.

Answering the following questions should give you the type of information required for selecting the best procedure or procedures:

❐ What is the general subject?

❐ From how many people will you need to obtain information?

❐ At how many locations are the people?

❐ How many people are available at the same time?

❐ How many levels of management and nonmanagement employees will be involved?

❐ How many degrees and types of information do the people represent?

❐ How technical is the subject?

❐ How controversial or political is the subject?

From How Many People Will You Need to Obtain Information?

This is really a two-part question. First you need to identify how many people are in the population who possess the information you want. Then you need to decide how many of them you should contact—all or just a portion.

The first part of the question should have been determined in the process of identifying possible areas of required training. However, you should review it to ensure it includes all sources.

Sometimes you may discover you can eliminate some of those initially considered. If they were not earlier identified, then that is something you need do.

Keep in mind the number may change as you pursue the investigation. Information you obtain may suggest new people to contact and allow you to remove others from the population.

If you have a large population, it is not readily available, or it is at several locations, you may want to just use a sample. If you do elect to use a sample, you need to ensure the sample represents all varieties of information. This means people from different locations, jobs, departments, levels of performance, seniority, etc. How many people should be in your sample and how they are selected should be the next question.

Most statistics books offer suggestions and formulas for determining the correct sample size for a population. Assuming all are at the same location and possess the same qualifications, the following table is one method:

Population	Sample
10–20	4–6
21–50	6–10
51–100	10–20
100 +	20%

For selection of the sample a random approach can be used. This helps eliminate a conscious selection of characteristics and contributes to more representative information. One method for random selection is to use random numbers. Here you assign consecutive numbers to each possible person and then, using a random number table (available in most statistics books), select the people for the sample.

For example, assume you assign fifty people each a number from one to fifty. You decided to use a sample of ten. From a statistics book table you used the first ten random numbers for a population of fifty: 18, 4, 31, 27, 9, 22, 45, 12, 39, and 41. The ten people with these assigned numbers were then selected for the sample.

One consulting group writes the names of all possible people on separate pieces of paper. These are then mixed, and the required number of names drawn. Once you have determined the procedures to use and the people to query, you are ready to take the next step in identifying training needs—collecting the appropriate information. The next few chapters will provide specific instructions in how to conduct many of the procedures.

PART THREE

Implementing
Specific Methods to
Gather Information

8

Standard Interviews

Interviewing is one of the most used of all management procedures. Managers conduct selection interviews, disciplinary interviews, performance interviews, and exit interviews. However, at least one study from the late 1990s discovered that in the majority of the firms where this was true, less than 30 percent of the managers conducting interviews had participated in any type of interview training.

> A manager at a Maryland company confided that he was required to conduct numerous selection interviews as part of the company's recruiting team, but he had never been trained in interviewing techniques or given any guidance. "I'm a manager, so I am supposed to know how to interview. All managers are supposed to know how to interview."

For identifying training needs, the interview is an information-gathering procedure. The specific information will vary, but in all cases you want to discover something. And it is not always an easy task.

Sometimes the person you are interviewing may not want to tell you what you need to know. Other times, the interviewee may not have the information you seek, and still at other times, your motives may be suspect. However, if you follow some basic rules and guidelines for preparing for and conducting an interview, you will greatly increase your chances of success.

Knowing Whom to Interview

In most cases, this is the individual who completed the questionnaire or otherwise contacted you that a training need might exist. There are situations in which the initial communication may direct you to an interview with someone else. For example, a manager may describe a problem his employees are having with materials received from another department. In such an instance, the majority of the information you require may be from that other department.

When you are identifying who it is you want to interview, keep in mind that if you need to talk to a number of people, it may be better to have a meeting with all of them at one time.

Planning the Interview

To be successful, an interview should be planned with a specific objective and identification of the information desired. As with any other management activity, to be successful you should first establish an objective. In creating your objective, keep in mind your primary purpose is to obtain information. As an example, your objective might be:

> To obtain the necessary information to determine the training required for a successful _____

As a part of planning for a needs identification study (see Chapters 5 and 6), you identified some of the specific areas where you might need information. In our example of the orientation program, a number of subject and sub-subjects were given. All of those represent areas in which you require information. Your overall objective is to obtain information for a new employee orientation training course, but the objectives for individual interviews may differ depending on whom you are interviewing. For example:

Interview Subject	*Objective*
A human resources professional	To identify the terms and conditions of the organization's health insurance program
A new employee	To discover what information about the organization would have assisted the new employee

Once an objective is established and the general subjects identified, you next need to develop your questions. Successful interviews do not just happen. They are planned and the questions predetermined and sequenced.

Designing the Questions

Questions should be designed to obtain the information you need. An excellent planning method is to list the information required and beneath each item the question or questions you will use to obtain that information.

For example, assume you are preparing to gather information to identify the training needs for a retail salesperson to learn the store's selling system. Two areas you'd be interested in are the types of sales and the return procedures. Perhaps the questions you have prepared to gather this information are as follows:

Types of Sales
❑ What types of sales are made in your department?
❑ Approximately what percent of total sales does each type represent?
❑ What are the most difficult types of sales to process?

Return Procedures
❑ What are the steps to process a return?
❑ How is a return authorized?
❑ What returns are acceptable?

One danger of not preparing your questions in advance is that you'll miss a key point. Another is that not having prepared questions can lead to confusing interviews that are either too short or too long. An interview is too short when the interviewer forgets what to cover, and too long when there is no plan to keep the interviewer focused.

For an information-gathering interview there are a number of guidelines to assist you in developing questions.

Be Sure the Questions Relate to the Interview Objective

By first listing the subject and then the questions, it is easy to determine if the questions will prompt the type of answers—and the information—you require. For example, assume you are investigating training needs for a supervisor's position. You know one of the required competencies for a supervisor is decision making, which is defined as the ability to consciously select an alternative from two or more. You have developed the following two questions:

1. What steps do you (i.e., the supervisor) follow to make a decision?
2. What was the poorest decision you ever made?

The first question will probably elicit an answer regarding the person's decision-making skills, but the second question, although related to decision making, will probably give more insight to the person's judgment. Actually, if the second question had a follow-up—What could you have done to make your poorest decision a good one?—you'd be even more likely to obtain the type of information you are seeking.

Avoid Questions That Are Answerable in One Word

Generally, one-word answers are of little assistance, and they put you in the position of asking the interviewee to explain or justify the answer. The interview becomes a type of interrogation. If you ask, "Do you feel the current training course is effective?" and you receive yes as an answer, you really do not have much information that will assist you. You have to then ask a "why" question, and generally "why" questions should be avoided. You will do better by framing your question as follows:

> How does the subject matter covered in the training course assist employees with their on-the-job performance?

Avoid Questions That Communicate a Desired Answer

Sometimes in attempting to place a question in a proper context, a desired or seemingly desired answer is communicated along with the question. For example:

> Our company's president believes that all new employees should attend a four-hour company orientation course. How do you feel about that?

Chances are the person will agree with company president even if she thinks the orientation should be longer or shorter. Or suppose you ask this question:

> We have always felt that, to be a successful, a supervisor must have strong leadership skills. How do you feel about that?

You will probably receive an answer that expresses agreement that leadership skills are important for a supervisor, rather than what the interviewee really thinks.

These types of questions control the input you receive. In fact, they often get you the answers you want rather than real information.

Structure All Questions Neutrally

You are trying to obtain information, so you do not want to appear to be defending or praising current training, or attacking or criticizing the interviewee. Instead of asking:

> What causes you to be so critical of the current training course?

You will do better by asking:

> What suggestions do you have for improving the current training course?

Use Questions That Encourage Application and Not Regurgitation of Facts

Asking "What is good management?" may get you a textbook answer. A better question is one that requires the interviewee to indicate her own thoughts regarding management in action. For example:

> What causes some managers to better motivate their employees than others?

Sequence Your Questions

Ask your questions in a logical order. You will begin your interview by stating its objective. The first questions should be a logical extension of that objective, and they should proceed in an order that makes sense to the interviewee. Jumping all around can confuse things and tends it reduce the depth of information you are given.

Give consideration to the difficulty in answering some questions. Begin your questioning with easily answered questions. Save the more difficult ones for later in the interview—when the interviewee is more comfortable with the process. You don't want to begin an interview with an employee by asking: "So what are the reasons your performance is failing?"

However, near the end of the interview, you might be able to ask a similar question:

> So, all things considered, what do you believe is causing you the greatest difficulty in meeting job standards?

Also, keep questions about one subject together and sequence them. For example, suppose you are seeking information about an individual's flexibility. You might ask the following questions— each after receiving an answer to the previous one:

❑ How do you react when your decisions are challenged?

❑ If your decisions were challenged, what would you do if asked to make a similar decision in the future?

❐ How many ways do you believe there are to make a decision?

Develop a Summary Question

This is not a necessity, but it assists in bringing the interview to a logical conclusion and provides the interviewee a way of summarizing his total responses.

A summary question should require a relatively short answer and allow the interviewee to provide an overall summary of the information. For example:

> All things considered, what three words best describe a successful supervisor at our company?

Or:

> In summary, what are the three most important requirements to succeed at your job?

Or:

> In conclusion, what are the major elements of a successful sales call?

Adopt an Interview Planning Form

Figure 8-1 is an Interview Planning Form. It is a useful device for planning your interview. The top half of the form is used to record the identifying information about the interview while the bottom half is used to list the subjects of the interview, the questions, and the interviewee's responses. As an example:

Objective: To identify the training needs of new inventory control clerks

Interviewer: Training Manager

Interviewee: Bill Johnson, Inventory Control Clerk

Time and Location: 3:00 P.M., Thursday, March 10 in Training Conference Room 3

Subject: Inventory Control Codes

Figure 8-1.

INTERVIEW PLANNING FORM.

Objective: _____

_____

Interviewer: _____

Interviewee: _____

Time and Location: _____

(The lines below are for listing the subject and questions, and for writing in the interviewee's responses.)

_____

_____

_____

_____

_____

_____

_____

_____

_____

_____

_____

_____

_____

_____

_____

_____

_____

_____

_____

_____

Questions:

What inventory codes does a new employee use during the first month of employment? _____

_____

What checks are there on inventory control code usage to ensure correctness? _____

_____

Figure 8-1 is a blank form you can copy and use for your own interviews.

Scheduling the Interview

The next step is to schedule the interview—establishing a time and location. Sometimes your initial analysis will require you to interview or obtain information from more than one person. In scheduling, you want to give consideration to the order in which you see people. Often the information gathered in one interview will assist you in preparing for the next one.

Select a Convenient Time

Be sure there is adequate time for the interview. You do not want to have to end the interview before asking all your questions or have to hurry through the last questions. Estimate how long your interview will last and then add 50 percent more time. It is better to finish early rather than to run out of time.

As a general rule for planning purposes, you will need fifteen minutes plus two minutes per question. So if you have identified twenty questions to ask, you will need fifty-five minutes (fifteen minutes minimum, plus two minutes for each of the twenty questions). Adding another 50 percent brings it to almost an hour and a half, so plan on a ninety-minute interview.

Next select a time. Consider the individual's job requirements. Some employees are available first thing in the morning. Others are very busy in the morning. Likewise, some people are free at the end of their day, and others are not. For some Monday is a very busy day. For others Monday is the slowest day of the week.

If you are unsure about the best time and day for an interview, call the person. Tell the person the subject of the interview and its planned length. Then ask the person what is a good time. You will always receive more cooperation when the interview is scheduled at a convenient time for the interviewee.

For your own schedule, be sure to allow enough time after the interview so that you can consolidate your notes. Generally, a time equal to the planned interview time is adequate.

Select a Location That Contributes to the Interview

Since you want to obtain information, a nonthreatening, neutral environment is conducive for that objective. Also, as with the time of the interview, you want a location convenient for the interviewee. Those thoughts should assist you in selecting a location.

The most nonthreatening and convenient environment for most people is generally their work area, but those locations often present privacy problems. A person's work area is subject to interruption—both by other people and the telephone. Also the interviewee's work surrounds him with reminders of what else is to be done.

Your office poses the same problems for the interviewee. It is where you are most comfortable but not the interviewee. Your office also displays the symbols of your work and position.

If possible, select another location, such as a small conference room or someone else's office. Your chances of maintaining privacy without interruption are much greater, and it is a neutral area for both of you.

However, avoid places such as an employee lounge, the lunch room, an open area where you can be seen and overheard by others, places with activity that is distracting, or a local restaurant. All of these lack privacy and, in addition, their atmospheres do not support the purpose of the meeting.

Prepare the Environment

The final step occurs just prior to the interview, and it is the preparation of the interview environment.

If you are meeting in the interviewee's office, you probably cannot prepare the environment (another reason for not using it). However, if you've selected another location, make sure you arrive before the interviewee so that you can prepare things to produce the best possible flow of information. For example:

❐ **Have the table or desk clear of unrelated items.** That indicates this interview is important. Other work has been put aside.

❐ **Arrange the chairs so that you can talk without a desk or table between you.** Desks can become barriers to open communications since they are symbols of authority. An excellent setup is two chairs set at an angle with a small table between them.

❐ **Be sure both chairs are of equal size and appearance, and that they're placed so that events outside the office are not visible and distracting.** Also be sure sunlight is not falling in either of your eyes.

❐ **Arrange to have no interruptions.** That might mean locking the door or posting a Do Not Disturb sign on it. If possible, turn off the ringer on the telephone or the telephone itself. If there is a PC in the office, turn it or the monitor off. Do not have a moving screen saver or some type of work product visible.

❐ **Do not use an audio or videotape recorder.** Tape recorders change the type of responses you receive. People are concerned about who else may listen to or view the tapes, so you will tend to get guarded answers. Also, do not use hidden tape recorders. Such actions always are found out, and then your credibility for future information gathering is diminished.

❐ **Keep the interview to just two people—you and the interviewee—unless it is a planned multiperson interview.** However, do not have someone else present to take notes or observe. It is not only distracting, but it causes the same problems as tape recorders.

Notifying the Interviewee

As mentioned previously, contacting the interviewee is a way of ensuring the time and day are convenient. It also allows you to check on the suitability of the location you've selected. If the interviewee has problems with any of these items, try to adjust the arrangements to meet the interviewee's concerns.

You want to call several days in advance. And you also want to be sure to state the objective of the interview. This gives the interviewee a chance to prepare as well. You will get more and better information in such circumstances.

Conducting the Interview

On the day and time for the interview, arrive a little early. Prepare the interview environment and have all of your materials at hand. Be fully ready to begin when the interviewee arrives.

State the Purpose of the Interview

Begin by restating the purpose of the interview. Be sure the interviewee understands why you are conducting the interview, the type of information you require and how it will be used.

Check for Questions

Before beginning to ask your questions, discover if the interviewee has any questions of her own, and answer them. Perhaps they will be about the process or where it may lead or who else you are interviewing. Whatever they are, not answering them can impede the interview, so deal with them up-front. Answer the person's questions to the best of your ability. If you do not know an answer, say so, and if appropriate offer to find the answer and report it to the interviewee. However, if you make that type of commitment, be sure to fulfill it.

If the interviewee asks if he will be directly quoted in any report, answer truthfully. If the interviewee does not want to be directly quoted or identified, respond truthfully. If you cannot grant the request, you may not receive the depth of information you are seeking. If an interviewee is concerned about being identified, discover the reasons. You may be able to easily alleviate concerns. However, if this is a real issue and problem, you may have to postpone or cancel the interview.

For example, you wish to do an interview with a salesperson to gain information that will help you identify the type of training new salespeople require. You might begin by saying:

Interviewer: The reason I have asked to meet with you is to obtain your thoughts and suggestions regarding the type of training our salespeople require. By meeting with you and several other salespeople, sales managers, and product managers, we hope to identify the specific needs new salespeople have. Those will then serve as a basis for developing a new sales training course.

So, that's the objective, but before I begin to ask my questions, what questions do you have?

Interviewee: I have one. My sales manager and I disagree about what type of training a new salesperson requires. My answers are not going to cause any problems for me with my sales manager, are they?

Interviewer: No. I am going to be interviewing a number of salespeople and sale managers. All of the information will be combined and a final report issued. All of you will be identified as participating in the process, but none will be quoted or credited for a specific piece of information.

Do you have any other questions?

Interviewee: No. I'm ready to begin.

Tell the Interviewee You Will Be Taking Notes

Before you actually begin asking any questions, tell the interviewee you will be taking notes.

There is a school of thought that says note-taking during an interview is threatening to the interviewee. However, post-interview discussions tend to suggest that for information-gathering interviews, most interviewees prefer that notes be taken. Or as someone once said:

> You know, I spent an hour in there talking about job require-
> ments, and the interviewer didn't write down one thing I said.
> I guess he didn't think it was important.

Take notes, but only notes. If you attempt to write everything the interviewee says, it will make for a long interview. Use key-words to summarize what the interviewee says. Take your notes openly. Do not attempt to conceal what you are writing. Studies have found that an interviewer can recall everything from an inter-view for the two or three hours following it as long as notes are available to jog the memory.

That is why it is important to schedule time immediately fol-lowing the interview to consolidate your notes. You can then also expand and detail your notes at that time. However, without key-word notes, it is sometimes difficult to recall all major items of information.

Do not write while the interviewee is talking. Wait until the in-terviewee has provided a full answer to your question. Then use a few keywords to summarize what was said. If you attempt to take notes while the interviewee is speaking, you cannot pay attention to how the interviewee is answering. Also, many people change their answers as they talk. That can cause you to continually cross out and rewrite. In addition, to use keywords you must first hear the complete answer to know what type of words to use to de-scribe it.

So ask your question. Focus your full attention on the inter-viewee as the answer is given. When the answer is completed, make your keyword notes.

Wait for Answers

When you ask a question, wait for an answer. Sometimes the inter-viewee may want to think before answering. Be patient. You will receive an answer or a request for clarification of the question. In the unlikely event that a minute or two passes without an answer, reask your question. However, do not offer clarification unless it is requested. If more time passes, reword your question. Then if the question is still not answered, you should determine if the interviewee understands your questions. You might say:

What can I add that will assist with the question?

How does my question relate to what you know of the subject?

Being patient and waiting for an answer is sometimes uncomfortable for an interviewer, It seems as if many minutes are passing when in fact it may only be a few seconds. However, in most cases the interviewee just wants to consider your questions before responding.

Do Not Comment on Answers

There are some interviewers who suggest that you should say things such as, "Good answer!" or "Very thoughtful!" or "Excellent!"

Their argument is that these comments are positive and supporting, and they will contribute to making the interviewee feel as if she is succeeding.

Maybe so, but when you make such comments to some answers and not others, it implies the answers that receive no comment are not as good as the ones that do. It also implies you are evaluating answers rather than collecting information.

You should not comment on the value of any answer. Just accept it and move on. This also means you do not react negatively or positively to answers. Even if you believe some responses are right or wrong, accept them and move on. If you feel compelled to say anything, use uncommitted phases and sounds such as, "Interesting," or "Hmm," or "I see. . . ."

Be Flexible

Even though you have prepared your questions, not all interviews go exactly as planned. Some answers may require follow-up questions. Other answers may open whole new areas to be considered.

Even the best-prepared questions sometimes receive answers that do not appear to relate to the question. If that happens, accept what you receive. You may have to develop a different question to obtain the information required. For example, you may have prepared the following question to obtain leadership information:

There are many different people who have been called leaders. Hitler, Patton, and Pope John Paul II are a few. All different people, but all called leaders. What did they have in common that made them leaders?

The question appears to be one that will obtain information regarding leadership, but you could receive an answer to it such as:

I believe the quality of a person's decisions are determined by the individual's past experience.

You may think the answer has nothing to do either with your question or leadership, but you asked a question and received an answer. You cannot now say, "Wait a minute. That is a leadership question, so give me a leadership answer." Instead accept what you received. You may have to develop a new leadership question during the interview.

You have a plan, but you do not become a slave to it. If responses open other areas for investigation that relate to your objective, pursue them. Remain flexible with your objective in mind and adjust your plan accordingly. In some instances, information may be given that will require you to conduct a follow-up interview.

Ask Your Summary Question and Explain What Will Happen Next

If you prepared a summary question, ask it as your final question.

During the interview you may have discovered that the interviewee has completely different objectives for the training than you do. You still need to remain neutral. Don't argue. Accept the information given. The training department's role is to provide the training required for the organization to meet its objectives. Training's role is not to defend courses that are not perceived as helpful.

Often such interviews will clear up misunderstandings as well as provide information for training. Whatever the case, you may want to conclude by telling the interviewee what will occur next. That may mean sharing information about:

- ❐ Who else you are going to interview
- ❐ Whether the interviewee will see your final report
- ❐ If the situation is not one that has training needs
- ❐ How the information just obtained will be used

Conclude the Interview

Again, answer any questions the interviewee may have at the conclusion of the interview. If you don't know the answers, tell the interviewee you will get back to him, but if you say that, be sure you do it.

Thank the interviewee for his time and say something like, "This has been most helpful. I have enjoyed speaking with you." However, do not use statements that communicate an evaluation of the responses, such as, "You have provided very good information," or "You have an excellent grasp of the situation." Keep things neutral and objective.

Handling the Interview Follow-Up

As soon as the interview is complete, finalize your notes of the interview. Expand the keywords you wrote down during the interview into more descriptive information. Identify any follow-ups now required and any information you promised to get back to the interviewee. Be sure to get such promised information back as soon as possible. If it will take more than a week or two, you should advise the interviewee of the delay.

Some Final Thoughts About Interviews

This chapter reviewed the approach for a typical information-gathering interview. However, there are other situations that are worth mentioning briefly:

- ❐ **Multiperson Interviews.** If you are interviewing more than one person at a time, prepare in the same way. However, during the interview, be sure to ask questions equally of all

interviewees. Also review the preparation steps and guidelines for meetings, since that is, essentially, what a multiperson interview is.

❐ **Panel Interviews.** If more than one interviewer is conducting the interview, prepare as you would for a normal information-gathering interview. Distribute the questions among
the interviewers and arrange for the order in which each
interviewer will ask questions. However, be advised that
panel interviews generally do not obtain as in-depth information as meetings and single interviews.

Chapters 9 and 10 will deal with specific interview techniques
that lend themselves to certain situations and other types of interviews.

Job Analysis Grid
Interviews

Although the interview is an excellent method for obtaining appropriate information for identifying training needs, one problem that can occur is the conscious or unconscious addition or deletion of information. In today's popular terminology, it's called "putting a spin on the facts." You may be told something that sounds good, makes the interviewee look good, or is a classic textbook answer. Other times, information an interviewee may (correctly or incorrectly) consider as being negative may be withheld. This may be intentional or accidental, but whatever the reason, it results in incomplete or inaccurate information. Consider this example:

A few years ago a study was conducted to determine exactly what competencies supervisors in a number of companies required. Later a follow-up evaluation was made to determine whether the studies accurately reflected the competencies required. The result of the study indicated the competencies were correctly determined. At that point, the results were communicated to the various companies.

In all but two companies, at least one senior manager disagreed with the results and claimed key competencies were missing. The most extreme example was a food processor in a western state. The initial work indicated that the company was very control-minded, or as one supervisor said, "The company has rules, and they don't want us mucking around with them."

So for that company, flexibility—the ability to adjust to changing conditions—was identified as an unneeded ability. In fact, inflexibility was closer to what was required for success.

When the president of the company saw the identified competence, he immediately demanded that flexibility be added to the list and given a high weight. He was the president, so the human resources director added the competence and used it as one of the selection criteria for supervisors.

The result—people placed in supervisory position who had high flexibility either failed or were fired or quit. Those with low flexibility succeeded.

The point of the story is that if you ask people to tell you what's required for success in a job, often they'll tell you what they want or think those success factors to be, or what sounds good, rather than what is reality. Or people in a position will often cite qualifications or performances that reflect what they perceive to be their individual strengths. They answer in terms of themselves rather than the job.

The problem, of course, is that the use of faulty information can result in training courses being designed to meet incorrect needs.

A North Dakota mutual funds company conducted a training needs analysis for employees in its contract fulfillment department. The investigation indicated that there was a need for personnel to learn techniques of PC operation, and an appropriate course was purchased and conducted. (They had been using terminals that each had a keyboard for data entry but no mouse, operating system, e-mail, or computation functions.)

However, there was actually no such training need. A month before the training needs analysis, the company's president had given a talk to all employees in which he said, "To progress in the future with this company, knowing how to operate a PC is a vital skill."

The president was giving her general view on future directions, but it impacted the employees and, in turn, the training needs investigation, even though the administrative department had no PCs and no plans to install them in the near future.

One method that can eliminate the contamination of information is the Job Analysis Grid technique. The method is an outgrowth of work done with a behavioral inquiry technique called the Repertoire Grid—a comprehensive approach for identifying specific human behaviors. The Job Analysis Grid is a version designed to identify job needs.

The method begins with a series of questions that do not appear to be directly related to the objective of the investigation. The questions elicit responses that are then used as a basis for questions directly related to the training need being considered. This approach produces very reliable information, something that is often difficult to ensure.

Actually, the Job Analysis Grid is a standardized form of interviewing. It is less direct than a traditional information-gathering interview, and it requires more time and an interviewer trained in the technique. Sometimes it is used in conjunction with information-gathering interviews as a cross-check.

The Job Analysis Grid is generally not used when the training need being investigated is to update an existing training course. However, when the investigation is for a possible first-time course, it can be an excellent method to determine basic needs. Often it is used as the first step when a series of methods are used—something that will be covered in Chapter 15 on combining methods.

The Technique

Let's assume you want to determine subjects for an orientation training program. You have scheduled an interview with a relatively new employee and have decided to use the Job Analysis Grid technique.

First, schedule a time, allowing at least an hour. Use a private location. (The same considerations covered in Chapter 8, on standard interviewing, are important—perhaps even more important, since the instructions for a Job Analysis Grid interview are more problematic than a traditional interview.) Then, to get started, you will need a stack of cards (three-by-five-inch cards without lines work fine) and three rubber bands.

The interview begins the same way:

1. State the objective, but be slightly less specific than in an information-gathering interview.

2. Check for interviewee questions.

3. Give a brief description of what will occur. You might say:

I am going to ask you a series of questions about your initial reactions to our organization, your department, and your job. I am going to record your answers on these cards. Then we'll use these cards to develop further insights into kind of information a new employee at our organization needs.

4. Check again for interviewee questions. Then begin to ask your questions (each of these questions can be modified as necessary to reflect the objective of the actual interview):

   ❐ What did you discover during your first month of employment that was a surprise to you?

   ❐ What are the three best features of working here?

   ❐ What are the three things you would most like to change?

   ❐ What would have helped you to have known before starting work?

   ❐ What three words best describe working here?

   ❐ If a new employee is dissatisfied with his or her job, what is the most likely reason?

As the employee answers each question, write the responses on the index cards—write one keyword per card. If a question produces multiple responses, use a single card for each response.

When all the questions have been answered, shuffle the cards and select three at random. Lay the three cards, face up, in front of the employee and ask:

Two of these cards have more in common than the other two. Which two have more in common?

When you receive the answer, remove the card that the interviewee identified as having the least in common with the other two. Then ask:

What is it these two have in common?

Here you have to wait for an answer and listen carefully. You may or may not receive an answer that is in terms of new employee orientation, but whatever you receive, write a keyword indicative of the response on a card. Again, if you get multiple responses, use one response card for each response.

You don't want to hurry this process. Give the person time to fully respond.

When the employee has completed the responses for the first three cards, reinsert the cards into the deck, reshuffle, and repeat the procedure with three other cards. Continue until you are no longer receiving new responses.

If you want to be very thorough, you can create a matrix table that indicates all possible three-card combinations. Number the backs of the cards and proceed in a way that provides all possible three-card combinations. Of course, you'll have a very large number of cards and it will greatly increase the time required to conduct the Job Analysis Grid, but it won't provide more useful input. Once you get the interviewee talking about the subject based on the initial response cards, you'll usually receive all the information you need.

A Typical Job Analysis Grid Interview

This section outlines the first part of an actual Job Analysis Grid interview conducted with a supervisor to identify the management competencies required for a supervisor's position. The actual responses are abbreviated as keywords written on index cards:

- ❏ What did you discover during your first month as a supervisor that was a surprise to you?

Responses	*Keywords*
Need to know employment procedures	Employment procedures
Some employees are not self-motivated	Motivation
Must have a daily plan	Planning

❐ What are the three best features of being a supervisor?

Responses	*Keywords*
Compensation	Compensation
Being in charge	Authority
Being a part of management	Management

❐ What are the three things you would most like to change?

Responses	*Keywords*
Hours	Work schedules
Pre-supervisory training	Training
Improve communications	Communications

❐ What would it have helped you to know before starting work as a supervisor?

Responses	*Keywords*
Employee histories	Employee histories
Payroll procedures	Payroll procedures

❐ What areas do you still not know?

Responses	*Keywords*
Disciplinary procedures	Disciplinary procedures
Interviewing	Interviewing

❐ If supervisors are dissatisfied with their job, what is the most likely reason?

Responses	*Keywords*
Cannot control employees	Controlling
No leadership	Leadership

After the interviewer collected and shuffled the cards, the first three that were displayed were:

❐ Controlling

❐ Disciplinary procedures

❐ Employment procedures

The supervisor selected "controlling" and "disciplinary procedures" as having the most in common. The supervisor commented: "Actually, all three have the same thing in common, but these two have the most in common."

When the supervisor was asked what they had in common, the keywords for the responses were:

❐ Controlling

❐ Oral communication

❐ Knowing disciplinary procedures

❐ One-on-one meeting skills

Since two of the responses were identical with earlier ones—controlling and disciplinary procedures—new cards were not made for them. Although communications had been mentioned, a card for "oral communications" was created. A card was also made for "one-on-one meeting skills."

The other comparisons produced similar responses, and at the conclusion of the comparisons, the interviewer had thirty-two cards.

Sometimes you have to interpret the responses. An interviewee may talk for several minutes about what is common between two of the cards. You need to listen closely and write the keyword or words that best describe what's being said. Sometimes the interviewee may not say the keywords you've chosen to use. Just be sure you are not writing what you wish was said. If you do that, you will be contaminating the information.

Concluding the Interview and Combining Results

The first part of the Job Analysis Grid interview produces a number of cards with responses. In our example the responses are primarily in terms of job competencies, since that's the information we're seeking in this case. However, there may be some responses that relate to other matters. For example, employee histories are not a competency. Nonetheless, use all the response cards that were created as you continue the interview.

When no new information is being offered, combine the new cards with the first deck and shuffle all of them together. Then lay all the cards from both decks out before the interviewee, face up. Staying with our example of seeking information on the competencies required for supervision, you would say:

> These are all of the things you mentioned. Consider them for a moment and then put them in order of importance as competencies a new supervisor requires for success at our organization.

When the interviewee has completed that task, ask:

> What competencies, if any, that a supervisor should possess for success are missing?

As you receive answers, write each answer on a new card. Then give the card to the interviewee and have the interviewee insert it at the appropriate point in his ranking. Continue until the interviewee is satisfied with the completeness and ranking of the competencies.

At this point, you need to record the rank order. You can do this by writing a number on each card (e.g., one for the first ranked, two for the second ranked, and so on) or making a separate list of the competencies. Now say:

> I want you to divide these cards into groups by placing them in separate piles. The three possible groups are: 1) Musts—

the competencies a new supervisor must absolutely have in order to function successfully; 2) Wants—the competencies a supervisor should have but can initially get by without, or one in which a person can be trained; and 3) Not Necessaries—the competencies a supervisor does not need to succeed. These are not competencies that the supervisor should not have. They just aren't required on the job.

Though there are three possible groups, you do not have to make three piles. You can have just two or one.

When the interviewee has divided the cards, be sure you know which group is which. Then collect the cards by groups, secure each group of cards with a rubber band, and identify it.

At the conclusion of the Job Analysis Grid interview, thank the interviewee, check if there are any final questions, and tell the interviewee what will happen next.

How Many Job Analysis Grid Interviews Should You Conduct?

Since it is a somewhat lengthy procedure and because final responses can be difficult to combine, the process is usually limited to a few interviews. Those results can then be confirmed through other procedures such as meetings and questionnaires. (Chapter 15 describes this combination of procedures in detail.)

If the population from which you are seeking information has distinct groups, you need to conduct Job Analysis Grid interviews with representatives from each group. For example:

❑ For a new employee orientation, you should probably interview at least two new employees, two supervisors of new employees, two managers of areas that hire new employees, and one or two people from human resources.

❑ To identify supervisory competence needs, you should probably interview at least two current supervisors, two managers of supervisors, and two employees who report to supervisors.

After you have concluded all your interviews, you need to combine the results by group. Figure 9-1 is an example of a grid results combining form that can be used for this purpose. You need to complete a form for each group of participants. If you conducted Job Analysis Grid interviews with managers, supervisors, and non-management employees, you need to complete three forms.

First, complete the upper portion of the form for the group. For example, assume you interviewed three managers regarding supervisor competence training needs. The upper portion of the form would appear as:

Subject:	Supervisor Competencies
Date:	August 19
Participant Group:	Managers
Number of Participants:	Three

Next, list the card responses from the first manager interviewed in the first column of the form. List the responses from the Must classification (if any), followed by the Want classification responses (if any), and finally, the Not Necessary classifications (if any).

The next column in Figure 9-1 (i.e., the column headed with the number 1) is used to record information gathered from the first manager interviewed. Here you then enter a number for each competency that's based on the classification given to the competency by Manager 1. The number for each classification might be:

6   Musts (i.e., the "absolutely necessary" competencies)

4   Wants (i.e., the "should have" group)

2   Not Necessary (i.e., the "not needed" group)

Now, take the second manger's cards. Using the same scale, write that participant's classification numbers after the competencies. If Manager 2 identified competencies the first one did not, add those competencies to the first column of the form, but leave the lines for those competencies blank in the first manager's column. If Manager 2 did not identify the same competencies the first

Figure 9-1.

GRID RESULTS COMBINING FORM (EXAMPLE 1).

Subject: _____   Date: _____

Participant Group: _____   Number of Participants: _____

Subject	1	2	3	Average
_____	___	___	___	_____
_____	___	___	___	_____
_____	___	___	___	_____
_____	___	___	___	_____
_____	___	___	___	_____
_____	___	___	___	_____
_____	___	___	___	_____
_____	___	___	___	_____
_____	___	___	___	_____
_____	___	___	___	_____
_____	___	___	___	_____
_____	___	___	___	_____
_____	___	___	___	_____
_____	___	___	___	_____
_____	___	___	___	_____
_____	___	___	___	_____
_____	___	___	___	_____
_____	___	___	___	_____
_____	___	___	___	_____
_____	___	___	___	_____

one did, leave the lines following those competencies blank for the second participant.

Continue in this manner, entering each manager's results in a separate column. In Figure 9-2, the form has been further completed with the addition of the subjects and rankings from the first manager interviewed. In Figure 9-3, the form has been further completed with the rankings from all three managers.

It is not uncommon for the participants to all have the same top-ranked inputs and to have differences in those ranked lower.

When all participants' responses have been entered into the form, total them and divide by the number of participants with a response for that subject. Figure 9-4 shows such a completed form.

When you have completed a grid results combining form for each group, the next step is to combine the information from all groups. To accomplish this you must first determine the relative weight of each group's responses. Since this is a requirement for all investigation methods used with a variety of groups, it is detailed in Chapter 16.

For now we are going to move on to another method for identifying training needs—the Need-to-Know Process.

Figure 9-2.

GRID RESULTS COMBINING FORM (EXAMPLE 2).

Subject: Supervisor Competencies   Date: August 19

Participant Group: Managers

Number of Participants: Three

Subject	1	2	3	Average
Leadership	6			
Controlling	6			
Oral Communication	6			
Flexibility	6			
Planning	4			
Organizing	4			
Written Communication	4			
Decision Making	4			
Employee Procedures	4			
Interviewing	4			
Discipline	4			
Initiative	2			

Figure 9-3.

GRID RESULTS COMBINING FORM (EXAMPLE 3).

Subject: Supervisor Competencies   Date: August 19

Participant Group: Managers

Number of Participants: Three

Subject	1	2	3	Average
Leadership	6	6	6	
Controlling	6	6	6	
Oral Communication	6	6	6	
Flexibility	6	4		
Planning	4	2	4	
Organizing	4	4	4	
Written Communication	4	2	2	
Decision Making	4	6	6	
Employee Procedures	4	6	6	
Interviewing	4	4	4	
Discipline	4	6	6	
Initiative	2		4	
Stress Tolerance		4		
Energy			4	
Thoroughness		4		

Figure 9-4.

GRID RESULTS COMBINING FORM (EXAMPLE 4).

Subject: Supervisor Competencies   Date: August 19

Participant Group: Managers

Number of Participants: Three

Subject	1	2	3	Average
Leadership	6	6	6	6
Controlling	6	6	6	6
Oral Communication	6	6	6	6
Flexibility	6	4		5
Planning	4	2	4	3.3
Organizing	4	4	4	4
Written Communication	4	2	2	2.7
Decision Making	4	6	6	5.3
Employee Procedures	4	6	6	5.3
Interviewing	4	4	4	4
Discipline	4	6	6	5.3
Initiative	2		4	3
Stress Tolerance		4		4
Energy			4	4
Thoroughness		4		4

10

The Need-to-Know Process

This technique is based on discovering exactly what a typical person to be trained needs to know in order to meet the objectives of the training. It is not applicable to every situation, but where it is, it produces an exact description of the training needs and a format that will provide an efficient and effective training course. The technique is exactly what its name implies—it is a method to discover what someone needs to know.

A Game of Chess

The Need-to-Know Process can be illustrated in the following examples.

A number of years ago an author was working on a book describing how to play chess. Most books that do this begin with a description of the chessboard, then describe the pieces along with their moves. The play starts with the first moves and proceeds through checkmate.

This author took a reverse approach. He began by describing the final move of the game—checkmate. He then worked back through the entire game. At each step he described what was necessary to get from the former step.

He developed this approach by sitting with someone who did not know the game, telling the person what she was to do, and then supplying whatever information she requested. In other words, he only told her what she needed to know to get to the game's objective.

The book followed that conversation. In fact, the last element of the book explained opening moves—the point at which most such books begin.

So, how did this author's technique work? Actually, quite well. In the preparation of the book, the author tested the approach and discovered that people learned faster and more completely than with traditional texts.

Later the technique was introduced as a method for developing programmed instruction. It identified what a typical student needed to know; what the student did not need to know, and what the student needed to have reinforced—exactly the type of information required to write a programmed instruction. In recent years the technique has been used to identify training needs for all types of training and educational programs and courses. To succeed the interviewer must know the contents of the proposed training and the job for which the training will be provided. The interviewer has to be able to answer all questions and know what information to provide at what points.

A Software Conversion

The following is a rather long story, but it describes the techniques and advantages of the Need-to-Know Process quite well.

> One of the country's leading mutual funds companies discovered it was necessary to change to a completely new software system. The one it had been using from its inception had performed well, but it was now limiting future expansion.
>
> After some research the company located a perfect system for its requirements—one that had the ability to expand with company growth.
>
> The system designers customized and debugged it. It was first installed and operated with new accounts to ensure it would meet the needs of the company and its customers. It was then time to convert. However, there were several gov-

erning factors. Parallel systems could not be run. Parallel systems are a procedure where a new system is installed and for a time both the new and old systems are simultaneously run. This continues until everyone is satisfied that the old system can be dropped. However, for technical reasons this could not be done at the mutual fund company. Running parallel systems was not a possibility.

Sometimes it is possible to install a new system in stages—converting partially at each stage. Because of the interrelationships among existing client accounts, this too was not an option for this company. All existing accounts had to be converted at one time.

The business was an ongoing one. From the client's viewpoint it was important that nothing must appear to change, and particularly because the company was dealing with its clients' investments, it was important that the clients remained confident in the company's operations and procedures. When the system converted, customer relations representatives had to behave as they had before and had to be able to completely interface with the new system.

The new system also required new hardware. The customer service representatives had been using terminals. These allowed access to information and recording of information, but not in real time. The recorded information was posted to the individual customer accounts at night.

Since stock markets can change in a few hours, this was seen as a disadvantage by clients. Moreover, competitive companies offered immediate real-time access for decisions. Making this change required replacing all the terminals with PCs.

A survey of existing customer service representatives discovered that only 55 percent of them were PC-literate to the degree required, and over half of those who were not PC-literate were deeply concerned about having to use PCs.

In total there were 570 customer service representatives who had to be trained to operate the new system. The company providing the new system estimated it would require eighty hours of training per employee. That would mean a total of 45,600 hours of training. Assuming there would be about fifteen participants per class, that was more than sixty weeks of training. Obviously, a shorter yet effective training approach was required.

The company decided to use the Need-to-Know Process to determine exactly what training was required—what the training needs of the customer representatives were.

A randomly selected group of twenty-five existing customer service representatives was chosen to participate in the study. All participants had been in their jobs long enough to know the procedures. Some were evaluated as excellent performers; some, as poor performers; most as typical performers.

The individuals conducting the Need-to-Know Process were skilled trainers (for the existing system) who had undergone the typical training provided by the system design company, so they were thoroughly familiar with the details of the existing system, the new system, and the customer service representative job. A final test was first developed for the training. The test was designed to ensure that someone passing it had all the information and skills necessary to operate the new system.

The trained people then conducted need-to-know interviews with the randomly selected customer service representatives. Each interview was one-on-one. The actual process went something like this: A room was provided with a PC on which the new software was loaded. The interviewee was brought into the room and the purpose of the procedure was explained. Next, any questions the interviewee might have were answered.

The interviewees were asked to talk as they proceeded, describing what they were thinking and trying to accomplish. The interviewer then administered the test that had been developed.

The first item on the test required the interviewee to report the current number of shares in a client's account and the current value of the shares. None of the participants knew how to perform the request, but as they talked and attempted to reason the procedure, the interviewer took notes. It was discovered that some steps were obvious, but for others information was required. When the participant identified a specific piece of information or action required, the interviewer provided it.

The process proceeded in this manner through all of the system's transactions. At the conclusion of each interview, the interviewer knew what the participant was able to do with no additional training and where in the process the participant needed additional information or instructions.

When the results of all twenty-five interviews were compared and combined, it was discovered there was a remarkable consistency among results. (This was true for both the group requiring PC training and the one not needing such training.)

Two training courses were created based on these results. One was for the PC skills required, and one was for the new system. The systems course based on the Need-to-Know Process information was twenty-four hours in length versus the eighty hours recommended by the system design company.

The PC course had been estimated as requiring two days. Based on the need-to-know information, the final course was four hours in length. The savings in time and cost were significant.

So what were the final results? How effective was the training? Over one weekend the system at the mutual funds company was changed to the new one. The following week there were no significant problems encountered by any of the trained customer service representative with the new system. There was a slight decrease in the number of clients dealt with each hour (a decrease that vanished within three days), and no mistakes were made to any customer account.

When to Use the Need-to-Know Process

The Need-to-Know Process is best used when a number of people are to be trained. However, conducting it with one person both identifies training needs and simultaneously trains the individual. It then becomes an individual coaching session.

The process can be used to teach a new subject as well as to make revisions to existing training. The mutual funds example is very typical of its use. An additional advantage to the process is that it can also be used to design the training course. The training then is conducted on the same need-to-know basis. That is also what happened at the mutual funds company.

> The mutual funds training was designed to be conducted using the Need-to-Know Process. For the new system training, the participants were brought into training rooms and seated at a PC. The trainer then began by asking the participants to report the current number of shares in a client's account and the current value of the shares—the same item that was the first request in the Need-to-Know Process.
>
> Again, the trainer's role was to supply information when it was requested. The training course proceeded in the same way through all elements of the new system with the trainer serving the role as an information provider and coach.

The Technique

To use the Need-to-Know Process, whoever will conduct it requires full knowledge of the ultimate training course content or job for which training is to be provided. Only with that knowledge will the person be able to answer questions and know when to supply required information.

The people to be interviewed in the process must be typical of those to be trained. If only a few are to be interviewed, they should be typical performers. If a number of people are to be interviewed, then you should have some from various levels of performance. All should have the length of service typical trainees will have.

If the training is for new employees, you do not want to interview those who have been in their jobs awhile. Likewise, if the training is for experienced employees, you do not want to interview those just joining the organization.

Planning

The first step is to identify exactly what the outcomes of the training are to be. Start with the overall outcome such as the ability to play chess or operate a new system. Then determine the specifics the trainee must have to accomplish to meet the overall outcome. (Chapter 17 will discuss how to write specific training objectives.) In effect you are preparing a "final exam" for the training course—an exam that, if passed, indicates the participant has learned everything the course was designed to impart.

Assume the training will be to learn how to operate a new piece of equipment. For planning a Need-to-Know Process, this final outcome should be subdivided into its basic elements so that the trainee will be able to:

- ❐ Turn on equipment
- ❐ Set equipment controls
- ❐ Operate equipment
- ❐ Troubleshoot
- ❐ Turn off equipment

The "final exam" would require the trainee to demonstrate competency in performing all of these actions. With this exam prepared and the necessary knowledge obtained, the interviewer is ready to conduct a Need-to-Know Process.

Implementation

With the planning completed, a participant is brought into a private location with whatever equipment and materials are required. The process then proceeds as follows, beginning with your explanation to a potential trainee:

> As you may know, our company is going to be introducing a new processing machine. It is one we believe will improve your job and increase your productivity. That is going to require training for all employees who will be using the equipment.

I have asked you here to spend sometime today to assist in determining exactly what is needed in the training. We will accomplish that by taking you through the operation of the new equipment. As that occurs, what you ask and tell us will assist in identifying what other employees need to learn.

How this works is that I will ask you to do something using the new equipment. You may or may not know how to do what I ask, but I want you to talk about what I ask and what you know. I want to hear your thinking process. If you have questions or need additional information, ask me. I don't expect you to be able to perform all the tasks I request, but that is the purpose of our meeting—to discover what you need to know. Now, are there any questions?

You will probably receive some questions. Answer them fully and be sure the participant is comfortable before beginning. Then say:

Please operate the equipment.

Be patient. Wait for responses. Listen to what the participant is saying. In most cases the first response will be, "How do I turn it on?"

You answer by supplying that information, and you record this question. You proceed in the same manner—providing information as required and making note of what is asked and what is provided. At the conclusion—when the participant has successfully demonstrated all the required outcomes, ask the participant for her/his reactions to the process and the new training. Record any additional information that may be of assistance, and thank the participant. You will then have not only identified the training needs, you will also have a training course outline and structure.

Developing Skill in the Need-to-Know Process

The easiest way to learn the Need-to-Know Process is to use it with a relatively simple task. For example, select a somewhat complicated form that requires completion. Give it to someone and ask him or her to complete it. In the process, you will discover what items on the form require no training, and what items require training.

With that information create a short training course that follows a similar flow and have someone participate in the training. Again, ask him to complete the form, but this time be prepared to provide information at the points identified in the interview.

Chapter 11 deals with the most used procedure for identifying the training needs of individual employees—performance standards and objectives.

11

Performance Standards

The most useful source of information for individual employee training need identification is some type of objective performance measurement. Such measures are comparisons of actual results an employee achieves with statements of the desired results from a job. Any differences can be considered gaps or individual employee training needs.

However, the performance measurement procedure is not one normally conducted by a training professional. Instead it is a function of professional management. A supervisor and the employee set performance standards, and performance collected and reviewed by them. It is the supervisor and employee who are identifying the training needs.

Usually training needs identified through performance standards require additional investigation to determine exactly what type of training is required to close any performance gap. That type of investigation is generally performed by a training professional using the performance measure as a starting point. It is therefore important to understand how the performance standards are established and how actual performance is measured. If your organization—like many—does not follow this process, that in itself could signify an urgent training need on how to measure employee performance.

A Definition of Performance Standards

The measures go by a variety of names: results, objectives, standards, and goals, but as long as they are objectively established and measurable, the names are not important. For our purposes we will consider the most common one used—standards of performance—and use that name for all such procedures.

Ideally every job has a set of performance standards. These are best defined as the conditions that will exist when the job is being satisfactorily performed.

Performance standards for a job generally do not describe the best possible performance. They describe the type of performance the job was designed to produce. When all employees in a department meet all their performance standards, the department should be also meeting its goals.

Generally, performance standards are extensions of a position's responsibilities. For example, the position description for a salesperson's job might have as a responsibility: "Obtain orders from new and current customers in assigned territory." That is not an uncommon responsibility. However, what does that mean? How many orders per year are required? What is the assigned territory? Who are new customers? Who are current customers? Performance standards for that responsibility should answer those questions and could be expressed as follows:

> To successfully fulfill the responsibility, the salesperson is to obtain at least $750,000 in orders per quarter of a year from new customers (customers who have not previously purchased from the company within the past two years) and current customers (customers who have purchased from the company within the past two years) in Ohio, Michigan, and Indiana.

The job responsibility requires a great deal of interpretation, but the performance standard is very specific. If both the salesperson and the manager know the performance standard in advance, they will both always know how well the salesperson is performing. There will be no surprises at the salesperson's annual performance review. Alan Hydrick, a management consultant, once remarked, "A surprise at a performance review is an indication of a manager's failure to communicate what level of performance is desired."

If the employee is not performing as required, an examination needs to be made to determine why. Perhaps it is some external force—the economy in the region dropped significantly after the standard was set, a new competitive product was introduced by another company, or perhaps it has something to do with how the employee is performing the job. For example, if the employee is not scheduling time correctly or makes an excellent presentation but cannot close a sale, both of these can probably be corrected through training. And, finally, if your organization does not use measurable standards of performance that in it self may be an area of training needs.

Types of Standards of Performance

Most standards of performance are written as positive statements to describe what type of results are wanted. An insurance office clerk might have a positively stated standard of performance such as: to process twenty-four insurance applications per hour. However, sometimes it is difficult to state what is wanted, but easier to state what is not wanted. Then a negative or zero standard can be established.

One of the country's major theme parks has employees assigned to greet people as they enter the park. A responsibility of that assignment is: "To welcome visitors to the park in a friendly manner." Writing a positive standard of performance for that responsibility would be very difficult. How do you describe "friendly"? It is easier to describe what is perceived as not being friendly by writing a negative standard such as: There shall be no more than two complaints regarding the employee's attitude in any one year.

Also, it is sometimes easier to describe what should never happen. This is called a zero standard of performance. For example, a production foreman may have the responsibility to operate a safe department. The easiest way to express a standard of performance for that responsibility may be to describe what should never happen: There are to be no instances during the year of an employee being injured due to a machine not having a safety guard in place.

Setting Standards of Performance

Standards should be set—agreed—by an employee and the employee's supervisor. They both know the job and what should be required. Usually, the supervisor prepares the initial standards. Then the supervisor reviews them with the employee. This sometimes leads to revisions to the standards.

Ideally, a set of standards is developed to which both the supervisor and employee can agree, but what if they can't agree? Ultimately, in that case, it is the supervisor who must determine the standards for an employee's position. It is the supervisor who is accountable for meeting department goals through the performance of the employees. The supervisor must ensure that each employee's standards are contributing correctly to that goal.

There should be at least one standard of performance for each position of responsibility. However, at times, you may have to have several standards to describe how one responsibility is to be fulfilled. If a standard cannot be established for a responsibility, it means there is no way of knowing when that responsibility is being satisfactorily performed. Under such circumstances, an employee cannot be held accountable for that responsibility. The responsibility should be eliminated or revised.

Measures

Each standard of performance requires at least two measurements. One is some type of quantifiable measure. For example:

❐ Twelve items per hour

❐ All applications

❐ 50 percent of customers

❐ No lost time

All of the above are some form of quantifiable measure. Unequivocal data can be collected to determine if they were met. However, words like enough, few, many, and adequate are not acceptable measures.

The second measure each standard of performance must contain is a measure of time. It can be either the time in which something is to occur or a due date such as:

❑ Per hour

❑ Quarterly

❑ Annually

❑ The current year

These are all types of time periods that can be used. The following are due date types of time measures:

❑ By the first Monday in each month

❑ Prior to May 17

❑ Three days after receipt

Some examples of standards that utilize both these measures are:

❑ Delivers two copies of the completed reports to the finance office by the fifteenth of each month

❑ Processes between twenty and twenty-five applications per hour

❑ Reduces annual employee turnover by 20 percent by June 18

❑ Has no lost time accidents this calendar year

When proper standards have been set and agreed, they should be written down and given to both the supervisor and the employee.

Performance Evaluation

Setting standards of performance is the first half of performance measurement. The second half is the comparison of employee performance to the standards. This generally takes the form of an annual performance review. However, in practice, reviews should occur more frequently than once a year.

If an employee is not performing to standard, waiting until the end of the year to discuss it with the employee may be too late to take corrective action. Also, if changes beyond the control of the employee are affecting performance, the standards should be revisited at that time.

The best approach is to establish a process for collecting and reviewing performance data throughout the year. Depending on the type of work, this may be a weekly, monthly, or quarterly activity. Such an approach allows the supervisor and employee to know how well actual performance relates to the standards.

> A Washington company requires each supervisor to review all her/his employees' performance to their standards each month. The supervisor is to meet with any employee not meeting standards to discover the reason and initiate corrective action. Included in this approach is a progress report on any annual standards.
>
> If an employee's performance misses standards for a second consecutive month, the supervisor is required to review the situation with the supervisor's manager. If the employee misses standards for a third consecutive month, the supervisor and manager must meet with the employee and then submit an action plan for correcting the employee's performance.
>
> Successfully assisting all employees to meet their standards is a part of the annual performance reviews of the supervisor and manager.

Another advantage of collecting performance data on a regular basis during the year is that it assists the annual performance review to be based on the entire year's performance. When performance data is not collected throughout the year, the annual review may only represent the employee's most recent performance.

The Annual Review

The actual annual review typically takes the form of an interview. This is a very important meeting of the supervisor and employee, and specific preparation is required.

Collection of Performance Data

First, the supervisor collects all performance data for each standard. If the data has been collected throughout the year, this is a relative easy task, but the important point is that the data used in the performance review represents performance during the entire evaluation period.

Review of Performance Data

When the data is collected, it should be compared with each standard to determine how well the standard was met. In the process, standards should be placed into three classifications: standards met, standards exceeded, and standards not met.

Standards met represent performance as desired. Standards not met almost always represent areas of performance that require improvement. Standards exceed most often represent better than desired performance (though sometimes exceeding a standard creates the need for training). For example, assume a customer service representative had the following standard of performance: to complete at least fifteen customer telephone inquiries per hour. The employee's actual performance during the month showed he had completed an average of twenty-four customer telephone calls. At first glance it appears the employee is performing better than expected. However, this employee had a second standard of performance: to have no instances during a month of customers recalling regarding the same problem. The employee's actual performance in this standard showed that sixteen customers called the company again to state that their earlier call was improperly dealt with by the employee.

So what first appeared as excellent performance in one standard takes on a whole different look when another standard is also considered. It then appears that customer problems are not being fully solved. This may reduce telephone time per customer and increase the number of customer calls per hour, but it is contributing to additional calls and customer dissatisfaction.

Employee Notification

The guidelines for establishing a time and location for the performance review are the same as those introduced for an information-gathering interview, and like the information-gathering interview, the employee should be given advance notice of the performance review. That allows the employee to be equally prepared.

If the employee and supervisor both have copies of the standards, they both know how the employee is performing. That being the case, the performance review will be able to concentrate on corrective actions.

The Performance Review Interview

The performance review interview should begin with a statement of its objective: to review performance to standard over the past year, create plans for closing any performance gaps, and establish standards for the next year.

Then the employee should be allowed to comment on her/his performance. This may supply information that creates a better understanding of performance to objective. It could result in changing the supervisor's initial thoughts on performance to some standards.

The supervisor should then review performance to standard and ensure the employee evaluates each standard the same way. Any difference should be discussed, but if the standards contain proper measure, there should be little disagreement. In most cases, differences in evaluation are caused by ambiguous measures or data collection.

The next step is to specify performance gaps and develop plans for closing them. As a general rule, three areas are about the most that can be successfully handled at one time. The most significant gaps or the gaps related to the most important standards and responsibilities should be the ones selected.

As with the setting of standards, having the employee agree to any development plan is ideal, but also as with standards, in the final analysis, the supervisor is the one who must establish the plan.

Standards of performance should be established for the next period. Often they remain the same, but new information and changing conditions may require new or revised standards.

The final element of the performance review interview should be a discussion of the employee's career plans. Those plans can contribute to any development plans and also directions the supervisor can provide.

Training Needs

The development gaps and any plans made for their correction are the type of information the training department requires in order to help. As mentioned in an earlier chapter, some organizations require their supervisors to notify the training department of any identified gaps. In other organizations training must contact the supervisors to discover if there are such gaps.

Objective performance measurement through the use of standards of performance is the best way to identify current employee individual training needs. It describes the difference between desired job performance and actual job performance. However, it usually requires an investigation to determine what is causing the problem. However, if standards are not properly set, if they do not contain quantitative and time measures, if performance data is not collected throughout the period, then they are not a good source. The training function needs to ensure all this before evaluating their input.

12

Meetings

When there are a number of people from whom to obtain information, and they are readily accessible, a meeting is often the most efficient approach to reach them. However, meetings can have some disadvantages.

If a meeting is not structured and conducted properly, and the participants are not selected correctly, meeting results often will not reflect the views of the group. Instead, the results may reflect those of an individual within the group. Meetings are dynamic, and they can take a direction and develop new approaches. If correctly run, they are an excellent method for obtaining useful information.

Information-Gathering Meetings

There are several types of meetings. For our purposes we are going to concentrate on the information-gathering meeting, and this chapter contains full instructions for planning such a meeting and conducting it.

As with all management activities, an objective is required. In this case, it should be a statement concerning what information you wish to obtain from the meeting. Here, your earlier planning should provide you with the basic direction.

The Meeting Participants

A major decision that will impact the success of the meeting is determining who should attend it. Who should attend? The simple answer is the people who have the information you desire. However, consideration has to be given to the numbers and group composition.

The Number of Participants

Information-gathering meetings need to be limited in size. Generally, having less than six attendees means individual interviews might have been more effective. More than fifteen attendees makes it difficult for everyone to participate. However, it is possible through the use of subgroups to work with a larger number of participants. Even so, the recommendation is to keep participation in the ten to sixteen person range. If, for some reason, it is absolutely necessary to have a larger number of participants, you should consider subgroup activities and a second leader.

The Type of Participants

One of the advantages of meetings is that they allow an exchange of ideas and information. To encourage such discussion, some thought has to be given to the type of people invited to any one meeting. As a general rule, you want people with somewhat similar degrees of information, interest in the subject, and a mix that does not prohibit or limit participation.

Include all appropriate people. If you know there are differing opinions on the subject, be sure your invitation is extended to those who hold varying opinions. This may allow you to resolve differing perceptions as well as to discover what, if any, are the real problems and training needs. Here are some general rules to follow.

Avoid Mixing Organization Levels Within One Group

Mixing organization levels can prohibit full discussion and participation. For example, someone might not want to be as open when his boss or someone higher in the organization is in the same room.

A Michigan-based, nonferrous metals manufacturing company was having a problem with its advertising. The president convinced the director of advertising to hold a meeting in which all those with recommendations for improvement could express their opinions.

The director brought such a group together and began the meeting by placing a tape recorder in the center of the conference table and saying, "*The* president wants to personally hear all the complaints about advertising, so please identify yourself and state your complaint."

Not surprisingly, little useful information was obtained.

You should also consider not having people in the same group who work together, but that is not always true. If the issue involves a department, having all of the department employees in the same meeting can be an advantage. On the other hand, if the problem has to do with internal relationships, separating the employees for an information-gathering meeting may be better. Keep in mind the purpose of the meeting is to gather information, so avoid any relationships among participants that may hinder obtaining information from all participants.

A Kentucky manufacturing plant was having difficulties with product quality. The plant manager was unsure whether the problem was a training issue or something else.

A meeting was called by the training manager to determine whether or not there was a training need. All members of department attended the same meeting. This included production workers and inspectors.

Eventually it was discovered the problem was due to faulty inspection procedures. However, the meeting degenerated into name calling and little was accomplished by it.

The Meeting Environment

You want to create an open atmosphere for the free flow of information. The best environment is one that's set up in a conference style. A large table with chairs around it is excellent. A classroom setting or chairs set in rows does not encourage open discussion. In such an arrangement the participants are not facing each other, and that itself will tend to limit participation. Also, that setting focuses attention on the leader or facilitator rather than on the participants.

The facility may determine the maximum number of participants for the meeting. If you use a conference table, all participants need to sit at the table. Avoid having some participants sitting at the table and others sitting in chairs at the side of the room.

Unless there is a specific reason for assigning seats, you create a more open atmosphere by allowing people to sit where they wish. If you do assign seats, prepare place cards and put them where you want people to sit. If you are not assigning seats and the participants are not known to each other, place a blank place card by each seat along with a marker.

You want a private location as well. You do not want interruptions, and you want participants to feel others are not listening. As with interviews, do not use recording devices or have someone taking notes. The meeting should have only participants and a leader—no observers.

The Facilitator or Leader

The real key to a successful meeting of this type is the leader or facilitator. That individual's role is to:

- ❏ Keep things on track and on schedule
- ❏ Lead the meeting to meet its objective
- ❏ Encourage full and open participation from all those attending
- ❏ Avoid conflicts
- ❏ Prevent any one person from dominating the discussion

To fulfill this role, the facilitator or leader needs to:

- ❏ Use proper questioning techniques
- ❏ Control the meeting
- ❏ Avoid content input
- ❏ Avoid having attendees raise hands to participate

The most important consideration for an information-gathering meeting facilitator or leader is not to be an expert. The meeting is called to obtain information from the participants. It is not a meeting for the leader to give information to the participants. You can assist in this role by avoiding symbols of authority such as:

❐ A stool for you but chairs for the participants

❐ A pointer

❐ Different dress

❐ A separate desk or table

Information-gathering meetings also tend to work better without time agendas. Certainly an objective is needed, and a length of time for the meeting should be established in advance. However, this type of a meeting is difficult to keep to a predetermined structure. If you finish an item early, the participants may feel they did not give it enough attention. If you go overtime with an item, that can be troubling to some participants.

General Rules for Conducting a Meeting

In advance, establish some general rules as to how the meeting will be conducted. The following are a few that are often used:

❐ No recording of what anyone says will be made or communicated.

❐ Only the results of the entire meeting will be shared with others.

❐ The only bad or silly question is the one not asked.

❐ All opinions are acceptable—there are no wrong opinions.

Notification

As with other activities to which employees are invited, give them some advance notice. Tell them when and where the meeting will be conducted and the general subject of the meeting. This provides participants an opportunity to prepare for the meeting.

Questioning

The question is the facilitator's key information-gathering meeting tool. Once the objective is explained and ground rules for the meeting set, questions comprise the majority of the facilitator's input. Through the proper use of questions, a facilitator can fulfill her/his role.

Here are some guidelines for a facilitator's questions:

❐ Use overhead questions—that is, questions asked of the entire group rather than an individual.

❐ Use questions that cannot be answered in one word.

❐ Avoid "why" questions.

❐ Begin any direct question—such as a question asked of a single individual—with that individual's name.

❐ Wait for an answer after asking a question. Sometimes it may take a few moments, but be patient. If necessary, walk to back of the room and repeat the question.

❐ Begin with a question you know can be answered. Speaking for the first time in a meeting is generally the most difficult activity for participants. If you ensure everyone can answer the first question, you can make it considerably less threatening.

Introductions

Even when you are sure the participants know one another, include introductions at the beginning of the meeting. This requires each participant to speak in this setting, and if you then move directly into questioning, you will get a faster response.

For introductions, always require at least four pieces of information from participants such as:

❐ Name

❐ Job title

❐ Length of service

❐ Question about the meeting and its purpose

If the participants do not know each other, you can include:

❏ Department

❏ Previous assignments

❏ Relationship to the subject of the meeting

Meeting Format

The basic format for conducting an information-gathering meeting is to:

❏ State the objective of the meeting.

❏ Describe the general rules.

❏ Be sure everybody knows everybody.

❏ Begin with a nonthreatening information-gathering exercise.

❏ Lead the meeting to its objectives and encourage equal participation.

❏ End with a summary of the information and a statement of what next will be done with the information from the meeting.

A Typical Meeting

The following is a scenario for a typical information-gathering meeting. This one was scheduled after the training department conducted its annual review of courses. The purpose was to discover why one course received varying evaluations. In the example, the information in standard format represents instructions to the leader. It is what is to be done during the meeting.

At the very outset, state the objective of the meeting and describe the general rules, then continue with introductions:

First, thank you for the valuable input all of you provided for our recent training review. Based on your input, I wanted to meet and discuss with you ways in which training can be more effective and of greater assistance to you and your employees.

The objective for this meeting is to review the effectiveness of (name of course). That is a course in which all of you have attending employees.

This meeting has been scheduled for two hours. If we discover we need additional time, we can always schedule a follow-up session.

The meeting is meant to be a forum for you to share ideas and information, so let's go over the general guidelines for how it will be conducted.

There will be no recording of what anyone says.

Only the results of the entire meeting will be shared with others.

The only bad or silly question is the one not asked.

All opinions are acceptable—there are no wrong ones.

There is to be no criticism of anyone's opinion—if you have something to contribute, say it.

You do not have to raise your hand. My role is to lead you through the process. I do not have the answers to the questions we will be considering.

So let's begin. I think you all know each other, but even so, let's take a few moments to introduce ourselves. What I want each of you to tell us is:

- ❐ Your name
- ❐ Your job title and department
- ❐ How long you have been in your current position
- ❐ How many of your employees annually attend the course
- ❐ And any questions you have about this meeting

Each person then introduces himself. Questions raised are answered or written on a chart pad so they can be answered later. Any cross-table discussion that developed is allowed to continue.

Let's begin with each of you writing on a piece of paper what you believe the course's objective should be. Do that in one sentence.

Give the participants time to write this one-sentence response, then move on to the next step:

Now write beneath the objective how satisfied you are that the course is meeting that objective. Use a one- to nine-point scale. One means you're dissatisfied, a score of five means neither dissatisfied nor satisfied, nine is very satisfied, but you may use any point on the scale.

Give everyone a moment to write this information down before saying:

Finally, write at the bottom of the paper how important such a course is to your operations. Write down whether it is not important, important, or very important.

In some instances, you can then have each participant read his answers as you request them, but in most cases the following statement seems to work better:

Now, fold your paper in half and give it to me.

Shuffle the papers—mix them up—and redistribute them.

Okay, let's see where we are. Each of you is to read the objective on your paper.

As they read the objectives, write the keywords from each on a chart pad or chalkboard. If there are differences, allow any discussion or questions that develop. When all are read, you can ask overhead questions such as:

❐ What are the differences?

❐ What are the similarities?

Next, have each participant read the rating number. Write these numbers in a column. Then have each participant read the importance. Write these in a column opposite the rating column. Have participants read the responses in the same order, so the importance is written next to the rating.

If no one feels the course is important, you need to discover why a course is being conducted if managers apparently do not want it. If there are differences in evaluations, you need to discover the basis for them. Depending on the rating numbers and importance you received, you may want to ask questions such as:

❑ What are the differences?

❑ What are the similarities?

❑ What is the basis for the differences?

❑ What results do you feel we should be achieving that we are not?

❑ What will make this course more effective for you?

❑ What additional information can you provide about any of these courses?

Keeping in mind the objective of the meeting, continue asking questions until you have obtained the information you need. At the conclusion of the meeting, tell the participants what you will do with the information, what will happen next, and whether another meeting is required.

Control Techniques

One more facilitator technique to consider is controlling the meeting. Basically you want to ensure:

❑ All attendees participate.

❑ No one is criticized for her or his opinions.

❑ No one dominates the meeting.

❑ The meeting is conducted within the scheduled time.

The following are some methods you may use in your role as facilitator role.

To encourage someone to speak:

❑ Make eye contact as you are asking a question.

❑ Have subgroups consider a question and appoint the non-speakers in each subgroup to report back.

❐ Resort to a direct question only if it's halfway through the meeting and someone has not yet participated. If you use a direct question, be sure it is one the individual should be able to answer.

To discourage someone from dominating the group discussion:

❐ Give the person an assignment such as writing input on a chart pad.

❐ Do not make eye contact with the person.

❐ Have subgroups consider a question. Assign all similar people to the same subgroup. When the subgroups report, call on that subgroup last.

To have the group let you speak:

❐ Encourage discussion by remaining seated. Then, when you stand, the group will give you their attention.

To avoid giving your opinion:

❐ Return the question to the asker by saying, "What do you think?" In this type of meeting structure, people asking questions of the facilitator generally have an answer.

❐ Relay the question to the entire group for answering.

To keep the group within time limits:

❐ Do not publish an agenda. This way the facilitator is the only one who knows the specific planned activities for the group. If time runs out before all are implemented, no one will know but the facilitator.

To limit criticism:

❐ Establish an atmosphere where all opinions are welcome and avoid both praise and criticism of what is offered. Generally, the participants will adapt to this style. However, in most cases where one participant criticizes another, the group will react.

❏   ❏   ❏

There is an alternative method to the meeting that can be used to gather information from a number of people, and that is a questionnaire. It is covered in the next chapter.

13

Questionnaires

Questionnaires are a relatively easy method for soliciting the type of information required to identify training needs. They are usually used when the population from which the information is sought is large and/or at several locations. Sometimes they are used in combination with other information-gathering methods as a way to involve more people in the process. Questionnaires lend themselves best to identifying organizational training needs since individual training needs rarely require information from more than one or two people.

Questionnaires are by their very nature less flexible than other methods of gathering information. They do not provide a way of adjusting to responses. Also, many people are not as forthcoming in writing as they might be in person. That may be because they are concerned about making a permanent record without knowing who may eventually read it. Other times it is because people are unable to express themselves as well in writing as through oral communications. Yet questionnaires are useful tools—particularly when you are revising an existing training subject or soliciting noncontroversial information.

Questionnaires also add credibility to the process and give people a feeling of involvement. For example, if you are investigating the training needs for a large population of employees at several locations and in several departments, you may be limited to the number of people you can interview and have attend meetings. A random sampling of the population for interviews and meetings may provide all the information you require, but the balance may feel left out of the process or ignored. If that occurs, it can create a negative reaction to the final results, or what is sometimes referred to as "malicious obedience." (Malicious obedience is performing a task as directed even when you know it is incorrect.) A questionnaire sent to everyone who was not interviewed or invited to meetings is a way of avoiding such negative reactions. It provides a method for all to participate in the process and allows everyone to communicate their thoughts. It creates a feeling that "they" were a part of the study.

This chapter examines two types of questionnaires: an information-gathering questionnaire and a job behaviors questionnaire.

Questionnaire for Information Gathering

In Chapter 2, a relatively simple information-gathering questionnaire was used to identify possible areas of training needs. The questions in that example requested "fill in" answers. The responder was asked to write in his answers, but the nature of the questions tended to limit the responses to one or two words each.

Other types of question-and-answer formats (with examples) are:

- ❒ **Objective Response.** These are questions that can be answered with a simple yes or no.

  Do new employees require information about benefits before beginning their jobs? ＿＿ Yes ＿＿ No

- ❒ **Multiple Choice.** Each question provides several possible answers from which to choose.

  How long should a new employee training orientation course last?
  ＿＿ 1 hour ＿＿ 2 hours ＿＿ 4 hours ＿＿ A full day

- ❒ **Scale Response.** Each question has a descriptive and/or numeric scale for responding.

  How important do you feel it is for new employees to participate in a company orientation program? Check one of the following:

☐ Very Important
☐ Somewhat Important
☐ Neither Important nor Unimportant
☐ Somewhat Unimportant
☐ Not Important

Or answer by selecting a number on a 1 to 9 scale (1 being Not Important, 5 being Neither Unimportant or Important, and 9 being Very Important).

❑ **Essays.** Written answers are requested in a format determined by the responder.

Describe what you feel should be the primary objective of a new employee orientation training course.

Objective, multiple choice, and scale response questions are generally the easiest for people to complete and tend to produce a high return rate. They are also the easiest for combining answers. You need to give some thought to such considerations in selecting the question format to use, although many times you will need to use several formats in the same questionnaire.

The majority of your questions may require objective, multiple choice, and scale responses, but you may have to consider an essay-type question or two to obtain all the information you require. Sometimes you may even include an essay question when one isn't required so that responders will feel their answers were not completely structured. For example, many people would like to be asked, "What additional subjects do you feel should be a part of a new employee orientation training course?"

New employee orientation training has been used several times as an example throughout this book. Figure 13-1 is an example of a questionnaire that was sent to all supervisors in a company to obtain their initial thoughts on what type of subjects should be included in such a training course. It used primarily multiple choice, objective, and scale response questions, but it did have one final essay question.

The questionnaire was sent to sixty-two supervisors. Forty-seven completed and returned the questionnaire. Of those returning the questionnaire, twenty-three answered the final essay question.

Figure 13-1.

ORIENTATION QUESTIONNAIRE.

We are currently developing an orientation program for all new employees. Its purpose is to provide an overview of the company, its mission, structure, and objectives; an explanation of its benefits; and an understanding of its employee policies and procedures. The orientation will cover all of the information new employees should know before reporting to their assignments.

To assist us in this effort, all supervisors are being asked to provide their thoughts on whether we should have such a program and, if so, what exactly should be included.

How important do you feel it is for new employees to participate in such a program? Circle one of the following numbers.

Very Important	Somewhat Important	Neither Unimportant nor Important	Somewhat Unimportant	Not Important
5	4	3	2	1

Regardless of your answer to the previous question, if a program is developed and offered to new employees, tell us what areas you think should be included.

Below are listed six possible areas. Each is followed by a scale. Circle the appropriate number on the scale to indicate how important you feel an area is for inclusion in the program:

	Very Important 5	Somewhat Important 4	Neither Unimportant nor Important 3	Somewhat Unimportant 2	Not Important 1
Company history	5	4	3	3	1
Company mission	5	4	3	3	1
Company structure	5	4	3	3	1
Company objectives	5	4	3	3	1
Employee benefits	5	4	3	3	1
Company policies/ procedures	5	4	3	3	1

Are there additional areas that you feel should be covered?
_____ Yes   _____ No

If you answered yes to the previous question, list the areas below and indicate (using a number from the above scale) how important you feel each one is for such an orientation program.

Area   Importance

_____   _____

_____   _____

_____   _____

_____   _____

    Below are listed the six areas again, with additional lines at the end of the list for you to add any additional areas you mentioned. In front of each is a short line. Indicate on those lines the relative importance of each by ranking them. Write a 1 on the line for the area you feel is most important; a 2 on the line for the second most important; and so on. You may only use a number once.

   ____ Company history

   ____ Company mission

   ____ Company structure

   ____ Company objectives

   ____ Employee benefits

   ____ Company polices and procedures

   ____ _____

   ____ _____

   ____ _____

How long (in hours) do you feel such an orientation program should last? _____

In the space below, write in anything else you feel will be of assistance in this endeavor.

One criticism of this type of questionnaire is that it tends to limit or control responses by providing predetermined areas for answers. In this example, those areas were determined by individual interviews and meetings with supervisors who were not sent a final questionnaire. As a result, the questionnaire confirmed the initial areas identified for the orientation and suggested two others that were later included.

The questionnaire's format made it relatively easy to combine answers; even the responses to the final essay question were easy to combine because they all tended to be one- or two-word subject names. Only three supervisors answering the final question gave lengthy answers.

When questions solicit answers that are written and lengthy, they become difficult to analyze and combine. However, they have the advantage of supplying more insight. For example, if your questionnaire was a first attempt at identifying information for an orientation course, it might be useful to ask a question that could yield more in-depth information; for example, "How would a new employee orientation course benefit the company and the employees?"

If an essay question is used and there are just a few responding, the answers can be read and combined relatively easily, but if there are numerous responses, you need some type of system for analyzing them. One approach is to identify the key elements in each response and give each a weight. Another is to record the frequency of each key thought. Other times it is possible to rate essay responses on a predetermined scale.

Questionnaires can also be implemented in two or more stages. For example, a questionnaire with fill-in and essay questions can initially be distributed. The information obtained from the responses can be combined and a more structured second questionnaire developed. When this approach is used, the first questionnaire may only go to a representative sample and the second questionnaire to the remainder of the population, or in some instances to the entire population.

For a new employee orientation training course, the first part of a two-part questionnaire might ask just three questions:

❏ How important is having a new employee orientation training course?

❏ What subjects should be included in such a course?

❏ What should the objective of the training course be?

The nature of the first two questions makes them relatively easy to combine responses. For the first question, you can use a scale and assign a number to each response. Then you can combine the numbers and calculate an average, as well as a range and frequency of responses.

For the second question, you can list the subjects, indicate the frequency with which a subject is mentioned, and then rank them by frequency.

The third question requires a bit more analysis, but generally you can develop an objective that includes all the important points.

In any event, consideration of how to combine the information from many sources should be a part of the questionnaire design.

There is one final thought regarding questionnaires of this type. Since their purpose is to gather information, you want to ensure they are not perceived as something else. Probably the greatest danger is that people completing the questionnaire will believe they are voting for or against something. Always keep the questions in a format that requests information and opinions, but not a positive or negative vote on an activity.

Information-Gathering Questionnaire Design

As with other information-gathering techniques, the starting point is to state the objective. Exactly what do you want the questionnaire to accomplish? Generally, your objective should be an initial part of the questionnaire. Tell the responder what the questionnaire is seeking and how it will be used. For example, assume the questionnaire is being used to obtain information for possibly revising an order-processing training course. It might begin as follows:

> We are currently reviewing the content of our order-processing training course for customer service representatives. By answering the enclosed questions, you can assist us and help to ensure the course will accomplish its objective—to train customer service representatives in how to use the order-processing system so that they are able to meet their standards of performance.

The next step is to list the areas where you require information and develop questions to obtain that information.

Keep in mind that you may have to use different questions for different groups regarding the same subject. For example, assume you are seeking information regarding training needs for an analysis of loan applications. There are two levels of application review, and both require an understanding of all information on the application. However, individuals who do the second review also need to know how to apply certain test formulas to the application information. The questions would therefore have to be different for each group.

Question Development

After you have selected the question format that will obtain the type of information you require, you need to develop the actual questions. Keep the questions and the possible responses simple. Do not word your questions to imply a correct answer. Do not use questions that can be interpreted as having more than one response. For example:

> Should both management and nonmanagement new employees be required to attend a new employee orientation course?
>
> ____ Yes   ____ No

It would be of more useful for information-gathering purposes (and less confusing to the reader) to ask two separate questions:

> How important is it for nonmanagement employees to attend a new employee orientation course? Select one of the following:
>
> 5   Very Important
> 4   Somewhat Important
> 3   Neither Important nor Unimportant
> 2   Somewhat Unimportant
> 1   Not Important
>
> How important is it for management employees to attend a new employee orientation course?
>
> 5   Very Important
> 4   Somewhat Important
> 3   Neither Important nor Unimportant
> 2   Somewhat Unimportant
> 1   Not Important

After developing your questions, sequence them in a way that leads the responder logically through the assignment. However, be careful that your question sequencing and responses do not imply correct or desired answers. Do not imply any values by the way questions are presented. For example, if you are giving a series of items in a list and requesting that the responder indicate how important each is, do not list the items in what you believe is a correct order. Mix them up.

Arrange questions and responses so a pattern of answers does not appear. Do not ask a series of questions that can be answered identically. If four questions in sequence tend to receive a 6 on a scaled response, the next question may also tend to be answered the same way. Mix up responses as well as questions.

To avoid patterns when the same scale is used for a number of questions, some questionnaire designers reverse the scales for every other question.

If you use a numerical scale for responses, always provide at least three possible responses: high, middle, and low. In other words, use a three-point scale. However, many people seem to prefer a scale of at least five points, but with a five-point scale, the end points are usually ignored and the middle three numbers used.

Some designers prefer a seven- or nine-point scale, and others prefer to allow decimals or fractions. With an odd-numbered scale, keep in mind it is still basically a three-point scale because answers will fall at the midpoint, above the midpoint, and below the midpoint. Adding numbers merely allows for a degree of variance above or below the midpoint.

Some questionnaire designers prefer an even-numbered scale—a scale with no neutral midpoint. They argue that such a scale forces the responder to make a positive or negative decision. Our experience is that an even-numbered scale tends to skew responses to the positive side, so we prefer an odd-numbered scale.

The questionnaire guidelines given thus far are for a basic information-gathering questionnaire. If you require a more complicated questionnaire or wish to be able to check consistency and reliability of responses, you should probably have your questionnaire designed by an expert in that field.

Demographic Information

Another design consideration is whether to have people identify themselves on a questionnaire. Generally, answers tend to be more open when such information is not required. Some designers include a line in the questionnaire for the person's name, but it's labeled as an optional response. Others mention in the initial instructions whether identifying information is required. If it is required, a reason is usually also given.

At times you need to know some demographics in order to correctly interpret the responses. For example, if you are questioning managers and nonmanager about requirements for a training course in the use of performance standards, responses will probably be framed in two different contexts. Knowing whether a responder was a manager or nonmanager will assist in interpreting the information.

In most cases, asking for data that's nonspecific to the individual will be seen as acceptable, but even then, you might want to make it optional. Depending on the subject, you could include questions about department or location, type of job, length of service, length of time in current position, level of education, and sometimes race, age, and sex—but only when necessary to understand responses by group. However, it is best not to request such information unless it is helpful. For example:

❐ Length of service can have a direct bearing on responses related to such training as a new employee orientation course

❐ Type of job can have a direct relationship to supervisory training

This type of information can best be obtained through multiple choice questions. Here's an example:

To which employee group does your job belong?
_____ Management
_____ Administrative
_____ Professional
_____ Sales

To which age group do you belong?

____ 18–25

____ 26–35

____ 36–45

____ 46–55

____ 56–65

____ 66 +

Initial Testing

Before actually distributing the questionnaire, conduct an initial test to ensure it will obtain the information you want and it won't be confusing to the people reading it. Consider having one or two people from your department complete it and tell you of any problems they encounter with the questions, instructions, or wording. You can then make any necessary revisions before actually administering it.

Behavioral Questionnaire

Another type of questionnaire that is often used in identifying training needs is a job behaviors questionnaire. It describes the type of behaviors required on the job. For example, let's assume you are trying to determine what type of training is needed for telephone sales representatives and you have identified the key competencies required for the job. Now you want to identify the correct behavior associated with each competency. For that purpose you can use a behavioral questionnaire.

Let's assume oral communications is one of the required key competencies. You were able to identify the worst possible oral communication—which is that customers on the telephone continually were unable to understand what the sales representative said to them—as well as the best possible oral communication— there are no complaints about misunderstandings. You now have two ends for a scale. That information can be presented on a questionnaire as follows:

What type of behavior is most desirable for a telephone customer service representative?

Customers on the telephone can't understand what the sales representatives are saying.	__ __ __ __ __ __ __ *(Place an X on this scale to indicate the response closest to your answer.)*	There are no complaints about misunderstandings.

This type of scaled response question can be developed for all types of job behaviors. However, they must have realistic anchor points for each end of the scale. If either is unrealistic, the scale cannot deliver accurate information.

Generally, the behavioral questions for a single competency are mixed with other competency questions throughout the questionnaire, so a pattern does not develop in the answers.

Like information-gathering questionnaires, behavioral questionnaires are often used in conjunction with other procedures.

Questionnaire Implementation and Administration

Generally, questionnaires are sent to the participants via mail, e-mail, or fax, and responses are returned after completion via the same delivery method. There is one potential problem with this approach. You are never confident as to who actually completed the questionnaire. There have been situations in which employees met as a group and decided on their answers. Other times, employees have asked someone else to complete the questionnaire for them. Either of these actions can confuse the results.

> A Minnesota-based sales organization sent questionnaires to its sales force regarding the current expense reimbursement procedure. One of the questionnaires did not seem to provide appropriate responses, so the individual completing it was called for some elaboration. That's when it was discovered that the salesperson gave the questionnaire to his wife to complete.

To eliminate such problems, some companies send a representative to the department and administer the questionnaires in-person, then collect the completed ones. Other companies ask employees to stop by the training department at their convenience to complete a questionnaire.

An increasingly popular approach is to present the questionnaire via a web site so that employees can access it from their own computer or on dedicated PCs at various convenient locations. The web browser–based questionnaire usually uses predefined or preprogrammed fields; people add information by typing in each field and submitting the page to a web server. The web-based approach often includes a server-side program that combines and reports all responses and, in some cases, generates and delivers a final analysis of training needs. For example, some suppliers offer questionnaires that accept information about a job from employees in the job as well as their supervisors. It weighs the information and then prepares a summary description and statement of what level of ability an employee needs in the competencies for the job. That report can then be used to develop a training course for new employees.

Results Tabulation

When you receive the completed questionnaires, you need to combine the responses. If you used objective, multiple choice, and scale response questions, this is relatively easy.

For objective questions and multiple choice questions, count the number of people responding to the question and to each possible answer. For example:

Question 4

Total number of people answering:	28
Number answering yes:	22
Number answering no:	6

For scaled response questions, total the responses and divide by the number of people answering the question to obtain an average scale rating. For fill-in and essay questions, you need a predetermined scoring system.

In addition, when combining answers, you may want to do it by groups. For example, you may wish to combine all management answers and calculate an average response and then do the same with the answers from nonmanagers.

You may also want to calculate total responses and responses by subgroup. As an example, consider the following question and the answers received:

How important is decision-making ability for success as a telephone customer service representative?

Total number of responses:	95
Telephone customer service representatives:	76
Supervisors of customer service reps:	13
Managers:	6

The responses, by group, are as follows:

Total responding:	Somewhat Important
Telephone customer service:	Very Important
Supervisors:	Somewhat Important
Managers:	Neither Important nor Unimportant

❐ ❐ ❐

There is one other type of written procedure to review—tests and assessments. They are the subjects of the next chapter.

14

Tests and Assessments

For our purposes, tests and assessments are different activities. Tests are standardized and objective measures of skills, knowledge, and competencies. They are standardized in that they are always administered under uniform procedures and conditions. This means the only variable is the individual being tested. Tests are objective in that their administration, scoring, and interpretation are independent of subjective judgments by the person implementing the test.

When tests are designed and administered correctly, they provide information about an individual's current skills, knowledge, and competencies in a format that can be compared to some standard. As such, they can be an accurate method for identifying certain characteristics.

Assessments, as the term is used in this book, are procedures designed to measure behaviors, but they are not in traditional "paper and pencil" test formats. Psychological interviews, job simulations, and assessment centers are considered assessments and are reviewed in this chapter.

Tests

Tests measure differences between individuals, and between individuals and some predetermined standard. A mathematics test purchased from a test publisher can report how an individual performs mathematical calculations as compared to all high school

217

graduates who have taken the same test. A test of chemistry can determine how many elements and symbols from the periodic chart an individual knows. A test of leadership can determine the degree of leadership competency an individual has as compared to the leadership requirements for a specific job.

Because of the supporting data that accompanies most tests, and their ability to assign a numerical or letter score to the results, they are often favored as identifiers of training needs. As one manager commented, "It seems so scientific. It makes my decision making easier."

> A Connecticut garment manufacturer contracted with a psychologist to test all management and professional candidates for positions with the company. The psychologist had developed the test used.
>
> A multipage report was sent to the company describing each individual's performance on the test. Near the end of the report a summary "grade" was assigned to the results. The grades were similar to school grades: A, B, C, D, and F.
>
> The company's management tended to focus on the grades. Asking for an individual's grade was easier than reading and interpreting the entire report. Candidates, even those hired, were referred to by their letter grades, and those grades often affected promotions even when actual job performance differed.

Although tests can be an effective and efficient method for identifying training needs, you have to ensure that they:

❐ Measure what you need to have measure.

❐ Are error-free.

❐ Are valid within your environment and your population.

❐ Are administered and scored properly, with a common understanding on how to interpret their results.

A Bit of History

Before the 1960s, tests were routinely administered by organizations to candidates for jobs and promotions. The results were used for making selection decisions and for identifying training and development needs. In the early 1960s, President John F. Kennedy initiated Executive Order 10925. Its basic purpose was to eliminate discrimination in employment, and it included specific requirements for tests used in making employment decisions. It required all tests to be job related, reliable, and valid.

Many organizations that had been using tests had never determined their job relatedness, reliability, and validity. Instead, they had accepted whatever the test publisher claimed. The new executive order required them to perform such studies. Many discovered that the tests on which they had based many decisions were actually not valid for such purposes.

> An Oregon-based manufacturer had used a short "learnability" test as a selection device for years. Anyone applying for any position was required to take the test.
>
> A score of twenty was needed to be hired as a production employee.
>
> After Executive Order 10925 was initiated, the company contracted an industrial psychologist to conduct a validation study for the test. The validation study discovered that people with scores above fifteen (which included the twenty score used for production employees) did not perform as well in production as those who scored between ten and fifteen. In effect, the company had been using the test to screen out the best potential employees and hire the poorest.

The original executive order covered companies doing business with the federal government. Later, the rules of Executive Order 10925 were expanded and incorporated into civil rights legislation covering many companies not doing business with the federal government.

Those rules still exist and actually are excellent guidelines for considering the use of any test, whether for selection or the identification of training needs.

Job Relatedness

Job relatedness refers to the elements of a job for which a test is used. This requires some evidence of what those elements are, so some type of job analysis has to be conducted. Actually, many of the methods used in identifying training needs can also be used to identify job requirements.

Validity

Validity refers to the relationship between a test score and another independent measurement. For example, if a job requires flexibility, and a test is used to measure flexibility, evidence is required that the test does in fact measure flexibility as required by that job.

There are six types of validity:

❑ Content validity (how well the test measures what it purports to measure)

❑ Construct validity (how well and completely the test measures various elements)

❑ Concurrent validity (how well the test measures someone's current performance)

❑ Predictive validity (how well the test predicts future performance)

❑ Criteria-based validity (validity that's calculated with some other measure)

❑ Face validity (how accurate a test appears)

Content Validity

This is a determination of how well the test measures its subject. For example, a test measuring mathematical achievement that only dealt with addition and subtraction would not measure all elements of what is normally considered mathematics. In such an instance, it would not have high content validity. However, if the test defined the mathematics it measured as just addition and subtraction, it could have high content validity.

Content validity is not something most organizations calculate, but independent test publishers often report it.

Construct Validity

Many tests measure complex behaviors. For example, leadership is not a pure and easily defined skill. It is constructed of many elements: communications, style, appearance, etc. Construct validity is a measure of how well a test identifies all of the elements of such a construct.

Construct validity is a calculation most often made by a test developer or publisher. Often it is reported in a manual accompanying a test.

Predictive Validity

In most cases, predictive validity is the best measure of a test's accuracy as used by an organization. However, many organizations prefer not to use it.

A predictive validity study requires the test to be administered but not used in any decision regarding the employee or candidate. For example, selection decisions are made without considering the test results. Later, when enough people have taken the test, been selected, and have enough time on the job to have ratable performance, the test is scored and its results compared to job performance.

The reason for not using the test results in the selection decision is to ensure it is not a self-fulfilling prophecy. Also, if the results are used, there is the possibility that you'll be screening out people at some levels of performance. A good predictive study requires a full range of performance.

Because of the necessity to wait a period of time (sometimes over a year) before calculating results, the process in not one many organizations are willing to undertake. Instead, concurrent validity is more commonly calculated.

An Indiana bicycle manufacturer decided to conduct a validation study of a test it was using to select quality control inspectors. Company managers gave the test to candidates for the position but did not see the results in making their selection decision. When the participant completed the test, the test administrator took it and left the room for ten minutes.

On returning the administrator said, "You have met our test requirements. Next is an interview."

A year later, the tests were scored and compared with the performance of sixteen people who had been selected for the position. The results indicate the test was a valid instrument for assisting in the selection decision. However, there was one interesting aspect of the validation study: One candidate had not completed the test. In fact, he had not answered a single question. The company's human resources manager commented, "I wonder what he thought when he was told he had met our testing requirements."

Concurrent Validity

Like predictive validity, concurrent validity is a comparison of test scores with actual job performance. However, in concurrent validity, it is current job performance and not future performance that is used. This means participants have to already be in the job.

The results of the comparison are projected for people not currently in the job. The assumption is that if the test accurately identifies performance of people currently in these positions, it should also identify how people not in those positions will perform if assigned to those positions.

Criteria-Based Validity

This is a term applied to any validity calculation using some independent factor such as job performance. Concurrent validity and predictive validity are both criteria-based validations.

Any criteria-based validity calculation is only as good as the accuracy of the independent measure that is used with the test. If job performance data is not accurate and free of errors, the resulting validity calculation is not something that ensures the test is a useful tool.

Face Validity

At times reports mention the face validity of a test, but face validity is not a real measure. Face validity means that the test appears to be valid. It appears to measure what it claims to measure.

Face validity has a use in supporting acceptance of test results, but it is only an opinion—an opinion that could be mistaken.

Calculations to Determine Validity

There are a number of statistical calculations to determine validity. The most commonly used produces a correlation coefficient. This is a number that expresses the relationship between two variables, such as a test score and job performance.

Correlation coefficients are reported on a scale with a range of $+1.00$ to -1.00. A correlation coefficient of $+1.00$ describes a perfect relationship between the two variables. In the case of one variable being job performance and the other being a test score, a $+1.00$ indicates that an individual receiving a high score on the test will receive a high job performance rating, and an individual receiving a low test score will have a low job performance rating. A test with a $+1.00$ correlation coefficient is an ideal instrument for selecting people or identifying individual training needs.

A correlation coefficient of -1.00 also describes a perfect relationship, but in reverse. It indicates an individual receiving a high score on the test will receive a low performance rating, and an individual receiving a low test score will have a high job performance rating. It is every bit as valid an instrument for selecting people or identifying individual training needs.

A zero correlation coefficient indicates there is no relationship between the two variables, so there is no basis for use of a test.

Not surprisingly, it is rare—extremely rare—that a test correlation coefficient of a $+1.00$ or a -1.00 is obtained. Tests and job performance are human behaviors. Human behaviors are constructed of many elements and are affected by many external conditions. However, correlation coefficients of less than 1.00 can be used.

An acceptable correlation coefficient is one that indicates the expressed relationship between the variables is not due to chance. That number is partially determined by the size of the population being studied and is expressed as a level of significance.

Levels of Significance

A level of significance indicates how confident you can be that a correlation coefficient represents a true relationship between the variables. The larger the population, the more likely the coefficient represents a true relationship. If you have only three people in a group, you want an extremely high correlation to assume validity. However, for a group of 100, a lower correlation is acceptable.

There are formulas for calculating levels of significance, but an easier method is to refer to tables found in most statistical and testing books. Using the size of the population and the correlation coefficient, you can discover what the level of significance is. Generally, these tables cover 95 percent and 99 percent levels of significance, although some include other measures. Most organizations desire at least a 95 percent level of significance.

Reliability

Reliability refers to the consistency of test scores obtained by the same individual. It is an indication of how free of errors the test is and whether someone taking the test can improve his score by repeating the test or coaching someone else in how to take the test. Reliability is not normally calculated by a test user. It is usually part of the test's design and included by the publisher in descriptive materials and manuals.

Levels of Tests

Tests are made available based on the qualifications of the user. The first level of tests requires the user to demonstrate a realistic need and some type of professional position. The second level requires evidence of general test training, similar to a master's degree in psychology. The third level consists of tests restricted to individuals specifically trained and certified in their use.

Throughout this book we have stressed validity and reliability of information. In this chapter, a closer look at these two concepts has indicated how they apply to tests, though similar consideration should be given to any other procedure you use as well.

Other procedures may not be eligible for statistical calculations, but you always want to ensure the information received is as error-free and accurate as possible.

Test Selection

If you are considering using a test to identify training needs:

- ❒ Be sure you have identified the requirements for a job. And be sure whatever job analysis method was used was error-free and accurate.

- ❒ Select tests that purport to measure the identified requirements, but be sure they are valid and reliable. If you will only be using the test once or twice, base your use on published validity and reliability information. If you plan to use the test on an ongoing basis, conduct a concurrent validity study and/or a predictive validity study.

- ❒ Keep records of the test's use and periodically recheck it for validity.

Guidelines for the development and use of tests are published by the American Psychological Association and Equal Employment Opportunity Commission (EEOC). Test publishers provide descriptive materials and administration manuals that provide validity and reliability information, and the *Mental Measurements Yearbook* (Lincoln, Nebr.: Buros Institute, 2001) describes the majority of tests.

Actually, test selection and validity studies are best done by a professional. If you do not have one on staff, you should contract one to perform these services.

Assessments

Assessments are procedures that are used to measure employee behaviors that can be the basis for determining training needs. Although not "paper and pencil" tests, they strive for validity, reliability, standardization, and objectivity. These include psychological interviews, self-testing devices, simulations, and assessment centers.

Psychological Interviews

Psychological interviews are the least standardized of these procedures since they depend on the skill of the interviewer. In most cases, the interviewer is a trained (and in many states, licensed or certified) psychologist. Sometimes, the interviews consist solely of one-on-one meetings conducted by the psychologist. Other times the psychologist may use paper-and-pencil tests or other tests along with the interview. Some create their own interview questions and approach. Others, such as those working for a consulting firm, follow a prescribed approach.

Psychological interviews evaluate behaviors and personal characteristics, and they tend to be conducted with management and sales professionals. Psychological interviews generally last about four hours (some run a full day and others only an hour or two). In any event, a half-day of a psychologist's time is not inexpensive.

If you use or are considering using psychological interviews, keep in mind that the same guidelines as recommended for tests apply. The interview needs to be conducted to meet identified job requirements, and whoever will be reviewing the report should be trained in its interpretation.

Self-Testing Devices

There are a number of self-testing devices currently being sold commercially. Many claim to provide a profile of an individual's job-related characteristics. They consist of a series of questions that the participant scores after completing. Then interpretative data about the scores is provided.

These tests are relatively inexpensive and have a great deal of face validity. However, many of them offer little, if any, evidence of validity or reliability. Even so, some organizations have elected to use these tests to identify training needs—some even use them to make selection decisions.

Self-testing devices are often an excellent tool for training classes, but they should not be used for other purposes unless they are job related, valid, and reliable.

Job Simulations

Some organizations identify training needs through performance in job simulations. These are standardized situations designed to duplicate a job's requirements, but in a controlled and standardized environment, such as flight simulations for pilot training.

The in-basket is one such simulation. It consists of typical mail someone in a job might receive. The participant is allowed to decide what to do with each item—discard it, respond to it, or send it to someone else. These decisions can be reviewed and training needs in competencies such as written communications, decision making, and administrative mail procedures identified.

Chemical manufacturers often use simulations of a processing control panel to assess how well employees react to various situations and then provide training as necessary. Telemarketing firms simulate the calls a telemarketer receives and then determine what training an employee requires based on how the calls were handled.

Some simulations include recording the participant's behaviors on video or audiotape. The participant reviews the tape and assists in identifying her training needs. Simulations have a great deal of face validity for participants.

Assessment Centers

Assessment centers are a form of simulation. They simulate a job through a combination of exercises that provoke required job behaviors.

Assessment centers are basically multiple evaluation devices. That is, they evaluate several people at one time, use a number of exercises on which to base the evaluation, measure several job competencies, and use a team of assessors.

The procedure was originally developed for management selection, but in recent years it has been increasingly implemented as a tool for identifying an individual's training and development needs. It also has been expanded to include evaluations of supervisory, sales, telemarketing, and customer service staffs.

Like simulations, assessment centers require observable behavior, so the process includes a number of exercises. A typical supervisory assessment center might employ the following exercises:

- ❐ Background questionnaire
- ❐ Interview
- ❐ Questionnaire covering typical supervisory problems
- ❐ In-basket (followed by a discussion of in-basket decisions)
- ❐ Social situations (e.g., a business luncheon)
- ❐ One or two leaderless group discussions (based on supervisor situations)
- ❐ Written self-evaluation

A supervisory assessment center might measure competencies such as:

- ❐ Leadership
- ❐ Planning
- ❐ Organizing
- ❐ Controlling
- ❐ Flexibility
- ❐ Stress tolerance
- ❐ Oral communication
- ❐ Written communication
- ❐ Decision making
- ❐ Judgment

Similarly, a salesperson assessment center might employ the following exercises:

- ❐ Background questionnaire
- ❐ Interview
- ❐ Questionnaire covering typical sales and marketing problems

- ❐ Preparation for a sales call
- ❐ Sales call
- ❐ Social situations (e.g., business luncheon)
- ❐ One or two leaderless group discussions (based on sales situations)
- ❐ Written self-evaluation

A salesperson's assessment center would likely measure competencies such as:

- ❐ Closing
- ❐ Product knowledge
- ❐ Group presentations
- ❐ Planning
- ❐ Organizing
- ❐ Questioning
- ❐ Flexibility
- ❐ Impact
- ❐ Stress tolerance
- ❐ Oral communication
- ❐ Written communication
- ❐ Customer need identification

An assessment center's exercises are interrelated, and they represent situations that are much like what someone in the position actually encounters. Some exercises require written communication and others oral communication. Some are individual focused and some are group oriented.

The assessors are usually operating managers who know the job for which assessment is occurring and have been trained in the assessment center process. They observe the participant's behaviors in the various exercises and then meet as a team to evaluate those behaviors in terms of the job's requirements.

Assessment centers, like other simulations, have a great degree of face validity. Also, when properly designed and administered, they have considerable predictive and concurrent validity. The one drawback often mentioned is their implementation cost and time requirements.

A supervisory assessment center requires one day of each the participant's time and at least two days of each assessor's time. Since assessment centers typically are conducted for twelve participants with a team of four manager assessors, that is a total of twenty person-days.

Assessment centers must be job related, valid, and reliable, and they are best purchased from an organization that has considerable experience in designing them. (There is an association of assessment center providers and users, but it does not include all sources. A search of current literature on the subject will identify some suppliers and users, and professional organizations such as AMA and SHRM may have lists or contacts.) They are usually provided with some type of job analysis and customization for your own organization.

We have now reviewed all of the individual methods that can be used to identify training needs, but sometimes a combination of methods is more effective. Chapter 15 considers that approach.

Combination Methods

The use of multiple information-gathering procedures is appropriate in many situations, and there are numerous possible combinations. The selection of which procedures to use depends on the objective, the subject, the population, and their locations. Perhaps the easiest overview of this approach is to examine a specific usage.

Company Demographics

The organization, a financial services firm, employed 2,180 people, of which 150 were first-level supervisors and thirty were managers of first-level supervisors. There were 1,500 employees who reported to the first-level supervisors. An additional 500 employees held professional, sales, and management positions. The company had two locations: one in New York and one in Minnesota. Employees were evenly divided between the locations.

The Objective

The company wanted to identify the competencies required for first-level supervision. Once identified, they could be used as a base against which each supervisor's performance could be compared and any training needs pinpointed. Management could also use the competencies as part of the requirements for selecting new supervisors and as a basis for developing a training program for them. So the objective was:

> To identify the competencies required, along with their relative importance, for success as a supervisor at the company.

The Plan

The project was considered to be of great importance to the company. The competencies identified were going to serve a number of purposes. The company wanted to ensure the results were accurate and error-free, and it wanted to include all appropriate people. It decided to use three information-gathering procedures:

1. **The Job Analysis Grid.** This procedure was selected as a way to ensure that the initial list of competencies (to be used at the meeting) was obtained with as little contamination as possible.

2. **Meetings.** Meetings provide a format for an interchange of ideas. Meetings were used to develop the main list because the rankings and ratings would be a group product.

3. **The Questionnaire.** A questionnaire was used as a check on the final list and a method of involving all managers and supervisors in the effort.

Job Analysis Grid Interviews

At each location two managers, two supervisors, and two employees reporting to supervisors participated in the Job Analysis Grid interviews. The results were combined and produced an initial list of twenty competencies. An initial definition was developed for each competency based on the input form for the grid interviews.

Meetings

The competencies initially identified by the Job Analysis Grid were used as the basis for a series of meetings. Two meetings were held at each location: one with supervisors and one with managers. The meetings produced a ranking and rating of the competencies. In addition, two other competencies were identified: nonverbal communication and delegation.

Questionnaire

To confirm the information already gathered and to ensure input from all supervisors and managers, a questionnaire was created and sent to everyone who did not participate in the grid interviews or meetings. Those results were combined with the previously obtained competencies.

Now let's examine the process, procedures, and results in more detail.

Initial List of Competencies

The twenty competencies identified by the Job Analysis Grid interviews were:

- ❏ Leadership
- ❏ Written Communication
- ❏ Oral Communication
- ❏ Planning
- ❏ Controlling
- ❏ Organizing
- ❏ Coaching
- ❏ Stress Tolerance
- ❏ Image
- ❏ Problem Analysis
- ❏ Disciplining
- ❏ Negotiating
- ❏ Listening
- ❏ Energy
- ❏ Thoroughness
- ❏ Accountability
- ❏ Decision Making
- ❏ Judgment
- ❏ Initiative
- ❏ Conflict Resolution

These competencies were listed in random order, with their definitions, for use in the meetings. Figure 15-1 is the document

Figure 15-1.

COMPETENCIES AND THEIR DEFINITIONS FOR AN EXAMPLE FINANCIAL SERVICES COMPANY.

Competency	Definition
_____ Oral Communication	Transferring a message by speech using appropriate gesticulations
_____ Flexibility	Adjusting to changing conditions
_____ Coaching	Working with an individual to improve job performance
_____ Decision Making	Consciously selecting the best alternative from two or more
_____ Leadership	Getting people to willingly accomplish objectives
_____ Accountability	Using delegated authority to meet assigned responsibilities
_____ Listening	Receiving correctly another's oral communication
_____ Stress Tolerance	Maintaining stability of performance under adverse conditions
_____ Problem Analysis	Identifying the real problem and obtaining the information necessary to solve it
_____ Initiative	Interjecting planned thoughts or actions into a situation
_____ Written Communication	Transferring a message through writing
_____ Conflict Resolution	Reducing tension between two or more people and arriving at a mutually satisfactory conclusion
_____ Planning	Outlining a course of action to achieve an objective
_____ Image	Projecting a positive initial and continuing presence
_____ Controlling	Ensuring the plan is followed and the objective met
_____ Stress Tolerance	Maintaining consistency of performance under adverse conditions
_____ Negotiating	Arriving at a mutually acceptable decision
_____ Energy	Starting a task enthusiastically and maintaining that enthusiasm until completion
_____ Organizing	Structuring assigned resources to fulfill a plan
_____ Disciplining	Correcting employee behaviors in a positive fashion

produced for use in the meetings. (Note: Each competency is preceded by a short line that will be used to rank the competencies during the meeting activities.)

Meeting Format and Results

The meetings were conducted in a conference setting. There were two chart pads with markers at the front of the room. A copy of the previously prepared list of competencies and definitions (Exhibit 15-1) was distributed to each participant along with note-taking pads and pencils. The meeting leader also used a meeting guide. In the example that follows, the information in standard format represents instructions to the leader. It is what is to be done during the meeting. The material that's italicized is a suggested script.

Example Meeting Guide

Begin with a statement of the meeting's objective and with introductions. Distribute the list of competencies to each participant and read each aloud, checking for questions. After reading the competencies and their definitions, and answering all questions, say:

> *Notice that each competency is preceded by a short line. In the next few minutes each of you is going to rank the competencies in order of what you believe their importance is for success as a first-level supervisor at our company. Write a one on the line in front of the competency you feel is most important; a two on the line of the next most important; and so on. You may only use a number once. No ties.*

Check for questions once again and then have the participants rank the competencies. This usually takes about ten minutes. Note that they can add subjects.

When everyone has completed this activity, say:

> You have just ranked all twenty competencies in order of their importance for success as a supervisor at our company. Now

you are going to have an opportunity to discover how the others in this group view the supervisor's job. I'm going to divide you into two groups.

Have everyone draw a line across the page to separate the subjects into two approximately equal groups—half above the line and half below the line—and say:

> You are going to meet in your groups and rank one-half of the competencies. Group one, you are going to rank the competencies above the line we just drew, and group two, you are going to rank the competencies below the line we just drew.
>
> This means that for your group work, you are going to forget the other competencies exist. You are only going to rank the ones on the page I have assigned your group.
>
> You are to make a list of your group's rankings. What is important in your group work is to express your feelings and discuss any differences, so do not make it a mathematical activity. Do not add your rankings and divide by the number in your group. That's not what the exercise is about.

Divide the participants into groups and start the process. Circulate among the groups as they work.

There is no specific time limit for this assignment, but it usually requires between ten and fifteen minutes.

When the groups have completed the assignment, reconvene the entire group. However, if one group finishes first, you can chart their rankings as the other group finishes.

When both groups have completed their assignment, have each read the competencies in rank order. Write the results on a chart pad or board in descending order of importance. Do not place the ranking numbers in front of the subjects. And write the lists on separate chart pads or side by side on the same pad. Do not have one list under another.

When you have the two charts, post them at the front of the room. Then on the chart pad write the numbers 1 to 20 in a column about six inches in from the left edge. Try to have all numbers on a single sheet.

So, what you have done is first individually ranked twenty management competencies in their order of importance for a supervisor at our company.

Then, in small groups, you discussed and ranked half of those competencies. But, obviously, where we are headed is the next step: We want to determine the ranking of all competencies.

We need a common understanding and agreement as to the importance of these competencies for success as a supervisor. So, regardless of you initial ranking, and regardless of your group's rankings and the other group's ranking, what do you believe to be the most important single competency for success as a supervisor?

This is an overhead question asked of the entire group, and it is a question everyone should be prepared to answer. However, it may take a minute or two before you receive a response.

You must wait for their response. If one does not come in a minute or two, ask your question again, but say nothing else. If you feel uncomfortable waiting for an answer, walk to the back of the room and sit there for a time to give participants a chance to think through their response.

Be patient. An answer will come, and it's important for the assessor training and for the operation of the assessment center that the participants develop the answer on their own.

Once you receive the first competency, write it after the number 1 on the chart pad. Then cross the competency off the small group's list.

Ask what is the next most important competency, and repeat the same procedure.

Once you receive the first competency, the group will provide the others without long waits. However, they may reach a point when they seem to have difficulty. If that occurs, allow them to tell you what the least important competency is—the twentieth competency.

Continue with this process (without a break) until all twenty competencies have been ranked. When all are ranked, remove the small group ranking charts from display.

Have the participants copy (in pencil) the rankings onto their note pads and say:

> You have now ranked the competencies in order of importance, but that doesn't tell us how important they are to supervisory success. For that we need to rate them.
>
> You are going to return to your small groups and rate the competencies. For your ratings, you will assign one of three letters to each competency.

Write the letters *M, W,* and *N* on a chart pad, along with these definitions, as you explain them.

> "M" is a must. This is a very strong statement. When you assign a must, you are saying that someone must possess the required degree of that competency to succeed as a supervisor. You are saying someone without the required degree of that competency cannot succeed as a supervisor.
>
> "W" is a want. This means you want a supervisor to have the required degree of this competency, but there is some flexibility. There may be an offsetting strength in another competency, or you may be able to provide training. The point is that it is possible to succeed without the required degree of the competency even though it's one that is wanted.
>
> "N" means not necessary. Here you are saying that the competency is not required. It is not that you want supervisors who lack this competency. It is just that it is not required for success as a supervisor.

Check if anyone in the group has questions. Be sure they understand the three rating letters and their definitions.

Tell the participants that they do not have to use all three ratings. They can use just one, or two, or all three of them.

Have the meeting participants return to their small groups and have each group rate all twenty competencies. When both groups have completed their ratings, reconvene the entire group.

Starting with the most important competency on the chart (ranked number 1), ask for the groups for their ratings. If both groups give the same rating, write it in the space in front of the competency. If the groups differ in their ratings, place a small check in front of the competency.

Proceed in this manner for all twenty competencies.

If they have agreed in their ratings for all competencies (an unlikely event), you have completed this activity.

More likely, the groups have disagreed on some of their ratings. If that occurs, revisit the competencies where there was a disagreement in ratings. Have the groups express the basis for their rating. Then have them decide on a final rating. If necessary, have them vote, but try to avoid that.

When all the competencies have a rating, review the list and make sure that all of the competencies rated Musts (if there are any) are ahead of the Wants and Not Necessaries, and that all of the Wants (if there are any) are ahead of the Not Necessaries. Explain to the group that if the competencies are in rank order of importance, the Musts have to be ahead of the Wants and the Not Necessaries, and the Wants have to be ahead of the Not Necessaries. If that is not the case, either the rating of those competencies or their rankings are incorrect.

In such an instance, allow the group to decide what to do.

If the participants ask how their rankings and ratings compare with other groups, tell them there are some differences, but none that are significant. Tell them that all groups see the job requirements similarly.

Have the participants copy down the final ranking list with ratings.

Example Questionnaire

The meetings added two competencies to the original list:

- ❑ Nonverbal Communication (transferring a message to another without the use of words)
- ❑ Delegation (passing authority to another)

After adding these two competencies to the other twenty, you would then develop and distribute a questionnaire to all managers and supervisors who had not participated in either the Job Analysis Grid interviews or the meetings. Figure 15-2 reproduces the questionnaire used at our example financial services company.

When all questionnaires were returned, the information from all three procedures—the Job Analysis Grid, the meetings, and the questionnaire—was combined. How to apply the combined information to produce a report of results is the subject of the next chapter.

Figure 15-2.

SUPERVISORY MANAGEMENT COMPETENCY QUESTIONNAIRE.

The Training Department is currently conducting several studies to identify the competencies required for success as a supervisor in our company. All supervisors and their managers are being asked to submit their thoughts.

Please complete this questionnaire indicating what you believe to be the requirements for a successful supervisor at our company. When all of the questionnaires are returned, the information from them will be combined into a profile of supervisor competency requirements. A copy will be sent to you, and the results will be used to identify training needs, create a supervisor-training course, and establish requirements for the selection of new supervisors.

It is not necessary to identify yourself. However, it will be of assistance to know whether you are currently a supervisor or manager.

On the lines below, write what you believe to be the primary function or purpose of a supervisor at our company. Write it in one sentence, beginning with the word "to."

To _____

_____

What percent of the requirements for a successful supervisor do each of the following categories represent? The percents assigned to all cannot total more than 100.

Management Competencies	_____%
Length of Company Service	_____%
Job Knowledge	_____%
Education	_____%
Total	100%

A list of the twenty-two management competencies and their definitions follows. Read all twenty-two competencies and their definitions, then rank them in order of importance for success as a supervisor at our company. Rank them by writing a ranking number on the short line proceeding the competency. Use a one for the most important, a two for the next most important, and so on. You may use a number only once. In the event you

(continues)

Figure 15-2.

CONTINUED.

believe one or more important management competency is not included in the list, add it on the lines provided, along with a definition, and include it in your ranking.

Competency	**Definition**
___ Oral Communication	Transferring a message by speech using appropriate gesticulations
___ Flexibility	Adjusting to changing conditions
___ Coaching	Working with an individual to improve job performance
___ Decision Making	Consciously selecting the best alternative from two or more
___ Leadership	Getting people to willingly accomplish objectives
___ Accountability	Using delegated authority to meet assigned responsibilities
___ Delegation	Passing authority to another
___ Listening	Receiving correctly another's oral communication
___ Stress Tolerance	Maintaining stability of performance under adverse conditions
___ Problem Analysis	Identifying the real problem and obtaining the information necessary to solve it
___ Initiative	Interjecting planned thoughts or actions into a situation
___ Nonverbal Communication	Transferring a message to another without the use of words
___ Conflict Resolution	Reducing tension between two or more people and arriving at a mutually satisfactory conclusion
___ Planning	Outlining a course of action to achieve an objective
___ Image	Projecting a positive initial and continuing presence
___ Controlling	Ensuring the plan is followed and the objective met

___ Stress Tolerance   Maintaining consistency of performance under adverse conditions

___ Negotiating   Arriving at a mutually acceptable decision

___ Energy   Starting a task enthusiastically and maintaining that enthusiasm until completion

___ Organizing   Structuring assigned resources to fulfill a plan

___ Disciplining   Correcting employee behaviors in a positive fashion

___ Written Communication   Transferring a message through writing

[Write in any additional competencies here]

___ _____   _____

    _____

___ _____   _____

    _____

___ _____   _____

    _____

___ _____   _____

    _____

Please indicate if you are a manager or a supervisor.

      _____ Manager   _____ Supervisor

PART FOUR

Concluding a
Needs Analysis

16

Combining Inputs and Reporting Results

Once you have collected all of the information required, the final step is to prepare a report that describes what, if any, training needs you identified. When the information was obtained from just one source, that is a relatively simple task. However, when there are multiple sources, the information has to be combined first. This chapter deals with methods of combining information and preparing training needs analysis reports.

Weighting Information Sources

Generally, information from different groups and individuals has different values to the process. In order to combine the information, those values have to be determined and applied. The values can be determined by considering:

❑ **The Relationship of the Group or Individual to the Employee(s) Being Trained.** Are they the ones to be trained? Do they supervise the people who are to be trained? Do they work for or with the ones to be trained?

❑ **The Relationship of the Group or Individual to the Training Subject.** Are they the ones accountable for the implementation of the training subject? Do they supervise those who are accountable for the implementation of the training subject? Do they work for or with those accountable for the implementation of the training subject?

☐ **The Group's or Individual's Knowledge and Experience with Implementation of the Training Subject.** What degree of knowledge or experience do they have with the training subject and its implementation?

☐ **The Procedures Used to Gather Information and Their Relative Accuracy.** In most cases there are no measurable answers to such questions. Instead, you have to answer the questions based on your knowledge and experience in the organization. You also have to consider the probable reliability and validity of the information. Actually, this should be done before beginning an investigation of possible training needs and then revisited after the investigation to determine whether adjustments are required.

Assigning Values

For example, let's assume you conducted a training needs identification for an individual employee who required performance improvement. In the process, you interviewed the employee and the supervisor. How do you evaluate the information from each?

Using the same philosophy as in determining performance standards, the supervisor probably has the most accurate information regarding the employee's performance, and the employee probably has information that provides insights into why standards are not being met.

Since it is the supervisor who establishes standards and measures performance, the supervisor's responses might be accepted at full value (100 percent). Although the employee may be able to provide excellent reasons for not meeting standards, the supervisor's input, as a rule, is used as the basis for identifying the specific subjects for training. The employees' information might be valued at 80 percent of the supervisor's information.

If the information gathering was undertaken to identify training needs for how to operate a new system, the greatest value might be placed on the information from the system designers and employees operating the system. In this situation, information from supervisors and managers might receive a lesser value, since they are removed from the actual system design and implementation.

When gathering information regarding the competencies necessary for supervisory success, the supervisors generally provide the most accurate information. They know what they are required to do and the competencies needed. Their managers provide the next most accurate information. The managers know what is to be accomplished, but they are not as knowledgeable about the specific skills required for supervisory work. Employees see the supervisor's job from an entirely different perspective. Their information is useful but not of great accuracy.

At times, senior managers have been involved in such information gathering. They are generally so far removed from the actual supervisor's accountabilities that the accuracy of their information falls between that of managers and employees.

When assessing competencies necessary for supervisory success, the following values might be assigned to the information obtained for each source:

Supervisors	100%
Managers	80%
Senior Managers	50%
Employees	50%

Another example concerns using various procedures. If you are collecting information for new employee orientation training courses and you used the Job Analysis Grid and questionnaires, the grid results are probably more accurate than the questionnaire. You might consider them at full value and the questionnaire information at 80 percent value. However, to apply these values and combine information, the responses must be in the same format.

Comparing Apples to Apples

Information must be in a similar form to combine. If numerical responses, such as ratings and rankings, or single words, such as competencies and subject titles, are collected they are in the same general format. For example, if the Job Analysis Grid identified twelve subjects for a new employee benefit training course, as well as rankings of those twelve from employee and supervisors, it is relatively easy to assign values and combine.

When information is received from several sources in other than a similar format, it is more difficult to combine the information. Sometimes it is possible to covert to a single format. For example, if several sources provided a single-word description of an activity, it may be possible to identify the key thoughts from each and record the frequency of their mention. However, at times the information can only be reviewed with values in mind and then some type of decision must be made for a final report. This may even necessitate revisiting some sources for clarification.

It is recommended that whenever information is being gathered from several people in the same group that it should be combined—generally as an average. That gives you a single measure for each group, but assumes that all people in the group have the same value of information. It is possible that at times different members of a group may have different values assigned to their information.

Combining Responses

Let's assume that the information you have is in numerical format and that it concerns the performance improvement needs of an employee, so you have information from the employee and the supervisor. Figure 16-1 shows an Information Combination Form that allows you to enter the numbers from two sources along with the value you have assigned each. For example, the same form appears in Figure 16-2 with competencies, numbers, and values added for two groups: supervisors and managers.

In the example in Figure 16-2, the average for each group is shown in the Number column opposite the Item (which in this case is a competency). The Value column has the value assigned to the group's average response. The value for the supervisors was 100 percent (or a value of 1 as shown on the form). The value for the managers was 80 percent (or 0.8 as shown on the form).

Figure 16-1.

INFORMATION COMBINATION FORM.

Item	Group: _____			Group: _____			
	Number	Value	Result	Number	Value	Result	Total
————————	——	——	——	——	——	——	——
————————	——	——	——	——	——	——	——
————————	——	——	——	——	——	——	——
————————	——	——	——	——	——	——	——
————————	——	——	——	——	——	——	——
————————	——	——	——	——	——	——	——
————————	——	——	——	——	——	——	——
————————	——	——	——	——	——	——	——
————————	——	——	——	——	——	——	——
————————	——	——	——	——	——	——	——
————————	——	——	——	——	——	——	——
————————	——	——	——	——	——	——	——
————————	——	——	——	——	——	——	——
————————	——	——	——	——	——	——	——
————————	——	——	——	——	——	——	——
————————	——	——	——	——	——	——	——
————————	——	——	——	——	——	——	——
————————	——	——	——	——	——	——	——
————————	——	——	——	——	——	——	——
————————	——	——	——	——	——	——	——
————————	——	——	——	——	——	——	——
————————	——	——	——	——	——	——	——
————————	——	——	——	——	——	——	——
————————	——	——	——	——	——	——	——
————————	——	——	——	——	——	——	——
————————	——	——	——	——	——	——	——
————————	——	——	——	——	——	——	——
————————	——	——	——	——	——	——	——

Figure 16-2.

INFORMATION COMBINATION FORM WITH SAMPLE VALUES FOR TWO GROUPS.

Item	Group: Supervisors			Group: Managers			
	Number	Value	Result	Number	Value	Result	Total
Leadership	15	1	___	17	.8	___	___
Oral Communication	12	1	___	10	.8	___	___
Planning	10	1	___	15	.8	___	___
Decision Making	9	1	___	11	.8	___	___

The next step is to multiply the numbers for each group by its assigned value and enter the result in the Result column for each group (as shown in Figure 16-3).

The final step is to calculate the average of the two group's Results, so you add the two Result figures for each competency and divide by two (since there are two groups). That has been done in the example in Figure 16-4.

Obviously, if you have more than two groups a form with more columns is necessary. However, the same approach is used. For

Figure 16-3.

INFORMATION COMBINATION FORM WITH RESULTS CALCULATED.

Item	Group: Supervisors			Group: Managers			Total
	Number	Value	Result	Number	Value	Result	
Leadership	15	1	15	17	.8	13.6	___
Oral Communication	12	1	12	10	.8	8.0	___
Planning	10	1	10	15	.8	12.0	___
Decision Making	9	1	9	11	.8	8.0	___

example, assume you have three groups: employees, their supervisors, and the managers of the supervisors. This time you have weighted them as follows:

Supervisors of the position   100%

Employees in the position at least six   85%
months

Managers of the supervisors   60%

Figure 16-4.

INFORMATION COMBINATION FORM WITH TOTALS.

Item	Group: Supervisors			Group: Managers			Total
	Number	Value	Result	Number	Value	Result	
Leadership	15	1	15	17	.8	13.6	14.3
Oral Communication	12	1	12	10	.8	8.0	10.0
Planning	10	1	10	15	.8	12.0	11.0
Decision Making	9	1	9	11	.8	8.8	8.9

When you are dealing with nonmeasurable responses, the task is more difficult. For example, assume you collected statements that describe the type of training required for salespeople and you were able to identify the responses with keywords. You then report the frequency, or how often the response is given, by keyword. You again calculate the average of each group and then multiply the average by the weighting—the value you have assigned the group—to get:

1.00   for the supervisors' averages

0.85   for the employees' averages

0.60   for the managers' responses

Then you would add the resulting number and divide by three (for the three groups).

Information gathered from all the procedures introduced in this book, except one, lend themselves to this type of combining. The one notable exception is when the information is developed by the Need-to-Know Process. By its very nature, this process accurately identifies the subject matter required by a typical learner, so unless there is a reason to modify it, no adjustment or weighting is required.

Reporting Results

So how do you report?

Generally, your first responsibility is to report to whomever initiated or requested the training needs analysis. That report can take two approaches. It can be a report of what was learned—what the training needs of the organization or individual are—or it can also include suggestions or recommendations for fulfilling those needs. Since identifying training to meet needs is the subject of Chapter 17, here we will deal solely with reporting any identified needs.

The report should contain:

❏ The reason or objective for the training needs analysis
❏ The methodologies used
❏ The population(s) contacted
❏ Any additional sources used
❏ The dates of the study
❏ The results

Because the person requesting the investigation had some reason for initiating it and probably some idea about what type of training was required, you should communicate the results to that person first. That person is also, in many instances, the one who decides whether to initiate any training. In some cases, you may be reporting that you have determined there was no training requirement, and that may come as a surprise for the person who requested the analysis. Consider this example:

> A Colorado candy manufacturer was experiencing difficulties in on-time shipments of products. The director of traffic asked the training department to determine what type of training needs the employees had. The director wanted to somehow fill those needs to improve performance.
>
> Training conducted a needs analysis and discovered the problem wasn't that the employees required training. The problem was being caused by delays in preparing shipping orders, and that was a system problem.
>
> The training department returned to the director to report its findings. The director disagreed with the results and decided to conduct his own training.

Other times, you may discover a disagreement with your report, as in this case:

> The manager of a utility company's repair department had an employee who she considered a very poor performer. The manager continually suggested various training for this employee, but he usually declined. Instead, he seemed to spend his time giving the manager suggestions on how to operate the department.
>
> The company initiated a program for the early identification of supervisor competencies and potential in nonsupervisors. The manager recommended her employee attend. The manager felt that receiving a report that indicated all the training this person needed might cause him to focus on his real problems.
>
> However, the report was not what the manager expected. The program evaluated the employee as having excellent supervisory competencies and recommended him for promotion.

The real problem was that the employee had better management skills than his manager and was quite vocal about what the manager should do, so the manager considered him a problem employee.

More often, though, you may discover that your report requires some adjustments to meet reality. For example:

A training needs analysis conducted for a Michigan automobile-parts manufacturer identified a need to train advertising personnel in the automobile-parts pricing system. When the report was shown to the director of advertising, he agreed, but decided that rather than train everyone in the procedures, he would assign people so that only a small number would deal with pricing issues. That reduced the number of people to be trained. As a result the training became an individual activity, whereas before a group course was recommended.

Once the report is prepared, it should be delivered in person or by mail. However, if done by mail, be sure to arrange an opportunity for the individual to ask questions, if necessary.

If the analysis was initiated by a group, a meeting may be the best way to deliver the report. A meeting can bring all appropriate people together and is a useful forum for answering all questions at one time.

There is no single format for a training needs analysis report. The report should be written in a format that meets the objective of the needs analysis. The balance of this chapter presents four sample reports. Each is from a different needs analysis, is in a different format, and varies in length.

- ❏ A short report of an individual employee's identified training needs.

- ❏ A more elaborate report of training needs identified for an existing supervisor through an assessment center.

- ❏ A report on the training needs and subjects for a new employee orientation training course.

- ❏ A report of a job analysis conducted to identify supervisory competencies for an assessment center in order to measure training and development needs. This last report example describes a combination of procedures.

None of these reports, presented in the next four sections, contain training recommendations. They are solely descriptions of the identified training needs.

Example 1: A Training Needs Analysis Report for Gloria Haver

At the request of Bill Armstrong, department manager, a training needs analysis was conducted for Gloria Haver, department employee reporting to Bill Armstrong. The objective of the analysis was:

> To determine specific training needs whose fulfillment will assist Gloria Haver in performing to job standard

Analysis

The analysis was conducted on June 17 and 18. The following methodologies and sources were used for collecting information:

- ❑ An interview was held first with Bill Armstrong and then with Gloria Haver.
- ❑ Performance reviews for Gloria Haver for the past three years, and her position's description and standards of performance, were obtained and reviewed.

Based on initial information, a standard test of mathematical ability was administered to Gloria Haver.

Results

Gloria's difficulties with meeting job standards appear to be caused by an inability to readily convert dimensions from metric to inches. This was confirmed by her scores on a standardized test of mathematical ability that included metric conversions.

Gloria Haver appears capable of learning better conversion techniques, and that should contribute to improved job performance.

Example 2: Morgan Company's Supervisor Assessment Center Report for Alice Larsen

Alice Larsen, currently a supervisor with Morgan Company in Tulsa, Oklahoma, participated in the company's supervisor assessment center on December 10.

The program was designed to measure the supervisor's management strengths and areas of needed improvement. Alice was requested to attend the program to obtain information that would assist her in her current position and in her individual career development.

The evaluation was based on twenty-one management competencies that have been identified as necessary for success as a supervisor at Morgan Company. The Morgan Company's Supervisor Assessment Center is a standardized, participative, multiassessment program designed to identify supervisory competencies and areas of needed improvement as demonstrated through individual performance. The program provides participants and their organizations with accurate information that can be used to improve current management performance and assist in preparing specific career plans and identifying development activities.

To produce these results, the program creates a simulated but realistic organizational environment using eight exercises:

1. An interview based on the competencies and information provided on a Background Information Form

2. A questionnaire containing management-related questions

3. An in-basket of supervisor problems, followed by an interview regarding each participant's decisions

4. A lunch meeting, during which each participant makes a short presentation on a management topic of his/her choice

5. A leaderless group discussion in which participants evaluate a promotion, as presented in a short videotape

6. A leaderless group discussion in which participants determine the competencies necessary for a supervisor's position and evaluate the qualifications of twelve candidates for such a position

7. A small group exercise in which participants reorganize a regional office

8. A self-evaluation questionnaire

A chairperson administers the exercises, and the performance of the participant is observed, recorded, and later evaluated by four Morgan Company managers who have been trained in the skills and techniques of the process.

The process requires each team member independently to arrive at an individual evaluation for each participant in each competency. The final evaluation is prepared by combining these individual evaluations. In virtually every instance, unless otherwise noted, the individual evaluations are consistent—that is, each evaluation team member independently has evaluated each participant the same way in each competency as the other team members. Where there is inconsistency—that is, where at least two of the evaluation team members differ significantly in their evaluations of a participant's management competency—the report indicates that difference.

The twenty-one management competencies that have been identified by a job analysis as necessary for success as a Morgan Company supervisor are as follows:

Competency	Definition
Leadership	Getting people to willingly accomplish objectives
Oral Communication	Transferring a message by speech using appropriate gesticulations
Flexibility	Adjusting to changing conditions
Decision Making	Consciously selecting the best alternative from two or more
Coaching	Working with an individual to improve job performance
Listening	Receiving correctly another's oral communication

Stress Tolerance	Maintaining stability of performance under adverse conditions
Team Participation	Working effectively with a group and being accepted as a part of that group
Accountability	Using delegated authority to meet assigned responsibilities
Problem Analysis	Identifying the real problem and obtaining the information necessary to solve it
Delegation	Passing authority and responsibility to another
Initiative	Interjecting planned thoughts or actions into a situation
Functional	Coping with the realities of a variety of situations
Handling Complaints	Accepting complaints and resolving them without conflict
Conflict Resolution	Reducing tension between two or more people and arriving at a mutually satisfactory conclusion
Assertiveness	Interjecting one's reactive thoughts or actions into a situation
Planning	Outlining a course of action to achieve an objective
Questioning	Obtaining desired information by asking questions.
Image	Projecting a positive initial and continuing presence
Controlling	Ensuring the plan is followed and the objective met
Written Communication	Transferring a message through writing

In the final evaluation, Alice's performance in each of the management competencies is rated according to the following categories:

❐ **More Than Enough.** Competencies in this category indicate that the individual's performance was above that typical of the competencies required for success as a supervisor at Morgan Company.

❐ **High Typical.** Competencies in this category indicate that performance was at the very high end of the range typical of the competencies required for success as a supervisor at Morgan Company.

❐ **Typical.** Competencies in this category indicate that performance demonstrated exactly the amount of the competencies required for success as a supervisor at Morgan Company.

❐ **Low Typical.** Competencies in this category indicate that performance was at the very low end of the range typical of the competencies required for success as a supervisor at Morgan Company.

❐ **Needed Improvement.** Competencies in this category indicate that performance was less than typical of the competencies required for success as a supervisor at Morgan Company.

❐ **Inconsistency.** A competency that falls in this category would have received significantly different evaluations from at least two members of the team. Since *inconsistency* refers to different evaluations obtained by the procedure, action should be taken to discover what caused the differences. However, for purposes of the report, it is important to indicate that there was a question regarding the reliability of the evaluations in this category and the probable reasons for the inconsistency.

Alice's ratings were based on her observable behavior in the program's exercises. Each assessor observed her on a number of occasions, but at different times and independent of the other assessors. To a large extent this approach contributes to the program's high reliability. The rating of her performance in each of the competencies is as follows:

Category/Rating	*Competencies Evaluated*
More Than Enough	Leadership
	Oral Communication
	Team Participation
	Accountability
	Problem Analysis
	Initiative
	Functional
	Assertiveness
	Planning
	Controlling
High Typical	Decision Making
	Stress Tolerance
	Handling Complaints
	Image
Typical	Flexibility
	Coaching
	Listening
	Conflict Resolution
	Questioning
Low Typical	Delegation
Needs Improvement	Written Communication
Inconsistency	Leadership
	Coaching
	Stress Tolerance
	Team Participation
	Handling Complaints
	Conflict Resolution
	Written Communication

When a participant performs significantly different at various points in the program, the differing performances produce different evaluations. This was what occurred in Alice's case. The assessors felt they had observed different degrees of performance in seven competencies during the program exercises. These competencies are therefore categorized as inconsistencies.

Example 3: Report of New Employee Training Needs for an Orientation Program

On January 7 and 8, information was gathered from possible employees on the need for a new employee orientation training course. The specific objectives of the study were:

To determine whether a new employee orientation training course would benefit employees and the company

To identify the subject matter for such a training course

To determine the appropriate length for a such a training course

Methodology

Several methods were used to gather information. The methods were conducted in the same sequence as follows:

❐ **Interviews.** Individual interviews were conducted with a number of employees. The interviews were of two types. One consisted of predetermined questions. The other was more free-flowing, but based on the conditions of employment that were to be measured.

❐ **Group Focus Meetings.** Two group focus meetings were held. These meetings began with individuals answering questions to be discussed. Each answer was written on individual cards (identified by individual), then the cards were collected and randomly redistributed. The group participants receiving the cards used the answers for initial input to the group discussions. This allowed others to contribute whether or not they had supplied the answers.

❐ **Written Questionnaire.** The group meetings concluded with individuals completing portions of a written questionnaire. The questionnaire was to be completed anonymously, and the optional demographic information requested was not specific enough to an individual to allow for identification.

Demographics

The demographics of the individuals participating in all of the groups are summarized in the following table:

Group	Number	Average Age	Gender	Human Resources	Management	New Employees
Total	40	35.2	23 male 17 female	6	14	20

Results

By using a questionnaire that solicited numerical responses, standardized responses were obtained that provide a statistical base for determining the desired information. The information obtained from the groups was weighted based on a predetermined set of values, as follows:

New Employees   100%

Management   80%

Human Resources   90%

Questions and Responses

1. Will a new employee orientation training course benefit the company?

	Yes	No
Employees	20	0
Management	12	2
Human Resources	6	0
Total Number of Responses	38	2

2. Will a new employee orientation training course benefit new employees?

	Yes	No
Employees	20	0
Management	10	4
Human Resources	6	0
Total Number of Responses	36	4

3. How long should a new employee orientation training course be?

	1 Hour	2 Hours	4 Hours	All Day
Employees	0	4	10	6
Management	1	5	6	2
Human Resources	0	1	2	3
Total Number of Responses	1	10	18	11

4. When should a new employee orientation training course be conducted?

	First Day of Employment	First Week of Employment	First Month of Employment
Employees	8	10	2
Management	10	4	0
Human Resources	4	0	2
Total	22	14	4

Subjects

The following subjects are recommended for the new employee orientation training course. They are listed in descending order of importance (i.e., the most important first, then the next most important).

Insurance

Health Insurance

Disability Insurance

Life Insurance

Dependent Coverage

Effective Date

Compensation

Pay Date

Overtime

Deductions

Form of Pay—Wire Transfer or Check

Time Sheets

Rule and Regulations

Hours

Absences

Lateness

Rules of Conduct

Dress Code

Benefits

Vacation

Paid Time Off

Retirement Plans

Educational Support

Company Organization

Key People to Contact

Senior Management

Organization Chart

Employee's Department and Manager

Performance Reviews

Company Mission

Company History

The subjects can also be divided into three groups. The first group would includes those subjects that *must* be covered by a new employee orientation training program. The second group would include those subjects that *should* be covered. The third group would include subjects to cover if there is time—in other words, they are not subjects a new employee has to be informed about during orientation.

Conclusion

The training needs analysis confirmed a need for a new employee orientation training course. It also identified specific subjects and timing for the training. Such a course is considered to be of benefit for both new employees and the company.

Example 4: Report of a Job Analysis Conducted for First-Level Supervisor Positions Within Calumet Financial

On October 30, information was gathered at the Chicago, Illinois location of Calumet Financial for an analysis of the company's first-level supervisory positions. The objective of the analysis was to identify the management competencies required for success as a first-level supervisor. That information would then be used as the basis for designing a supervisor assessment center for Calumet Financial.

This report contains the results of the job analysis. Within it the following terminology is used:

❐ **Supervisor** refers specifically to a first-level supervisor.

❐ **Manager** is the position to which a first-level supervisor reports.

❐ **Employee** is anyone in a nonmanagement position.

Methodology

Information was collected in two basic settings: interviews and group meetings. The methodologies used were the Job Analysis Grid, individual questionnaires, and group decision discussions.

Interviews

Interviews were conducted with two current supervisors, two current managers, and three current employees.

The Job Analysis Grid was used during the interviews. This technique is designed to obtain reliable information about a position's competencies with minimal contamination from the interviewer's input. The technique is executed in three stages. In stage one, questions are asked regarding position performance. In stage two, the competencies required for that performance are identified. In stage three, the identified competencies are ranked and rated with respect to their relationships to supervisor success.

Group Meetings

There were two separate group meetings: a meeting with six current supervisors and a meeting with seven current managers.

The first activity in each group meeting was completion of a Management Questionnaire. This questionnaire, which was answered by each participant, sought the following information:

☐ Function of the supervisory position within Calumet Financial

☐ Relationships of various qualifications to supervisor success

☐ Relationship of the times spent on management and nonmanagement activities

☐ Ranking and rating of twenty-nine management competencies

☐ Identification of any additionally required management competencies

The twenty-nine management competencies supplied by the questionnaire were based on the most-often-identified supervisor management competencies from past job analyses. Each competency was accompanied by its definition. Group meeting participants were allowed to add competencies and include them in their rankings and ratings. Ultimately, the participants added five competencies to the original list of twenty-nine. The complete list (i.e., thirty-four competencies in total) follows:

Competency	*Definition*
Team Participation	Working effectively with a group and being accepted as a part of that group

Functional	Coping with the realities of a variety of situations
Creativity	Developing new alternative solutions to problems
Stress Tolerance	Maintaining stability of performance under adverse conditions
Controlling	Ensuring the plan is followed and the objective met
Questioning	Obtaining desired information by asking questions
Leadership	Getting people to willingly accomplish objectives
Written Communication	Transferring a message through writing
Organizing	Structuring and arranging resources to accomplish a task
Handling Complaints	Accepting complaints and resolving them without conflict
Assertiveness	Interjecting one's reactive thoughts or actions into a situation
Energy and Drive	Starting a task enthusiastically and maintaining that enthusiasm until completion
Public Speaking	Giving an oral presentation to a group of four or more people
Persuasiveness	Converting others to a point of view or obtaining a commitment from them
Professionalism	Demonstrating the skills and knowledge required to successfully practice in a selected field
Accountability	Using delegated authority to meet assigned responsibilities

Image	Projecting a positive initial and continuing presence
Decision Making	Consciously selecting the best alternative from two or more
Flexibility	Adjusting to changing conditions
Problem Analysis	Identifying the real problem and obtaining the information necessary to solve it
Delegation	Passing authority and responsibility to another
Planning	Outlining a course of action to achieve an objective
Conflict Resolution	Reducing tension between two or more people and arriving at a mutually satisfactory conclusion
Thoroughness	Staying with a task once begun until the desired degree of completion
Meeting Management	Leading a group to accomplish a predetermined objective
Oral Communication	Transferring a message by speech using appropriate gesticulations
Initiative	Interjecting planned thoughts or actions into a situation
Listening	Receiving correctly another's oral communication
Identifying Needs	Determining the individual requirements of another
Coaching	Working with an individual to improve job performance
Feedback	Recognizing positive behavior and communicating ways to improve it
Corporate Savvy	Doing the politically correct thing

Interpersonal   Communicating with others in a manner that
Communication   develops rapport and trust

Projects   Completing technical projects

Once the competencies were ranked and rated by the individual participants on the Management Questionnaire, the participants were divided into two small groups. Each group was assigned one-half of the competencies for ranking. Following the small group work, the entire group was reconvened so that it could rank and rate all the competencies.

Rankings required the participants to place the competencies in descending order of importance for supervisor success. Then one of the following three ratings was assigned to each competency:

Must   A competency that an individual must possess
                       in the required amount to succeed as a
                       supervisor

Want   A competency that an individual should possess
                       in the required amount to succeed as a
                       supervisor, but that can be present to a lesser
                       degree if offset by other competencies

Not Necessary   A competency that is not required in order to
                       succeed as a supervisor

During the information-gathering process, a question was raised as to whether process would identify the competencies required by current supervisors or a desired type of supervisor. The job analysis was based on what is needed by current supervisors performing their job as desired. This allows the assessment center to identify more of a competency than is required and less of a competency than is required. In addition, the design creates a profile that can be adjusted for specific supervisor positions and changing supervisor needs.

The information collected in the interviews and group meetings was entered into and compiled by a computer program that applied predetermined weights to the various information sources. In addition, the interview information was used as a control to cross-check competencies.

Results

The results identified qualifications for supervisor success, evaluated time spent on management versus nonmanagement activities, and produced a ranking and rating of management competencies.

Qualifications

The results yielded the following weights of various qualifications for supervisor success:

Qualifications	Weights
Length of Company Service	5.2%
Knowledge of Employees' Work	25.5%
Education	10.7%
Management Ability	58.6%

Time

The relationship between a supervisor's time spent on management versus nonmanagement activities was:

Management   58%

Nonmanagement   42%

Management Competencies

Competencies were listed in rank order (with the competencies most important for supervisor success listed first) and then grouped by their ratings. Although twenty-nine competencies were initially supplied, and the participants identified an additional five, only thirty-three are ranked and rated. One competency, Interpersonal Communication, is not included. The analysis indicated its definition was covered by other competencies. If it had been included in the list, it would have been near the end and rated as Not Necessary.

In reviewing the rankings and ratings, it is important to remember that only management competencies were evaluated. Competencies for nonmanagement activities, such as those related to the actual work of an area or specific professional skills, were not ranked and rated. The reason is that the analysis was conducted for the purposes of designing a supervisor assessment center to measure the management aspects of the position. The competencies, and how they were grouped according to their ratings, are listed as follows:

Musts

❐ Leadership

❐ Oral Communication

❐ Flexibility

❐ Decision Making

❐ Coaching

❐ Listening

❐ Stress Tolerance

❐ Team Participation

❐ Accountability

❐ Problem Analysis

❐ Delegation

❐ Initiative

Wants

❐ Functional

❐ Handling Complaints

❐ Conflict Resolution

❐ Assertiveness

❐ Planning

❐ Questioning

❐ Image

❐ Controlling

❏ Written Communication

❏ Professionalism

❏ Thoroughness

❏ Energy and Drive

❏ Organizing

❏ Persuasiveness

❏ Meeting Management

❏ Creativity

❏ Identifying Needs

Not Necessary

❏ Public Speaking

❏ Feedback

❏ Corporate Savvy

❏ Projects

Recommendations

The competencies identified by the job analysis are all ones that can be measured by an assessment center. However, a one-day assessment center best measures performance in no more than twenty competencies, so it is recommended that the top-twenty competencies be used for designing the assessment center exercises and evaluating participant performance. They are:

Musts

1. Leadership
2. Oral Communication
3. Flexibility
4. Decision Making
5. Coaching
6. Listening
7. Stress Tolerance
8. Team Participation

9. Accountability

10. Problem Analysis

11. Delegation

12. Initiative

Wants

13. Functional

14. Handling Complaints

15. Conflict Resolution

16. Assertiveness

17. Planning

18. Questioning

19. Image

20. Controlling

In addition to the top-twenty competencies, the assessment center will also be designed to measure:

- ❐ **Overall Management Ability** (i.e., the overall rating of a participant's first-level supervisory management ability based on all assessment center performance)

- ❐ **Management Potential** (i.e., the current management level at which the participant can perform successfully without additional training and development)

Conclusion

The job analysis was successful in identifying management competencies to be used as the basis for a supervisor assessment center. The next step is approval of the competencies to be used. However, if any competencies are added, they must be ones that can be accurately measured by observable performance in assessment center exercises.

The first run of the supervisor assessment center will include a validation study of the process. That study will yield:

- ❏ The relationship of each competency to supervisor success.
- ❏ The reliability of the center in evaluating the competencies.
- ❏ The consistency of the assessors in evaluating the competencies.
- ❏ The accuracy of the assessment center in identifying overall management ability (provided current supervisors are the participants and appropriate job performance data is supplied).

It is important to note two other items of information gained from the job analysis. Management ability accounts for 58.6 percent of the qualifications needed for success as a supervisor, and the management portion of the job requires 58 percent of a supervisor's time. In selecting supervisors and evaluating their on-the-job performance, areas other than management and management competencies (i.e., areas that round out the supervisor's qualifications and time commitment) must be also considered.

17

Transferring Training Needs to Training Objectives

The final goal of a training needs analysis is the identification of specific training requirements to fulfill the identified needs. Actually, the training requirements are sometimes included in the report, along with the identified training needs, but at other times it becomes a second report. When these have been accepted by the client, approved or revised, the needs and requirements can be turned over to someone to determine the training required to fulfill the identified needs.

The person conducting and reporting the training needs is not always the individual who develops or recommends the training. However, at the least, the final step in a training needs analysis should be to translate the identified needs into objectives. Then those objectives can be used to develop or select a training approach.

In this chapter, we will first examine translating training needs into training objectives. Then we will do an overview of the types of training and considerations in recommending training methods.

Training objectives serve two main purposes:

❐ They describe what is to be learned or taught.

❐ They describe how you will know when training is successful.

279

Behavioral Objectives

Let's start with a few definitions. Training objectives are generally called behavioral objectives. Sometimes they are referred to as learning objectives. Whatever they are called, they are descriptions of what is to be learned through training. One definition of learning is a change in behavior. Two other useful definitions to keep in mind are:

❐ Behavior is a person's visible actions.

❐ Concluding behavior is a behavior that can be observed and measured at the completion of something.

Using these definitions a training objective becomes a description of the specific concluding behavior a learner can demonstrate and have measured at the conclusion of training.

Behavioral objectives are the keys to successful training. If developed properly, they are both specific and measurable, so they not only provide guidelines for designing and conducting training, they also provide the basis for measuring the results of the training. Furthermore, they are an effective way of clearly communicating what a training course is expected to accomplish.

If behavioral objectives are not included in the report of identified training needs, they should be communicated after the needs have been accepted or revised. They too require approval by the appropriate person before initiating the development or selection of a training methodology. You need to ensure that what the training will be designed to accomplish is what is wanted and needed. For example, take the following statement:

The employee needs to be trained to improve telephone techniques.

It is not as clear as this statement:

At the conclusion of the training the employee will be able to handle or answer twelve incoming telephone inquiries an hour, bringing at least ten to a successful resolution without transferring the callers to others for answers.

Communicating in such a specific, unambiguous fashion allows the client to make a decision on whether or not to proceed with training. A behavioral objective describes exactly what the training proposes to accomplish, and it allows the client to indicate any disagreement he may have and request any desired revisions.

Writing Behavioral Objectives

Writing behavioral or learning objectives is almost the same as writing performance standards. Like performance standards they should be measurable. Measurable means that they contain some form of description that can be quantified. For example:

- ❐ At the conclusion of training the learner will be able to assemble and disassemble all class B products, each within fifteen minutes.

- ❐ At the conclusion of training the learner will be able to answer 85 percent of incoming mail inquiries without having to contact other departments for information.

- ❐ At the conclusion of training the learner will be able to enter all new account information for forty to fifty applications per hour.

In the first and third behavioral objectives cited above, a part of the measure is time. However, behavioral objectives only require a time element for measurement. They do not require a time element with respect to the length of training, although such a time requirement may become part of the ultimate training design. With these types of measurements, the concluding behavior of someone completing the training can be quantified.

Unfortunately, many training objectives do not meet these criteria. Here are three behavioral objectives used in three training programs:

- ❐ At the conclusion of training the learner will be able process a typical number of insurance applications.

- ❐ At the conclusion of the training the learner will be able to sell the company's products.

❐ At the conclusion of the training the learner will be able to operate a PC.

All three of these examples use words for measures— "typical number," "sell," and "operate"—that require interpretation: Does typical number refer to the average number processed by all employees, or the average processed by the best-performing employees? Does sell mean making a presentation, obtaining an order, or something else? Does operate refer to turning a PC on and off, booting it up, or using a specific software?

These three examples could have been made specific:

❐ At the conclusion of the training the learner will be able process an average of twenty-four insurance applications an hour with no more than a 2 percent error rate.

❐ At the conclusion of the training the learner will be able make a sales presentation of all the company's products and close sales with an average order rate of ten per week.

❐ At the conclusion of the training the learner will be able to operate a PC using Lotus 1-2-3 spreadsheet and perform all functions specified in the software manual.

You should avoid nonmeasurable words; for example:

Instead of:	*Use:*
to know	can describe
to understand	can apply
to use	can list

Each of the words in the second column can be demonstrated through the learner's behavior. The learner can be required to provide a description. The learner can be required to apply by demonstrating use, and the learner can create a list.

There should be a behavioral objective that relates to every training need. For example, assume the following training need was identified: "To be able to complete construction permit requests." A behavioral objective for the training could be: "At the conclusion of the training, the learner can demonstrate the ability to complete all areas of a construction permit request form without mistakes."

At times, one behavioral objective may relate to more than one identified training need, and at other times it may require more than one behavioral objective for a single training need. However, if you cannot identify a behavioral objective for a training need, you probably cannot provide the appropriate training. How would you know when you had succeeded?

A convenient method for communicating the relationship between training needs and training objectives is to list the behavioral objective(s) beneath the training need(s). For example:

❑ The training need is for the employee to be able to locate requested parts from inventory.

❑ The behavioral objective is that at the conclusion of training, the learner will be able to locate 90 percent of total stored parts by searching the inventory base on the computer. No part shall require over four minutes to locate.

Finally, as with performance standards, behavioral objectives should be written and agreed upon by the trainer and learner. If both know and accept the need for the training and the planned outcomes, the training will be far more successful.

Sequencing

It helps to sequence behavioral objectives for reporting and communicating purposes. There are two ways to accomplish that. One is to sequence them in the order they are implemented on the job. For example:

❑ Answer all incoming telephone calls by the third ring, beginning each telephone conversation with the approved opening procedure.

❑ Answer all inquiries or refer the caller to someone who can.

The second approach is to sequence them by importance. For example:

❏ Answer all inquiries or refer the caller to someone who can.

❏ Answer all incoming telephone calls by the third ring, beginning each telephone conversation with the approved opening procedure.

In many cases, both sequencing methods are provided to the training designer and the client.

Types of Training

You should be aware of the types of training your organization currently uses. *The Trainer's Dictionary* (Amherst, Mass.: HRD Press, 1993) is a book of some 200 pages that describes types of training. We are not going to attempt to cover all of them. Instead, for our purposes, we will concentrate on the ones most used and the ones that cover the broadest spectrum. These are:

❏ **Group Training.** Group training involves three or more individuals who participate in a common learning activity generally led by a group facilitator.

❏ **Coaching.** Coaching is one-on-one job training. Generally it includes demonstration, lecture, and observation of practice.

❏ **Mentoring.** This is a process in which experienced employees are assigned to assist newer employees through guidance. Sometimes it is a formal approach, at other times it is informal. It is also used to introduce employees to a company's culture and environment.

❏ **Self-Paced Learning.** This is any learning activity in which the learner determines the speed at which the material is covered. Generally, it is an individualized form of instruction, but it can be used with groups with the speed set either individually or by the group.

❏ **E-Learning.** This is a term used to describe learning activities conducted from the user's desktop via the Internet or e-mail. As such, it is generally an individual learner activity.

❏ **Computer-Assisted Instruction.** This is delivery of training via a computer. Again it is generally individualized. It can include programs on modeling, simulation, practice, and knowledge.

❏ **Distance Learning Training.** This describes instruction in which the teacher is geographically separated from the learner. Connection can be via satellite or phone line with the instruction delivered to a PC or to a room specially equipped with video or audioconferencing equipment.

❏ **Self-Study.** Self-study refers to learning activities initiated and participated in by an individual. Programmed instruction, computer-assisted instruction, and reading assignments can all be self-study activities.

❏ **Simulations.** These are controlled and standardized representations of a job, activity, or situation used as a basis for developing skill in dealing with the bases of the simulation.

❏ **Lectures.** These are structured oral presentations delivered for the transfer of information.

❏ **Job Assignments.** Job assignments place an individual into an actual job, generally for a limited period of time, for which the primary goal is for the individual to learn all or part of the job.

❏ **Job Rotation.** This is similar to job assignment but generally includes several assignments in a preplanned order or the exchange of jobs with another person.

Who Conducts Training

Along with the types of training you must consider who conducts the training. Typically courses are conducted by:

❏ **Supervisors.** These are the people who manage the people being trained.

❏ **Human Resources.** These are the professionals in the human resources department. If training is a function of the HR department, it is treated separately.

❏ **Operating Department Employees.** These are the employees of the department for which an individual is to be trained.

❏ **Training Department Personnel.** These are generally training professionals employed by the training department. Their strengths are their skills and knowledge of training techniques and procedures. The most-often-heard criticism of such people is that they lack specific job or operational knowledge. Some organizations assign their trainers to specific areas—sometimes even to temporary work in the operating departments—to overcome such weaknesses.

☐ **Operating Department Personnel on Temporary Assignment to Training.** These are people who usually have excellent job knowledge but often lack training skills. Many organizations use this approach since it gives greater credibility to the training sessions, and the operating personnel on such an assignment benefit greatly from the experience and learning of training techniques.

☐ **External Professionals.** These are usually training consultants, supplier employees, or university professors. Generally, they are used when the required degree of knowledge or skill is not available within the organization. These people usually are excellent trainers, but they can be expensive to use. If they offer similar classes on a regular basis, consistency may be lost if the same external person is not conducting all classes.

☐ **External Organizations.** Local schools and professional organizations often conduct registration programs in general subjects.

Knowing the types of training currently being used by your organization and who conducts each training type allows you to indicate initially what can be done. However, in some cases the training will have to be designed and/or obtained elsewhere.

Selection of a Training Method

Once approved by your client, the training needs analysis and behavioral objectives form the basic information required to design or obtain a training course. At times it may be obvious what training should be recommended. For example, if you have identified basic written communication training needs, and your organization conducts a written communication training course that covers those needs, that is the recommendation. However, other times it may not be as obvious. That, then, becomes an assignment for a training course developer.

Developing a training course and evaluating an existing one are beyond the scope of this book. However, there are several basic considerations with which you should be familiar:

❏ Value

❏ Content

❏ Measurement

❏ Availability

❏ Timeliness

Value

When you conducted the training needs analysis, it was recommended that you calculate the training's value. If you have that information—even if only an estimate—all you need to do then is calculate the costs of various training methods.

At its simplest, value equals benefit minus cost. However, to perform the calculation, both benefit and cost must be expressed in the same terms. They can be expressed in a number of ways: time, dollars, efficiency, and production. For example:

❏ **Benefit.** This training will increase production 10 percent per month if all employees in the department are trained. That represents $20,000 in increased production.

❏ **Cost.** Conducting a training course for all employees in the department will cost $30,000.

❏ **Value.** On an annual basis the value is $210,000 (calculated as $240,000 [$20,000 × 12 months] minus $30,000).

A value calculation may not always be exact, but it provides an estimate that will assist in determining the training to recommend. Sometimes, particularly when there is just one employee to train, there may be greater value in sending the employee to an external course than to purchase one for internal use. Other times when there are a number of employees to train, but only one time to train them, an external consultant with an existing course may be the best value approach. To estimate costs consider:

❏ The purchase price, design cost, or registration fee

❏ The employee's time to be trained

❏ The instructor's time

❏ The cost of consumed materials

❏ The cost of any equipment

❏ The facility costs

❏ The number of current employees to be trained

❏ The number of future employees to be trained

❏ The frequency of required training

❏ Miscellaneous costs, such as licensing fees, transportation and lodging, meals and discounts for repeat sessions.

Most of these consideration were factors in gathering information for the training needs analysis, so the major requirement is to convert them to similar units.

Content

You need to ensure the content of a course is what is required. Often titles of subjects can be misleading. For example, you may have identified an employee's need to improve his oral communications skills. A course offered at the local community college may have that title. However, you could be seeking presentation skills and the course could be covering vocabulary building.

You need to read descriptions, definitions, and outlines of any training course you are considering. At times, the course may not be exactly what is required, but you may be able to supplement the training internally.

Measurement

Training should be measurable. You should be able to determine whether or not it was effective. This requires behavioral objectives and a method for measuring them. Some training courses supply measurements. Other times you may have to develop them yourself or purchase a separate measuring tool.

Availability and Timeliness

Is the training available? Some courses are only conducted sporadically. Some courses may have prerequisites that may preclude your use. Some may no longer be offered. Some may only be conducted at inconvenient locations. Along with availability, timeliness is a consideration. Can the course be conducted in time to meet organizational needs?

18

Considering External
Services and Products

Several times in this book the possible use of external products and services has been mentioned. Generally, such services and products are provided by:

❏ Consultants who conduct training needs analysis and products

❏ Publishers who provide training needs analysis procedures

In this chapter, we will examine some steps to consider when selecting such services and products and whether they are correct for your situation.

Yours or Ours?

One of the first questions you need to ask is whether or not you have the personnel capable of conducting the training needs analysis, and if they have the necessary time available. This means you have to examine the qualifications and schedules of internal people. However, there are two additional considerations concerning using internal people—both political in nature.

Whoever conducts a training needs analysis should be an objective, neutral person. Sometimes, there are no employees who can meet that requirement. Even if an employee is objective and neutral but is perceived otherwise, it is the perception that becomes the reality. If an employee's motives are suspect, chances are the results will also be questioned. The second consideration has to do with how an external person's qualifications are related to those of the organization's employees. At times, a stranger's work is more accepted than that of someone who is known in the organization. In fact, a well-known consultant once said, "I am usually hired because no one in the company knows me. They accept my credentials, but when they begin to call me by my first name, my magic is gone."

However, there are some organizations that have a "not invented here" reaction to externally obtained products and recommendations. In such organizations, only the work performed internally is accepted.

If you decide, for whatever reasons, that you need to obtain external assistance, there are several approaches you can use to help ensure the selection is qualified for your assignment.

Locating External Assistance

Generally, individuals and firms providing training needs analysis services classify themselves as management or training consultants. Sometimes industrial psychologists perform such services, but there are numerous other possible titles such as organizational consultants, organizational psychologists, and development advisors. The following are sources for such services (listed in no particular order):

❒ **The Yellow Pages.** Look under the listings of consultants, management consultants, psychologists (industrial or organizational), and training. You will find that some listings show the areas of specialization.

❒ **The Internet.** Use key words such as "consultant, training, industrial psychologist and organizational psychologist. More and more individuals and firms are establishing web sites. You may discover exactly the expertise you require.

❒ **The Public Library or Bookstores.** There are several directories of consultants. Probably the best known is the *Directory* *of Management Consultants,* published by Kennedy Publications and Consultants News (Fitzwilliam, New Hampshire). Another is *Consultants and Consulting Organizations* published by The Gale Group (Detroit, Michigan).

❑ **Professional Associations.** Organizations such as the American Management Association (New York, New York); the American Society for Training and Development (Alexandria, Virginia); and the Society for Human Resource Management (Alexandria, Virginia) generally will not recommend consultants, but usually can supply a list of people and firms in your area.

❑ **Universities or Colleges.** If there's a business school in your area, contact one of departments specializing in organizational development or a similar topic. They may be able to provide names of professionals in your area, and at times, names of professors who also supply such services.

❑ **Other Organizations.** If you know of an organization that has conducted a similar activity, give them a call. They may be able to give you names of who they used and others they considered.

❑ **Your Professional Services.** If your organization uses professional services such as labor lawyers, benefits consultants, search firms, and accountants, they may be able to supply names. Sometimes, they have people on staff who perform such work. At other times, they may have come in contact with such firms at other clients.

How to Select an Outside Service Provider

Assuming you have obtained several names of possible individuals and firms, how do you determine which to use? Here are some considerations:

❑ **Check references.** Talk to former clients. Ask how satisfied they were with the services. Check such things as cost, staying within quote, validity and reliability of results, on-time delivery, credibility, and thoroughness. If you obtained the name from another organization or one of your other professional services, ask them for a reference. As a general rule, ask for the last three clients for whom similar services were provided. Then call those clients. Explain your projects and ask if they would recommend the individual or firm for it.

❏ **Visit the individual's or company's office.** The office can tell you a great deal about how the work is accomplished. It communicates the degree of organization, equipment, and support personnel. One caution, there are independent practitioners who work out of an office at home. Many of these people are excellent at what they do, so do not discount them for lacking a formal separate office and staff.

❏ **Talk to more than one service provider.** Each meeting with a prospective service provider will be educational. You will not only learn about them but also more about your project through their questions and suggestions. Be prepared for these meetings. Have your questions ready and have available all of the answers and materials someone will need in order to give you a proposal. When you meet the consultant, state your objective and give any necessary background information. Then turn the meeting over to the consultant. Let her ask the questions she needs. You will discover how thorough the person is, how well your need is understood, and the approach the person uses. After all the person's questions have been answered, you can then ask yours. You'll want to know:

   ❏ Can they do the work?

   ❏ What is the cost?

   ❏ What approaches and methods will be used?

   ❏ How much time will it require?

   ❏ When will it be completed?

   ❏ What will be the deliverables on completion?

   ❏ What reliability and validity is there to the process and resulting information?

   ❏ For whom has similar work been performed?

❏ **Require a written proposal.** Ask for a written proposal that describes how the project will be approached, when it will be completed, and what it will cost. Describe the degree of detail you expect. Written proposals allow for easy comparisons. Also, they provide documentation of all aspects of the project. Read all proposals carefully. Raise questions about any item you feel is not covered and request any additional information you feel is required.

❑ **Confirm details.** Be sure you understand when the project will be complete, what you will receive at the conclusion of the projects, what the total costs will be, and how expenses are billed and documented.

❑ **Check costs.** If you are unsure of the going rate for such work, check with other organizations or compare rates among proposals. Determine if expenses require your prior approval; over a certain amount they likely should. Also, be sure expenses are invoiced as actual and not "marked up." An exception here is based on your organization's payment practices. If you pay within thirty days of invoicing, expenses should be actual. If you take longer, a charge is not unreasonable.

❑ **Check credentials.** Be sure what you are told is correct. If an individual claims some type of certification or specialized training related to the work, check it. If an individual tells you he is a licensed psychologist, confirm it. Such information is a matter of public record, and every so often you will discover a claim of credentials that is false.

❑ **Check payment time.** It is not unreasonable for an initial payment at the time work is begun, and if the project continues for several months, interim payments are reasonable. However, the final payment should not be required until the project is completed and all materials and information are delivered to you. The final payment should be of significant size to assist in ensuring completion.

Contracting

Once you have made your selection, get all the details in writing: cost, expenses, invoicing procedures, payment times, delivery times, and work schedule. Be sure the project as presented will meet your objectives. You might also want to include a statement of confidentiality regarding the information obtained about your organization and employees. Such a statement can prohibit disclosure of that information to third parties including journal articles and presentations to other clients.

One condition often added to such documents is a statement that the individual or firm conducting the training needs analysis is prohibited from delivering any training resulting from the study. The reason for this is to remove any motivation for recommending specific training. Actually, this requirement sometimes results in a change upward in the price of the training needs analysis or the firm declining your project.

Both parties should sign the document to indicate their agreement to its terms and conditions. Since such a document is binding on the organization, your internal legal department or external legal counsel should review it.

Products

If you are considering products to purchase and use rather than services, many of the previous suggestions still apply—particularly if you are considering a product offered by a consultant or consulting firm. However, in most instances, you will probably be dealing with a publisher, and you may be limited to reviewing literature.

❏ **Read sales and administrative materials.** Most publishers provide descriptive sales literature. Sometimes it is very complete, but other times it makes general claims with little documentation. Obtaining an administrative manual can often solve this potential problem. Also, some publishers have validity and reliability studies available on request.

❏ **Talk to a representative.** Depending on the cost of the product and your potential volume, a representative may meet with you. Other times it may be possible to meet with a representative at the publisher's offices. If the product is going to be used on an ongoing and extensive basis, ask if the publisher provides internal validation services.

❏ **Visit conventions.** There are several appropriate national conventions and regional meetings in the training and organizational development fields. Often, these include vendor booths. If the timing is right for you, you can meet with several publishers in one day, compare their products, obtain prices and literature, and ask questions.

❐ **Check the library and bookstores.** Mentioned earlier in this book was the *Mental Measurements Yearbook* published by Gryphon Press (Highland Park, New Jersey). If the product you are considering is any form of a test, it may be described in that book. There are also other books describing and overviewing specific training needs analysis procedures.

❐ **Review certification requirements.** Some publishers require one or more employees to be certified in a product's use. Sometimes such requirements are legitimate to ensure proper implementation and interpretation. Other times, the requirements appear designed more for the publisher to charge more and ensure resales. Some publishers even require annual fees to stay accredited, so if certification is required find out what it costs and if there is an annual fee. Generally, avoid products that require certification unless there is a logical reason and the cost is not excessive. Also, be sure to discover the actual repeat costs of any product requiring certification.

❐ **Be cautious of interpretation by mail.** There are some products that require they be returned to the publisher for scoring and interpretation. Generally, these should also be avoided unless they provide a logical reason for the approach. However, this caution does not apply to a service that will machine-score tests for you.

❐ **Check everything.** As with services, and using the same approaches, check references, claims, prior users, and costs.

Summary

Whenever you are embarking on an activity that can affect the employment of others, you want to be confident you have taken the appropriate precautions to ensure the information is valid and reliable. Otherwise, you will be making decisions based on faulty information, with the result that you may end up spending a great deal of time, money, and other resources and not accomplish the objective.

Procedures, Summaries, and Checklists

We have now covered all elements of identifying training needs. We began with a review and analysis of your current training function. Next, identifying areas of possible training requirements and planning how to investigate them were described. Then, a number of training need identification procedures were detailed, along with how to combine and report the information gathered. Finally, considerations for using external services and products were overviewed.

At this point, you have an understanding of what is required for a successful training needs identification effort, how to initiate one, and the tools at hand to implement such a project.

In this section, implementation is presented in guideline format. The guideline format is an outline of the key steps and considerations. Each step is followed by questions that serve as a checklist for implementation. It provides a convenient way to review how to use the methods covered in this book. However, if you need to refresh you memory on the "why" of things, you will need to return to the original chapters in which the materials were introduced and described.

Analyzing Your Training Department's Effectiveness

❏ Identify the important areas of your training function.
❏ Have you listed all areas of your training function? Consider the twelve provided:

- ❐ Training organization
- ❐ Training personnel
- ❐ Employee training
- ❐ Employee development
- ❐ Remedial training
- ❐ Organizational development
- ❐ Communications
- ❐ Training facilities
- ❐ Identifying training needs
- ❐ Training design and development
- ❐ Training delivery
- ❐ Assessment and measurement
❐ Have you defined each area?
❐ Have you determined how important each is to your training function's success?

Determine How Your Training Function's Performance Is Perceived

❐ Have you contacted other areas of the organization for their evaluations of the training function's effectiveness?

❐ Have you used a similar scale for collecting perceptions?

❐ Have you compared ratings and identified differences?

❐ Have you discovered the basis for any differences?

❐ Have you followed up to obtain further information where required?

❐ Have you planned or taken action to correct any differences?

❐ Have you prioritized such the actions you have decided to take?

Investigate How Well Training Is Using Assigned Assets and Controlling Costs

❐ Have you completed a form similar to the cost comparison and asset matrix provided in this book?

❑ Were you able to answer all the questions?

❑ Did you take action to discover answers you did not know?

❑ If so, have you compared the results with other training organizations and the expectations of your organization?

Analyzing Your Training Department's Organization

Review Your Training Function's Mission Statement

❑ Does your training function have a mission statement?

❑ Is the statement clear and direct?

❑ Does it describe the purpose of the training function in the organization?

❑ Have others contributed to its development?

❑ Is the statement in writing?

❑ Has it been communicated to all training function employees?

❑ Has it been communicated to the balance of the organization?

❑ Does the balance of the organization agree with the statement?

❑ Is it regularly reviewed for currency?

Review Your Training Function's Organization Chart

❑ Does it include all positions in the functions?

❑ Are proper guidelines for organization chart construction being adhered to?

❑ Are all reporting relationships indicated?

❑ Are all key result areas covered?

❑ Has the organization chart been distributed to all training function employees?

❑ Has the organization chart been distributed to all other functions within the organization?

❑ Is it regularly reviewed for currency?

Review Your Training Function's Position Descriptions

❑ Is there a position description for every position in the training function?

❏ Does every position description agree with the organization chart?

❏ Has every employee been give a copy of her/ his position description?

❏ Have the position descriptions been checked to ensure they follow good principles of organization: delegation, span of control, and unity of command?

❏ Is position description regularly reviewed for currency?

Create a Mission Statement for Your Training Function

❏ Has it been written in one sentence beginning with the word "to?"

❏ Is the statement clear and direct?

❏ Does it describe the purpose of the training function in the organization?

❏ Have others contributed to its development?

Identify the Training Function's Key Result Areas

❏ Have the key result areas for the training function been identified?

❏ Does each key result area describe a major activity of the training function?

❏ If all are satisfactorily performed, will the training function fulfill its mission?

❏ Are there any key result areas also assigned to another organization function?

Create an Organizational Chart for Your Training Function

❏ Does a position box containing the position's title represent every position in the training function?

❏ Are multiple positions with the same title represented by a single position box, with the number of positions indicated in the box beneath the title?

❑ Is every position box (other than support staff position boxes) connected by one line from the top of its box to the bottom of another position box—the one to which it reports?

❑ Are support staff positions connected to their supervisor's position box by a line from the side of its position box?

❑ If a position supervises other positions (except support staff positions), is it connected to those position boxes by a line from the bottom of the supervisor's position box to the tops of their position boxes?

❑ Does the organizational chart indicate levels of accountability by the position box's location on the chart?

Create Position Descriptions for Your Training Function

❑ Is there a position description for every job in the training function?

❑ Does every position description have an objective written in one sentence, beginning with the word "to"?

❑ Does every position description indicate the position's title, the title of the position it reports to, and the titles of any positions reporting to it?

❑ Does the position description indicate when it was prepared?

❑ If there is an incumbent in the position, did that individual contribute to the position description's development?

❑ Are job responsibilities listed in descending order of importance?

❑ Are job responsibilities each written in one sentence, beginning with a verb?

❑ Have job responsibilities been checked to ensure the position has been delegated the necessary authorities to accomplish them?

❑ Are all position descriptions written?

❑ Does the employee in that job agree with the position's description?

❑ Do all position descriptions cover all of the training department's key result areas?

❐ Have all position descriptions been reviewed for span of control and unity of command compliance?

Identifying Possible Areas That Need Training

Learn About Possible Training Needs

❐ Is there a procedure for learning about areas with possible training needs?

❐ If yes, has that procedure been communicated to the balance of the organization?

❐ If any new activities occur (e.g., new equipment or systems purchases, changes in workflow, or reassignment of responsibilities), is there a system for ensuring the training function is notified of possible resulting training needs?

Conduct an Annual Training Survey

❐ Does the training function annually conduct a survey of internal clients to identify areas of possible training needs?

❐ If yes, does the survey:

   ❐ Request evaluations of existing training courses?

   ❐ Request identification of future training needs during the year?

   ❐ Request identification of future training needs beyond the year?

   ❐ Request information on any individual employee requiring training?

❐ Does the training department automatically receive any employee gaps identified as part of an annual performance review?

❐ Does the training department request information on any employee's performance gaps from managers and supervisors on a regular basis?

❐ Is the information you receive about possible areas of training needs reviewed in a timely fashion?

❑ Are the people who provide information about areas of possible training needs given feedback about what the training department is doing with the information?

❑ If received information is not clear or complete, does the training function initiate some process to obtain additional information (e.g., interviews, questionnaires, or meetings)?

❑ If the training function does not believe the issue is a training one, does it communicate that to whoever sent the information?

❑ Are all areas of possible training needs prioritized for implementation of a training needs investigation?

❑ Is there a predetermined basis for prioritizing areas of possible training needs, such as by their importance and urgency?

Planning to Identify Training Needs

Decide What You Need to Know to Determine the Necessity for a Training Needs Investigation

❑ Have you described what you require in terms of:

    ❑ Training subject(s) and sub-subjects?

    ❑ Importance of the training, using some type of a scale?

    ❑ Urgency or time requirements for the training?

    ❑ Current training population?

    ❑ Potential training population by year?

    ❑ Frequency of training (based on to numbers of people to be trained, size of training group, and availability)?

    ❑ Subject review and update timing to ensure relevance?

    ❑ Required results of the training for the learner?

    ❑ Content information sources (such as performance reviews) for the:
        Training designer
        Supervisors or managers of the people to be trained
        People to be trained (an equally good source)
        Senior managers (for organizationwide training)
        Department heads (for departmentwide training)

Vendor (if it relates to equipment or systems)
Operational staff member in that area (if it relates to a specialized area within the organization)

Identify the Individual to Conduct the Training Needs Analysis

❏ Does the person know the content of the subject?

❏ Is the person familiar with any existing training in the area?

❏ Does the person have the required training need identification skills?

❏ Is the person perceived as neutral, objective, and competent?

Prepare a Schedule of Who to Contact

❏ Have you identified who to contact for what information?

❏ Are the people to contact listed in sequence?

❏ Is the sequence based on some logical progression of information?

Procedures for Identifying Training Needs

Determine What Type of Basic Information-Gathering Procedure to Use

❏ How many people are in the population with information?

❏ At how many locations are the people?

❏ How available are they?

❏ How many should be involved?

Select a Specific Information-Gathering Procedure

❏ Have you considered the advantages and limitations of each of these various types of procedures:

Individual

- ❐ Interview
- ❐ Performance review
- ❐ Need-to-Know Process
- ❐ Job Analysis Grid
- ❐ Job analysis
- ❐ Task analysis
- ❐ Job sampling

Group

- ❐ Conference
- ❐ Focus group
- ❐ Workshop
- ❐ Teleconferencing/audioconferencing

Written

- ❐ Information-gathering questionnaire
- ❐ Survey
- ❐ Computer-based questionnaire
- ❐ Self-report
- ❐ Testing and assessment
- ❐ 360-degree and peer review

Other

- ❐ Experts
- ❐ Specialized techniques
- ❐ Combination of two or more techniques

❐ In making your selection, did you consider:
  - ❐ What is the general subject?
  - ❐ From how many people will you need to obtain information?
  - ❐ At how many locations are the people?
  - ❐ How many people are available at the same time?
  - ❐ How many levels and types of employees will be involved?
  - ❐ How many degrees and types of information do the people represent?

❏ How technical is the subject?

❏ How controversial or political is the subject?

❏ How soon must the information be obtained?

❏ How much will it cost to use the procedure?

Standard Interviews

Identify the Person(s) to Be Interviewed

❏ Have you identified all people who have appropriate information?

❏ Have you properly sequenced the people?

Plan the Interview

❏ Have you established a clear objective for each interview?

❏ Have you identified the specific information to obtain from each interview?

❏ Have you developed questions for each element of the information you require?

❏ Have you designed questions that follow the guidelines?

  ❏ Questions should be not answerable in one word.

  ❏ Questions should not communicate a desired answer.

  ❏ Questions are structured neutrally.

  ❏ Questions encourage application and not regurgitation of facts.

  ❏ Questions should be sequenced in a logical order with the easiest ones first.

❏ Have you considered developing and using a summary question?

❏ Are your questions written?

❏ Are your questions followed with space for notes?

Schedule the Interview

❏ Have you selected a location for privacy and neutrality?

❏ Have you selected a time convenient to you and the interviewee?

❏ Have you scheduled enough time for completing the interview?

❏ Have you scheduled time following the interview for completing your notes?

❏ Have you allowed the interviewee to suggest time and location?

❏ Have you given the interviewee advance notice of the interview?

❏ Did you tell the interviewee the objective of the interview?

Prepare the Interview Environment

❏ Did you arrive early and prepare the environment?

❏ Is the desk or table free of unrelated materials?

❏ Are chairs positioned to eliminate any barrier to communication?

❏ Do you have all materials with you?

❏ Did you arrange for no interruptions?

Conduct the Interview

❏ Did you begin by stating the interview objective?

❏ Did you check for and answer any interviewee questions?

❏ Did you tell the interviewee you would be taking notes?

❏ When you asked a question, did you wait for an answer?

❏ Did you focus your full attention on the interviewee during the answers?

❏ Did you follow up any new areas suggested by responses?

❏ Did you check for any needed clarification?

❏ Did you ask a summary question?

❏ Did you again check for and answer any interviewee questions?

❏ Did you tell the interviewee what would happen next?

Complete Your Notes

❏ Did you finalize your notes immediately after the interview?

❐ Did you identify any areas in which you had to "get back" to the interviewee?

Job Analysis Grid Interviews

Schedule the Interview

❐ Have you selected a location for privacy and neutrality?

❐ Have you selected a time convenient to you and the interviewee?

❐ Have you scheduled enough time for completing the interview?

❐ Have you scheduled time following the interview for completing your notes?

❐ Have you allowed the interviewee to suggest time and location?

Prepare for the Interview

❐ Have you obtained a deck of three-by-five-inch cards?

❐ Do you have three rubber bands?

❐ Do you have at least two pencils?

❐ Have you prepared your initial questions such as:

    ❐ What did you discover during your first month of employment that was a surprise to you?

    ❐ What are the three best features of working here?

    ❐ What are the three things you would most like to change?

    ❐ What would have helped you to have known before starting work?

    ❐ What three words best describe working here?

❐ If a new employee is dissatisfied with his/her job, what is the most likely reason?

❐ Will your initial questions obtain answers that can be expanded into the subject of your interview ?

❐ Do your initial questions not request the specific information you are seeking?

Conduct the Interview

❒ Did you begin by stating the interview objective?

❒ Did you check for and answer any interviewee questions?

❒ Did you ask your initial questions and record responses with key words—one word per card?

❒ When you asked a question, did you wait for an answer?

❒ Did you focus your full attention on the interviewee during the answers?

❒ After all initial questions, did you have the interviewee identify the two cards with most in common from various three-card displays?

❒ Did you record responses regarding the two selected cards with key words—one word per card?

❒ Did you stop providing the three cards when there seemed to be no more new information?

❒ Did you shuffle all cards and have the interviewee place them in order of importance?

❒ Did you ask the interviewee if anything was missing and if so, add a card of it?

❒ Did you introduce and explain three categories of classification?

    ❒ Must

    ❒ Want

    ❒ Not necessary

❒ Did you have the interviewee place the cards into separate categories?

❒ Did you collect and bind the cards by category?

❒ Did you conclude by again checking for and answering any interviewee questions?

❒ Did you tell the interviewee what would happen next?

Combine Multiperson Results

❒ If more than one person was interviewed, did you calculate an average result by group?

The Need-to-Know Process

Identify Exactly What the Outcomes of the Training Are to Be

❏ Have you clearly stated what someone is to be able to accomplish after the training?

❏ Have you prepared a "final exam" that includes all desired outcomes?

❏ If someone passes the final exam, does it indicate training for that person is not required?

Select Someone to Conduct the Need-to-Know Interview

❏ Is the person knowledgeable of the subject of the training?

❏ Has the person been trained in all aspects of the new training?

❏ Is the person knowledgeable of any existing training in the subject?

Select a Person(s) for the Interview

❏ Is the person's length of service in the current position typical of that for employees to be trained?

❏ Is the person's job performance typical of that for employees to be trained?

❏ Is the person's education and experience typical of that for employees to be trained?

Conduct the Need-to-Know Interview

❏ Did you begin by stating the interview objective?

❏ Did you check for and answer any interviewee questions?

❏ Did you describe the approach?

    ❏ The interviewee is not expected to know all the answers to your questions.

    ❏ The interviewee should describe reactions to questions.

    ❏ The interviewee should ask for anything he/she needs to know in order to accomplish a task.

❏ Did you ask questions from the final exam and write the person's answers?

❏ Did you provide information when requested?

❏ Was any provided information limited to just what was requested?

❏ Did you record interviewee's requests and actions:

   ❏ What information was requested?

   ❏ When was information requested?

   ❏ What were the tasks the interviewee could not accomplish without additional information?

   ❏ What tasks could the interviewee accomplish without additional information?

❏ Did you conclude by again checking for and answering any interviewee questions?

❏ Did you tell the interviewee what would happen next?

Performance Standards

Review Performance Standards for Job Relatedness and Accuracy

❏ Does each position responsibility have at least one performance standard?

❏ Does each performance standard include some type of objective, quantitative measure?

❏ Does each performance standard include an item period to date for completion?

❏ Have the performance standards been agreed upon by the employee and the supervisor?

❏ Are the performance standards in writing?

Do a Performance Evaluation

❏ Is data pertaining to actual performance completed throughout the time period?

❐ Is actual performance to desired performance reviewed individually by the employee and supervisor prior to any meeting?

❐ Is the performance review meeting scheduled at a convenient time and appropriate location?

❐ Is the employee given advance notice of the meeting?

Conduct a Performance Review Meeting

❐ Does the meeting begin with a review of standards met or exceeded?

❐ Is the employee given an opportunity to provide information regarding missed standards?

❐ Are differences in desired and actual performance identified and referred to as development gaps?

❐ Are no more than three development gaps selected for improvement during the next time frame?

❐ Are performance standards adjusted as necessary for the next time frame?

❐ Does the supervisor perceive as her/his responsibility assisting the employee to close development gaps?

❐ Does the supervisor regularly notify the training function of any identified employee development gaps?

Meetings

Establish an Objective and Type of Meeting

❐ Have you identified the information to obtain through the meeting?

❐ Have you determined the type of meeting to meet your objective?

  ❐ Conference

  ❐ Focus group

  ❐ Workshop

  ❐ Teleconference/audioconference

❐ Are appropriate facilities available?

❐ Have you determined how many participants the meeting can effectively have?

❐ Have you determined how many sessions to conduct?

Select Meeting Participants

❐ Have you considered participant locations?

❐ Have you considered participant knowledge regarding subject matter?

❐ Have you considered participant levels?

Prepare the Meeting Room

❐ Do you have all required equipment and materials?

❐ Does the room setup support the type of meeting you will conduct?

Select a Meeting Leader

❐ Do you have someone skilled in conducting such a meeting?

❐ Is the person knowledgeable about the meeting subject?

❐ Will the person be perceived by participants as being objective?

Notify Participants

❐ Was advance notification given to the participants?

❐ Were the participants told in advance the subject/objective of the meeting?

❐ Would any premeeting assignment help?

Conduct the Meeting

❐ Did the meeting start with a statement of its objective?

❐ Were all participants requested to introduce themselves?

❐ Were overhead questions primarily used?

❐ When direct questions were used, did the leader begin with the person's name?

❐ Did the leader use questions that cannot be answered in one word?

❐ Did the leader avoid "why" questions?

❐ Did the leader wait for an answer after asking a question?

❐ Did the leader obtain equal participation?

❐ Did all participants contribute?

❐ Did the leader maintain an objective approach?

❐ Did the leader avoid supply content?

❐ Did the leader avoid symbols of authority? That is, did the leader avoid:

  ❐ Requiring participants to raise their hands to participate?

  ❐ Using a stool or chair different for those of the participants?

  ❐ Using a pointer?

  ❐ Wearing different dress?

  ❐ Using a separate desk or table?

❐ Did the meeting reach its objective in the allotted time?

❐ Did the leader explain what would happen next?

Questionnaires

Select a Questionnaire Format

❐ Have you determined the type of questionnaire you need?

  ❐ Information-gathering

  ❐ Behavioral

❐ Do you require the individual to identify him/herself on the questionnaire?

❐ Have you determined any identifying information by group?

  ❐ Department

  ❐ Location

  ❐ Type of job

  ❐ Length of service

  ❐ Length of time in current position

  ❐ Level of education

  ❐ Race

  ❐ Age

  ❐ Sex

❐ Is all demographic information to be requested necessary to interpret results?

Develop the Questions for an Information-Gathering Questionnaire

❐ Have you selected the type of responses your desire?

    ❐ Objective

    ❐ Fill-in

    ❐ Essay

    ❐ Multiple choice

    ❐ Scale

❐ Have you considered how to combine answers in selecting the type of responses?

❐ Have you considered what you need to know in selecting the type of responses?

❐ If using a scale, have you determined the number of points on the scale?

❐ If using a scale, does it have a neutral position as a possible selection?

❐ If all questions are objective, multiple choice, or scale responses, is an opportunity provided for additional information?

Develop the Questions for a Behavioral Questionnaire

❐ Have you identified all behaviors you wish to include?

❐ Have you defined each behavior?

❐ Have you identified the two extremes of each behavior on the job?

❐ Have you written enough questions to cover all aspects of each behavior?

❐ Have you developed a scale with anchor points for each behavior question?

Administer the Questionnaire

❐ Will you administer the questionnaire by mail, computer, or in a meeting?

❐ Who will score the questionnaire?

Tests and Assessments

Determine the Appropriateness of a Test

❒ Does the test measure the characteristics you need measured?

❒ Is job analysis information available?

❒ Does the test deal with an identified aspect of the job?

❒ Is there a person qualified to administer, score, and interpret the results?

❒ Is the test available to you?

Determine Other Forms of Assessment

❒ Are other forms of assessment conducted by the organization?

❒ Is there a form of assessment currently available that is suitable to your needs?

Ensure Test Validity

❒ Is there evidence of the test's validity?

❒ Is there evidence of the test's validity with respect to the subject of you investigation?

❒ What type of validity has been calculated?

❒ If a criterion-based validity was calculated, is there evidence of the accuracy of the criterion?

❒ Is there evidence of other studies regarding the test and its use such as reliability, content validity, and construct validity?

Ensure Proper Use

❒ Has everyone receiving the results been trained in how to interpret them?

❒ Have the credentials and qualifications of anyone administering or conducting a test or other assessment device been checked?

Combination Methods

Consider Multiple Procedures

❐ Will using more than one procedure contribute to more accurate information?

❐ Do the locations and number of people require multiple procedures?

❐ Will the credibility of the process be improved by using multiple procedures?

❐ Is the information obtainable through multiple procedures comparable/combinable?

Combine Multiple Procedure Information

❐ Have you established in advance how information from multiple procedures will be combined?

❐ Have you considered whether the quality of information differs by procedure?

❐ If different procedures provide different qualities of information, have you created a method for weighing them?

Issue Report

❐ Has a report of the training needs investigation been prepared?

❐ Does the report include:

   ❐ The objective?

   ❐ The dates of inquiry?

   ❐ The methods used?

   ❐ A description of the population?

   ❐ The resulting training needs?

❐ Is the report sent to the person requesting the training need investigation?

❐ Did someone meet with that person to answer questions and discuss results?

❒ Does that person have the authority to accept, revise, or reject the report?

Transferring Training Needs to Training Objectives

Create Behavioral Objectives

❒ Has each identified training need been translated into a behavioral objective?

❒ Does each behavioral objective include a quantifiable measurement?

❒ Are all behavioral objectives written?

❒ Have behavioral objectives been sequenced for communicating?

Consider Types of Training to Fulfill Behavioral Objectives

❒ Do you know the types of training currently conducted by your organization?
  ❒ Group training
  ❒ Coaching
  ❒ Mentioning
  ❒ Self-paced learning
  ❒ E-learning
  ❒ Computer-assisted instruction
  ❒ Distance learning training
  ❒ Self-study
  ❒ Simulations
  ❒ Lectures
  ❒ Job assignments
  ❒ Job rotation

❒ Do you know the advantages and limitations of each type of training offered by your organization?

Consider Who Conducts Training

❏ Do you know who currently conducts the training offered by the organization?

   ❏ Supervisors

   ❏ Human resources

   ❏ External experts/consultants

   ❏ Operating department employees

   ❏ Training department personnel

   ❏ Operating department personnel on temporary assignment to training

   ❏ External professionals

   ❏ External organizations

Consider the Training Method

❏ Have you determined the value of a training method (value equals benefit minus cost)?

❏ Has each element for the value calculation been described in the same terms?

❏ Are the elements of the value calculation actual or estimates?

❏ Does the value calculation consider urgency, importance, cost of materials and equipment, time required, and number of current and future employees to be trained?

Considering External Services and Products

Consider an External Service

❏ Can an external expert provide a service you cannot?

❏ Will an external expert's results be acceptable?

❏ Will an external expert have more credibility than internal people?

Locate an External Expert

❒ Have you:
  ❒ Checked the yellow pages?
  ❒ Checked the Internet?
  ❒ Checked the public library or bookstores?
  ❒ Checked with professional associations?
  ❒ Checked with universities or colleges?
  ❒ Asked another organization for guidance?
  ❒ Asked one of your professional services for recommendations?

Evaluate an External Expert

❒ Have you:
  ❒ Checked references?
  ❒ Visited the individual's or firm's office?
  ❒ Talked to more than one external expert and asked the following questions:
  Can you do the work?
  What is the cost?
  What approaches and methods will be used?
  How long will it require?
  When will it be completed?
  What will be received on completion?
  What reliability and validity is there to the process and resulting information?
  For whom has similar work been performed?

Require a Written Proposal

❒ Have you read each proposal?
❒ Have you identified differences and similarities between proposals?
❒ Have you identified the one that best meets your requirements?
❒ Have you ranked the proposals as to degree of acceptability?
❒ Have you identified proposals that do not meet your requirements?

❏ Have you obtained any additional information required for evaluating proposals?

Select an External Expert

❏ Have you checked and confirmed all details such as:
   ❏ Costs?
   ❏ Credentials?
   ❏ Payment times?
   ❏ Time schedule?
   ❏ Completion date?
❏ Will you consider an expert as a provider of any resulting training?
❏ Do you have a signed agreement describing all terms and conditions?

Consider Using an External Product

❏ Is there an external product that can fulfill your needs?
❏ Does the product have validity and reliability information?
❏ Are descriptive materials available?
❏ Have you read all sales and administrative materials?
❏ Have you met with a representative?
❏ Were all your questions satisfactorily answered?

Consider Other Sources of Products

❏ Have you visited appropriate conventions and regional meetings?
❏ Have you checked the library and bookstores?
❏ Have you reviewed appropriate journals?

Evaluate External Products

❏ Is certification required?
❏ If certification is required, what is the charge?
❏ If there is a charge for certification, is it a one time or annual charge?
❏ What is the cost of reorders?
❏ Are there any limitations on use of the product?

Appendix: Forms

This Appendix contains all of the forms introduced in the book. They can be copied for your use. The same forms are also available on the disk that accompanies the book and can be printed from the disk for use or modified to meet your specific requirements.

List of Forms

1. Training Activities
2. Your Training Activity Perceptions
3. Training Department Survey
4. Training Rating Comparison
5. Training Activity Priority List
6. Department Employees' Rating Comparison
7. Internal Clients' Rating Comparison
8. Cost Comparison-Analysis
9. Asset Comparison Matrix
10. Key Result Area/Position Form
11. Position Description Preparation Form
12. Annual Training Review
13. Annual Employee Performance Survey
14. Training Needs Analysis Report
15. Training Needs Information Planning Form
16. Interview Planning Form
17. Grid Results Combining Form
18. Information Combination Form

TRAINING ACTIVITIES

_____ Training organization—the mission of the training function, its internal structure, and internal and external relationships

_____ Training personnel—the selection, qualifications, and motivation of department employees

_____ Employee training—training in requirements of specific job or organizational activities

_____ Employee development—training in requirements for future jobs and broadening of abilities for a current job

_____ Remedial training—training conducted to correct inadequate basic skills such as mathematics, reading, speaking, and writing.

_____ Organizational development—improving communication and understanding throughout the organization in order to produce effective, functioning teams; establishing or changing to a desired culture; and responding to changing conditions

_____ Communications—internal and external communication of the training department's abilities, results, and offerings

_____ Training facilities—the physical space and equipment allocated to conduct training

_____ Identifying training needs—determining the training required by individual employees and the organization

_____ Training design and development—creating, structuring, or obtaining a training program to meet specific objectives or outcomes

_____ Training delivery—implementation of training to meet specific needs and objectives (e.g., courses, programs, self-study, etc.)

_____ Assessment and measurement—using valid and reliable methods to determine the current abilities of an individual and the results of training activities

Total points = 100

YOUR TRAINING ACTIVITY PERCEPTIONS

Activities	Your Ratings	Your Perception of Department Employees' Ratings	Your Perceptions of Internal Clients' Ratings
Training Organization			
Training Personnel			
Employee Training			
Employee Development			
Remedial Training			
Organizational Development			
Communications			
Training Facilities			
Identifying Training Needs			
Training Design and Development			
Training Delivery			
Assessment and Measurement			
Overall Department			

TRAINING DEPARTMENT SURVEY

TO: (group or type of employee)

The training department is currently conducting an audit of its performance. As one of our (clients/department employees), your perceptions will be of considerable assistance with this project. Please take a few moments to complete this form and return it. No identification is requested.

The following are the categories of training and the definitions we are using. Read each one and then rate how well you feel our training department is performing in that category. The questions ask for your perceptions—what you think—not necessarily information based on an evaluation of factual performance criteria.

For your ratings, use a nine-point scale (1 = Low; 5 = Typical; and 9 = High). Select a single number from that scale for each rating. Write the number on the line in front of the category. If you do not have any idea as to how well training is performing in a category, place an "X" on the line for that category.

_____ Training organization—the mission of the function, its internal structure, and internal and external relationships

_____ Training personnel—the selection, qualifications, and motivation of department employees

_____ Employee training—training in requirements for specific job or organizational activities

_____ Employee development—training in requirements for a future job and broadening of abilities for a current job

_____ Remedial training—training conducted to correct inadequate skills, such as in math, reading, or writing

_____ Communications—internal and external communication of the department's abilities and offerings

_____ Identifying training needs—determining the required training of individual employees and the organization

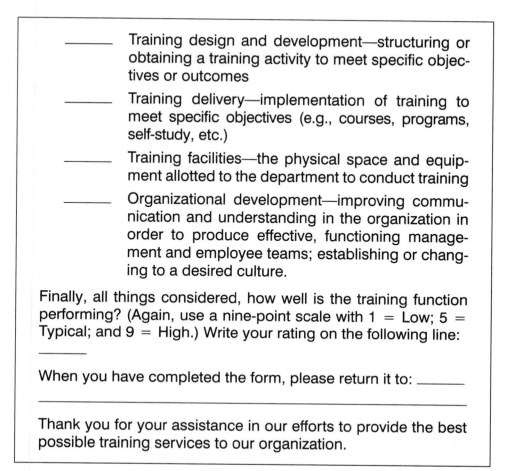

_____ Training design and development—structuring or obtaining a training activity to meet specific objectives or outcomes

_____ Training delivery—implementation of training to meet specific objectives (e.g., courses, programs, self-study, etc.)

_____ Training facilities—the physical space and equipment allotted to the department to conduct training

_____ Organizational development—improving communication and understanding in the organization in order to produce effective, functioning management and employee teams; establishing or changing to a desired culture.

Finally, all things considered, how well is the training function performing? (Again, use a nine-point scale with 1 = Low; 5 = Typical; and 9 = High.) Write your rating on the following line:

_____

When you have completed the form, please return it to: _____

_____

Thank you for your assistance in our efforts to provide the best possible training services to our organization.

TRAINING RATING COMPARISON FORM

Activities	Your Rating	Average Department Employee's Rating	Average Internal Client's Rating	Degree of Agreement
Training Organization				
Training Personnel				
Employee Training				
Employee Development				
Remedial Training				
Organizational Development				
Communications				
Training Facilities				
Identifying Training Needs				
Training Design and Development				
Training Delivery				
Assessment and Measurement				
Overall Department				

TRAINING ACTIVITY PRIORITY LIST

Activities Requiring Improvement   Rating

1. _____   _____

2. _____   _____

3. _____   _____

4. _____   _____

5. _____   _____

6. _____   _____

7. _____   _____

8. _____   _____

9. _____   _____

10. _____   _____

Activities with Low Rating Agreement   Agreement

1. _____   _____

2. _____   _____

3. _____   _____

4. _____   _____

5. _____   _____

6. _____   _____

7. _____   _____

8. _____   _____

9. _____   _____

10. _____   _____

(continues)

Activities Requiring Further Investigation	*Agreement*	*Rating*
1.		
2.		
3.		
4.		
5.		
6.		
7.		
8.		
9.		
10.		
11.		
12.		
13.		
14.		
15.		
16.		
17.		
18.		
19.		
20.		

DEPARTMENT EMPLOYEES' RATING COMPARISON

Activities	Your Perception of Department Employees' Rating	Average Department Employee's Evaluation	Degree of Agreement
Training Organization			
Training Personnel			
Employee Training			
Employee Development			
Remedial Training			
Organizational Development			
Communications			
Training Facilities			
Identifying Training Needs			
Training Design and Development			
Training Delivery			
Assessment and Measurement			
Overall Department			

INTERNAL CLIENTS' RATING COMPARISON

Activities	Your Perception of Internal Clients' Ratings	Average Internal Client's Evaluation	Degree of Agreement
Training Organization			
Training Personnel			
Employee Training			
Employee Development			
Remedial Training			
Organizational Development			
Communications			
Training Facilities			
Identifying Training Needs			
Training Design and Development			
Training Delivery			
Assessment and Measurement			
Overall Department			

COST COMPARISON-ANALYSIS

1. What is the annual cost of operating the training department? $ _____

2. What percent of the organization's total income or sales does the cost of operating the training department represent? (Total Training Operating Costs/Organization's Total Income for the Same Period × 100) _____%

3. What percent of the organization's total operating costs does the cost of operating the training department represent ? (Total Training Operating Costs/Organization's Total Operating Costs for the Same Period × 100) _____%

4. What is the dollar value of the organization's assets assigned to the training department? $ _____

5. What percent of the organization's total capital investment do the training assets represent? (Total Training Operating Assets/Organization's Total Assets × 100) _____%

6. What percent of the organization's total employees are in the training department? (Total Number of Training Employees/Organization's Total Number of Employees × 100) _____%

7. What percent of training's employees are management, professionals, and administrative? (Total Number of Each Group of Training Employees/Total Number of Training Employees × 100) Management _____% Professionals _____% Administrative _____%

8. What is the ratio of training employees to the total number of employees in the organization ? (Total Number of Organization Employees/Total Number of Training Employees) _____

Answers to these questions provide a basis for comparing your training department with the training departments in other organizations of your size, in your industry, and in your geographic area.

ASSET COMPARISON MATRIX

For this analysis your assets are considered to be employees, budget dollars, equipment, and time. Use numbers for employees, dollars for budget, numbers for equipment, and hours for time, or you may use percents for any or all.

If an activity does not apply, place an X on the appropriate lines. If some people, budget dollars, equipment, or time is assigned to more than one activity, use partials numbers. For example, an employee assigned to both remedial training and employee training could be entered as 0.5 in each. You may want to enter the actual time consumed by the activity rather than the time assigned.

Activity	Employees	Budget	Equipment	Time
Organization	_____	_____	_____	_____
Personnel	_____	_____	_____	_____
Employee training	_____	_____	_____	_____
Employee development	_____	_____	_____	_____
Remedial training	_____	_____	_____	_____
Organizational development	_____	_____	_____	_____
Communications	_____	_____	_____	_____
Facilities	_____	_____	_____	_____
Identifying training needs	_____	_____	_____	_____
Training design and development	_____	_____	_____	_____
Training delivery	_____	_____	_____	_____
Assessment and measurement	_____	_____	_____	_____

KEY RESULT AREA/POSITION FORM

Key Result Area	Position Title

POSITION DESCRIPTION PREPARATION FORM

Position Title: _____   Date: _____

Department: _____   Reports to: _____

Supervises: _____

Position Objective:

To _____

_____

Responsibilities:

1. _____

_____

2. _____

_____

3. _____

_____

4. _____

_____

5. _____

_____

6. _____

_____

7. _____

_____

8. _____

_____

ANNUAL TRAINING REVIEW

TO: (Group or type of employee)

The Training Department is currently reviewing all existing training activities to ensure they are meeting their objectives and identifying additional training requirements. Your input will be of considerable assistance in this effort, so please answer the following questions and return the completed form.

1. List below the courses the Training Department is currently conducting for your department and employees, and then indicate how satisfied you are with the results of each course. Use a three-point scale to indicate satisfaction (1 = Not Satisfied; 2 = Satisfied; 3 = Very Satisfied).

Training Course   **Satisfaction with Results**

_____   _____

_____   _____

_____   _____

_____   _____

_____   _____

_____   _____

2. List below any of your department's individual employees who have specific training needs to improve current job performance.

_____

_____

_____

_____

_____

(continues)

3. *List below any additional training that you or your employees require. Please list in order of need (the most needed first, and so on).*

_____

_____

_____

_____

_____

4. *List below any training requirements you believe will develop within the next year.*

_____

_____

_____

_____

_____

5. *List below any other areas in which training can be of assistance to you and your employees.*

_____

_____

_____

_____

_____

ANNUAL EMPLOYEE PERFORMANCE SURVEY

To: (Manager/Supervisor)

With the annual performance reviews of your employees now completed, the Training Department is interested in learning of any areas in which it can be of assistance to improve employee performance. Please complete this form by identifying such individuals in need of assistance. Upon its receipt, someone from the training department will contact you for more detailed information.

In the space below, list any employees in your department who have performance gaps that training might be able to assist in closing. After each name, indicate what you believe to be the urgency of obtaining such assistance. Use this rating system: 1 = Most urgent; 2 = Sometime in the next three months; 3 = Sometime in the next six months.

Employee	Urgency
_____	_____
_____	_____
_____	_____
_____	_____
_____	_____

During your performance reviews you may have also learned of employees with career or other objectives that could be provided assistance through training. Please indicate those employees on the following lines. Once again, indicate how urgent you believe it is to receive such assistance.

Employee	Urgency
_____	_____
_____	_____
_____	_____
_____	_____

TRAINING NEEDS ANALYSIS REPORT

Training Subject(s)

_____

_____

_____

_____

Content Information Sources

_____

_____

_____

_____

Importance of the Training

_____

_____

_____

_____

Urgency of the Training

_____

_____

_____

_____

Current Training Population

_____

_____

_____

_____

_____

Potential Training Population

_____

_____

_____

_____

_____

Frequency of Training

_____

_____

_____

_____

_____

Subject Review and Update

_____

_____

_____

_____

_____

TRAINING NEEDS INFORMATION PLANNING FORM

Training Subject: _____   Date: _____

Information	Who to Contact	Sequence	Method

INTERVIEW PLANNING FORM

Objective: _____

_____

Interviewer: _____

Interviewee: _____

Time and Location: _____

(The lines below are for listing the subject and questions, and for writing in the interviewee's responses.)

_____

_____

_____

_____

_____

_____

_____

_____

_____

_____

_____

_____

_____

_____

_____

_____

_____

_____

_____

_____

GRID RESULTS COMBINING FORM

Subject: _____   Date: _____

Participant Group: _____   Number of Participants: _____

Subject	1	2	3	Average
_____	___	___	___	_____
_____	___	___	___	_____
_____	___	___	___	_____
_____	___	___	___	_____
_____	___	___	___	_____
_____	___	___	___	_____
_____	___	___	___	_____
_____	___	___	___	_____
_____	___	___	___	_____
_____	___	___	___	_____
_____	___	___	___	_____
_____	___	___	___	_____
_____	___	___	___	_____
_____	___	___	___	_____
_____	___	___	___	_____
_____	___	___	___	_____
_____	___	___	___	_____
_____	___	___	___	_____
_____	___	___	___	_____
_____	___	___	___	_____
_____	___	___	___	_____
_____	___	___	___	_____
_____	___	___	___	_____

INFORMATION COMBINATION FORM

Item	Group: _____			Group: _____			
	Number	Value	Result	Number	Value	Result	Total
_____	___	___	___	___	___	___	___
_____	___	___	___	___	___	___	___
_____	___	___	___	___	___	___	___
_____	___	___	___	___	___	___	___
_____	___	___	___	___	___	___	___
_____	___	___	___	___	___	___	___
_____	___	___	___	___	___	___	___
_____	___	___	___	___	___	___	___
_____	___	___	___	___	___	___	___
_____	___	___	___	___	___	___	___
_____	___	___	___	___	___	___	___
_____	___	___	___	___	___	___	___
_____	___	___	___	___	___	___	___
_____	___	___	___	___	___	___	___
_____	___	___	___	___	___	___	___
_____	___	___	___	___	___	___	___
_____	___	___	___	___	___	___	___
_____	___	___	___	___	___	___	___
_____	___	___	___	___	___	___	___
_____	___	___	___	___	___	___	___
_____	___	___	___	___	___	___	___
_____	___	___	___	___	___	___	___
_____	___	___	___	___	___	___	___
_____	___	___	___	___	___	___	___
_____	___	___	___	___	___	___	___
_____	___	___	___	___	___	___	___
_____	___	___	___	___	___	___	___
_____	___	___	___	___	___	___	___

Index

administrative assistants, 48, 49
American Management Association, management competencies study of, 2–5
American Psychological Association, 225
annual reviews, 186
apples to apples, comparing, 249–250
assessment centers, 227–230
assessment(s), 129, 225–230
  definition of, 225
  job simulations as, 227
  psychological interviews as, 226
  self-testing devices as, 226
asset comparison matrix, 41
associations, professional, 293
audioconferences, 125
authority
  delegation of, 56–57
  lines of, 48
availability of training, 289

basic skills, 1, 66–67
behavioral objectives, 279–289
  clarity and specificity of, 280–281
  and people/entities conducting training, 285–286
  purposes of, 279
  and selection of training method, 286–289
  sequencing, 283–284
  and type of training, 284–285
  writing, 281–283
behavioral questionnaires, 128, 213–214
behavior (term), 280

career objectives, 77
certification requirements, 297
classroom meetings, 125
clients
  definition of, 14
  external, 4
  internal, 4
coaching, 284
colleges, 293
combining responses, 250–255
communication
  of behavioral objectives, 280–281

in meetings, 192
  need for, 82–83
comparing apples to apples, 249–250
computer-assisted instruction, 284
concluding behavior, 280
concurrent validity, 222
conferences, 124
construct validity, 221
Consultants and Consulting Organizations, 293
contacts list, 113–114
content information sources, 110–111
content validity, 220
contracting, 295–296
conventions, 296–297
correlation coefficients, 223
cost-benefit analysis, 287
cost comparison analysis, 40
costs
  estimating, 287–288
  of outside services providers, 295
criteria-based validity, 222

data, performance, 186, 187
delegation, 56–57
demographic information (on questionnaires), 212–213
department meetings, 74
departments, 69, 73
Directory of Management Consultants, 292–293
distance learning training, 285
dotted lines (on organizational charts), 49

economic influences on training needs, 2
EEOC, *see* Equal Employment Opportunity Commission
effectiveness of training function, 15, 17–39
  others' perceptions of, 19–39
  your perceptions of, 15, 17–19
e-learning, 284
employees
  assigning values to information from, 248–249
  effectiveness of training department as perceived by, 19, 21–22
  failure of, to meet performance standards, 182–183

employees (*continued*)
  identifying training needs of, 100–101
  as initiators of training needs identification
    process, 64
  training needs of individual, 74–79
  see also new employees; performance re-
    views
Equal Employment Opportunity Commission
  (EEOC), 225
equipment, addition of new, 72–73
essay questions, 205, 208
Executive Order 19025, 219
exit interviews, 71
external clients, 4
external consultants, as initiators of training
  needs identification process, 64–65
external organizations, 286
external professional trainers, 286
external services and products, 291–297
  contracting with, 295–296
  deciding whether to utilize, 291–292
  locating, 292–293
  and planning for needs identification, 130
  and purchase of products, 296–297
  selecting, 293–295

face validity, 222–223
facilitators, meeting, 194–195
focus groups, 74, 125, 264
follow-up memos, 39
frequency of training, 108–109
function (term), 13–14
future training needs, assessing, 87

government requirements/regulations, 73
group training, 124–127, 284

human resources professionals, 285

identification of competencies project (case
  example), 231–243
  example of questionnaire in, 239–243
  initial list of competencies in, 233–235
  meeting format and results in, 235–239
  objective of, 231–232
  plan for, 232–233
identification of training needs
  group procedures for, 124–127
  of individual employees, 86–87, 100–101
  individual procedures for, 119–124
  and need for communication, 82–83
  number of people needed for, 132–134
  and performance measures, 189
  performance survey for, 88, 89
  persons/entities conducting, 65, 111, 113
  persons initiating, 64–65
  planning for, 103–117, 232–233
  procedures for initiating, 65
  procedures used for, 119–134
  sample report on, 258
  training review questionnaires for, 88, 90–91
  training survey as tool for, 83–87
  unanticipated requests for, 81–82
  written procedures for, 127–130
importance of training, determining, 106–107
individual training needs analysis proce-
  dure(s), 119–124
  interviews as, 120–121
  job analysis as, 123–124
  Job Analysis Grid as, 123

Need-to-Know Process as, 122–123
  performance reviews as, 121–122
  task analysis as, 124
information-gathering meetings, 191
information-gathering questionnaires, 127–
  128, 204–213
  design of, 209–213
  for new employee orientation training,
    205–209
  question-and-answer formats for, 204–205
  question format in, 204–205
information sources, weighting, 247–248
initial testing, 213
initiation of training needs identification,
  64–65
internal clients
  definition of, 4
  effectiveness of training department as per-
    ceived by, 19, 21–22
Internet, finding external services via the, 292
Interview Planning Form, 143–145
interview(s), 93, 95–97, 120–121, 137–154
  concluding, 153
  exit, 71
  follow-up questions in, 39
  follow-up to, 153
  guidelines for conducting, 148–153
  for information gathering, 137
  multiperson, 120, 153–154
  and notification of interviewees, 147–148
  panel, 120–121, 154
  performance, 121
  performance review, 188–189
  planning for, 138–139, 143–145
  psychological, 226
  questions for, 139–143
  in sample report on job analysis for first-
    level supervisor positions, 268–269
  in sample report on training needs for new
    employees, 264
  scheduling of, 145–147
  selecting individuals for, 138
  and selection of interviewees, 138
  see also Job Analysis Grid technique

job analysis, 123–124
job analysis for first-level supervisor positions, sample report on training needs for,
  268–277
Job Analysis Grid technique, 123, 155–169
  in case example, 232
  combining results from, 164–169
  concluding interview using, 162–163
  example of interview using, 159–162
  forms used in, 165, 167–169
  procedure for using, 157–159
job assignments, 285
job relatedness (of tests), 219–220
job responsibility, 82
job rotation, 285
job sampling, 124
job simulations, 227, 285

Kennedy, John F., 219
key result areas, 45–47, 51, 52

leaders, meeting, 194–195
learning objectives, *see* behavioral objectives
lectures, 285

levels of significance, 224
libraries, 292, 297
lines of authority, 48
location(s)
  for interviews, 146–147
  for meetings, 193–194

management competencies, AMA study of, 2–5
managers
  assigning values to information from, 249
  definition of, 4
  as initiators of training needs identification
    process, 64
measures
  of standards of performance, 184–185
  of training results, 288
meeting(s), 124–126, 191–202
  in case example, 232, 235–239
  control techniques to use in, 200–202
  department, 74
  environment for, 193–194
  facilitator/leader of, 194–195
  format for, 197
  guidelines for conducting, 195–197
  identifying training needs through, 97–100
  information-gathering, 191
  making introductions in, 196–197
  notification of, 195
  participants in, 191–193
  questioning in, 196
  in sample report on job analysis for first-
    level supervisor positions, 269
  scenario of typical, 197–200
memos, follow-up, 39
Mental Measurements Yearbook, 225, 297
mentoring, 284
methods of operation, changes in, 72
mission
  training, 6
  of training delivery manager, 54
mission statement, 44–45, 55
multiperson interviews, 153–154

Need-to-Know Process, 122–123, 171–179
  learning how to use, 178–179
  planning for, 177
  procedure for using, 176–178
  when to use, 175–176
negative performance standards, 183
new employees
  Job Analysis Grid technique with, 163
  sample report on training needs for,
    264–268
new equipment, addition of, 72–73
The New York Times, 2
notes, taking interview, 149–150

objectives, training, *see* behavioral objectives
one-on-one job training, 284
online questionnaires, 128–129
operating department employees, 285, 286
opinion surveys, 74
organization
  definition of, 13
  need to know the, as recognized training
    need, 68–69
  training needs of the, 67–74
organizational chart (for training depart-
    ment), 46–52

organizational studies, 74
orientation training, 68–69
outsourcing, *see* external services and prod-
    ucts
outsourcing of training, 17

panel interviews, 120–121, 154
peer reviews, 130
performance review interview, 188–189
performance reviews, 75–76
  employee notification of, 187–188
  and performance standards, 185–186
performance standards, 181–189
  definition of, 181–182
  investigating failures to meet, 182–183
  and job responsibility, 182
  measures of, 184–185
  and performance evaluation, 185–188
  and performance standard interview,
    188–189
  positive vs. negative, 183
  setting, 184
  and training needs, 189
  types of, 183
performance surveys, 88, 89
planning to identify training needs
  in case example, 232–233
  and deciding on required information ele-
    ments, 104–111
  and deciding on who will conduct identifi-
    cation process, 111, 113
  investigation phase of, 113, 117
  training needs analysis report for, 111, 112
population, training
  current, 107–108
  potential, 108
position descriptions (for training depart-
    ment), 51, 53–58
predictive validity, 221–222
procedures, training needs identification, 66
products, purchasing, 296–297
professional associations, 293
professional trainers, 6–7
psychological interviews, 226

questioning (during meetings), 196
questionnaire(s), 92–94, 203–216
  behavioral, 128, 213–214
  in case example, 233, 239–243
  implementation/administration of, 214–216
  information-gathering, 127–128, 204–213
  limitations of, 203
  online, 128–129
  in sample report on training needs for new
    employees, 264
  web browser–based, 215
questions (interview), 139–143
  asking "why," 140–141
  and communicating a desired answer, 141
  encouraging application when asking, 142
  from interviewee, 148–149
  and interview objective, 140
  maintaining neutrality when asking, 141
  sequencing of, 142–143
  summary, 143

recognized training need(s), 67–71
  need to know a department as, 69
  need to know the organization as, 68–69

recognized training need(s) (*continued*)
  need to learn specific job requirements as, 69–71
references, checking, 293–294
reliability (statistics), 224
report(s) (of results), 255–277
  adjustments to, 257
  elements of, 255
  on job analysis for first-level supervisor positions (example), 268–277
  on new employee training needs (example), 263–268
  on supervisor assessment center (example), 259–263
  on training needs analysis (example), 258
requested training needs, source(s) of, 71–74
  changes in jobs/systems as, 72
  department performance as, 73
  government requirements as, 72–73
  new equipment as, 72–73
responses, combining, 250–255
responsibility for training, 15, 17
results
  reporting, *see* report(s)
  required, 110
reviews, performance, *see* performance reviews

scheduling, interview, 145–147
selection process, 76
self-paced learning, 284
self-reports, 129
self-study, 285
self-testing devices, 226
significance, levels of, 224
simulations, 285
span of control, 58
specific job requirements, 69–71
staff departments, as initiators of training needs identification process, 64
standard interviews, *see* interview(s)
standards of performance, *see* performance standards
subject of training
  detailed description of, 104–106
  review and update of, 109–110
sub-subjects, 105–106
succession plans, 77–79
summary questions (in interviews), 143, 152–153
supervisors, 55
  assigning values to information from, 248, 249
  definition of, 4
  Job Analysis Grid technique with, 163
  and performance review interview, 188
  sample report on assessment center for, 259–263
  training conducted by, 285
surveys, 128
  performance, 88, 89
  training, 83–87

task analysis, 124
teleconferences, 125
testing

employee, 76–77
  initial, 213
tests, 129, 217–225
  changing attitudes toward, 218–219
  function of, 217–218
  job relatedness of, 219–220
  levels of, 224–225
  levels of significance of, 224
  reliability of, 224
  selection of, 225
  validity of, 220–223
360-degree and peer reviews, 130
timeliness of training, 289
time requirements, 107
training delivery manager, 54
training department personnel, 285–286
training function
  activities of, 14–16
  effectiveness of, *see* effectiveness of training function
  increasing importance of, 1
  mission of, 44–45
  ultimate mission of, 6
training method, selection of, 286–289
training needs
  definition of, 66
  identification of, *see* identification of training needs
  of individual employees, 74–79, 100–101
  of the organization, 67–74
  planning to identify, *see* planning to identify training needs
  and training objectives, *see* behavioral objectives
training needs analysis report, 111, 112
training objectives, *see* behavioral objectives
training review analysis, 88, 90–91
training surveys, 83–87

unanticipated requests to investigate training needs, 81–82
unity of command, 49, 57–58
universities, 293
urgency of training, 107

validity, test, 220–223
value of training, estimating, 287–288
values, assigning, 248–249

web browser–based questionnaires, 215
weighting (of information sources), 247–248
workshops, 125
writing behavioral objectives, 281–283
written proposals (from outside service providers), 294–295
written training needs analysis procedure(s), 127–130
  behavioral questionnaires as, 128
  information-gathering questionnaires as, 127–128
  online questionnaires as, 128–129
  self-reports as, 129
  surveys as, 128
  tests/assessments as, 129
  360-degree and peer reviews, 130

Yellow Pages, 292

zero standards of performance, 183